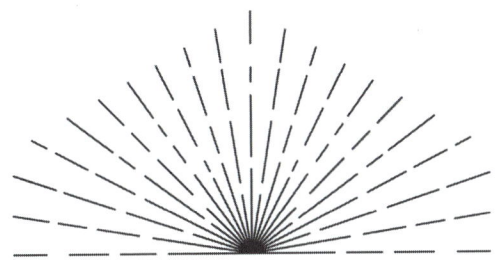

THE FUTURE OF EVANGELICALISM IN AMERICA

EDITED BY
Candy Gunther Brown and Mark Silk

Columbia University Press
New York

Columbia University Press
Publishers Since 1893
New York   Chichester, West Sussex
Copyright © 2016 Columbia University Press
All rights reserved

Library of Congress Cataloging-in-Publication Data
The future of evangelicalism in America/edited by Candy Gunther Brown and Mark Silk.
  pages cm.—(Future of religion in America)
  Includes bibliographical references and index.
  ISBN 978-0-231-17610-1 (cloth : alk. paper) — ISBN 978-0-231-17611-8
  (pbk. : alk. paper)— ISBN 978-0-231-54070-4 (e-book)
  1. Evangelicalism—United States—Forecasting. 2. Christianity—21st century.
    I. Brown, Candy Gunther, editor.   II. Silk, Mark, editor.
      BR1642.U6F88 2016
      280′.4097301—dc23
         2015034509

Columbia University Press books are printed on permanent and durable acid-free paper.
This book is printed on paper with recycled content.
Printed in the United States of America

c 10 9 8 7 6 5 4 3 2 1
p 10 9 8 7 6 5 4 3 2 1

COVER DESIGN: Catherine Casalino

References to Internet Web sites (URLs) were accurate at the time of writing. Neither the author nor Columbia University Press is responsible for URLs that may have expired or changed since the manuscript was prepared.

Contents

Series Editors' Introduction: The Future of Religion in America
Mark Silk and Andrew H. Walsh   vii

Introduction
Candy Gunther Brown   1

1 American Evangelicalism: Character, Function, and Trajectories of Change
   Michael S. Hamilton   18

2 Sound, Style, Substance: New Directions in Evangelical Spirituality
   Chris R. Armstrong   54

3 The Emerging Divide in Evangelical Theology
   Roger E. Olson   92

4 Evangelicals, Politics, and Public Policy: Lessons from the Past, Prospects for the Future
   Amy E. Black   124

5 The Changing Face of Evangelicalism
   Timothy Tseng   158

   Conclusion
   Candy Gunther Brown   203

Appendix A: American Religious Identification Survey: Research Design   225

Appendix B: American Religious Identification Survey: Future of Religion in America Survey   228

Appendix C: American Religious Identification Survey: Typology of Religious Groups   231

List of Contributors   237
Index   239

The Future of Evangelicalism in America

THE FUTURE OF RELIGION IN AMERICA

THE FUTURE OF RELIGION IN AMERICA
Series Editors Mark Silk and Andrew H. Walsh

The Future of Religion in America is a series of edited volumes on the current state and prospects of the principal religious groupings in the United States. Informed by survey research, the series explores the effect of the significant realignment of the American religious landscape that consolidated in the 1990s, driven by the increasing acceptance of the idea that religious identity is and should be a matter of personal individual choice and not inheritance.

Series Editors' Introduction: The Future of Religion in America

Mark Silk and Andrew H. Walsh

What is the future of religion in America? Not too good, to judge by recent survey data. Between 1990 and 2015, the proportion of adults who said they had no religion—the so-called Nones—increased from the middle single-digits to more than 20 percent, a startling rise and one that was disproportionately found among the rising "millennial" generation. If the millennials remain as they are, and the generation after them follows their lead, one-third of Americans will be Nones before long. To be sure, there are no guarantees that this will happen; it has long been the case that Americans tend to disconnect from organized religion in their twenties, then reaffiliate when they marry and have children. It is also important to recognize that those who say they have no religion are not saying that they have no religious beliefs or engage in no religious behavior. Most Nones in fact claim to believe in God, and many engage in a variety of religious practices, including prayer and worship attendance. Meanwhile, nearly four in five Americans continue to identify with a religious body or tradition—Christian, for the most part, but also Jewish, Muslim, Hindu, Buddhist, Sikh, Baha'i, Wiccan, New Age, and more. How have these various traditions changed? Which have grown and which declined? What sorts of beliefs and practices have Americans gravitated toward, and which have they moved away from? How have religious impulses and movements affected public policy and the culture at large? If we are to project the future of religion in America, we need to know where it is today and the trajectory it took to get there.

Unfortunately, that knowledge is not easy to come by. For nearly half a century, the historians who are supposed to tell the story of religion in

America have shied away from bringing it past the 1960s. One reason for this has been their desire to distance themselves from a scholarly heritage they believe to have been excessively devoted to Protestant identities, perspectives, and agendas. Placing Protestantism at the center of the story has seemed like an act of illegitimate cultural hegemony in a society as religiously diverse as the United States has become over the past half century. "Textbook narratives that attempt to tell the 'whole story' of U.S. religious history have focused disproportionately on male, northeastern, Anglo-Saxon, mainline Protestants and their beliefs, institutions, and power," Thomas A. Tweed wrote in 1997, in a characteristic dismissal. Indeed, any attempt to construct a "master narrative" of the whole story has been deemed an inherently misleading form of historical discourse.

In recent decades, much of the best historical writing about religion in America has steered clear of summary accounts altogether, offering instead tightly focused ethnographies, studies based on gender and race analysis, meditations on consumer culture, and monographs on immigrants and outsiders and their distinctive perspectives on the larger society. Multiplicity has been its watchword. But as valuable as the multiplicity approach has been in shining a light on hitherto overlooked parts of the American religious landscape, it can be just as misleading as triumphalist Protestantism. To take one prominent example, in 2001 Diana Eck's *A New Religious America: How a "Christian Country" Has Become the World's Most Religiously Diverse Nation* called for an end to conceptualizing the United States as in some sense Christian. Because of the 1965 immigration law, members of world religions were now here in strength, Eck (correctly) claimed. What she avoided discussing, however, was the relative weight of the world religions in society as a whole. As it turns out, although twenty-first-century America counts millions of Muslims, Hindus, Buddhists, Jains, Sikhs, Taoists, and adherents of other world religions in its population, they total less than 5 percent of the population. Moreover, Eck omitted to note that the large majority of post-1965 immigrants have been Christian—for the most part Roman Catholics. Overall, close to three-quarters of Americans still identify as Christians of one sort or another.

While there is no doubt that the story of religion in America must account for the growth of religious diversity, since the 1970s substantial changes have taken place that have nothing to do with it. There is, we believe, no substitute for comprehensive narratives that describe and assess how religious identity has changed and what the developments in the major religious institutions and traditions have been—and where they are headed. That is what the Future of Religion in America series seeks to provide. For the series, teams of experts have been asked to place the tradition they study in the contemporary American context, understood in quantitative as well as qualitative terms.

The appropriate place to begin remapping the religious landscape is with demographic data on changing religious identity. Advances in survey research now provide scholars with ample information about both the total national population and its constituent parts (by religious tradition, gender, age, region, race and ethnicity, education, and so on). The Lilly Endowment funded the 2008 American Religious Identification Survey, the third in a series of comparable, very large, random surveys of religious identity in the United States. The survey is a major source of information for this series. With data points in 1990, 2001, and 2008, the ARIS series provided robust and reliable data on American religious change over time down to the state level that are capable of capturing the demography of the twenty largest American religious groups. Based on interviews with 54,000 subjects, the 2008 Trinity ARIS has equipped our project to assess in detail the dramatic changes that have occurred over the past several decades in American religious life and to suggest major trends that organized religion faces in the coming decades. It has also allowed us to equip specialists in particular traditions to consider the broader connections and national contexts in which their subjects "do religion."

The ARIS series suggests that a major reconfiguration of American religious life has taken place over the past quarter-century. Signs of this reconfiguration were evident as early as the 1960s, though not until the 1990s did they consolidate into a new pattern—one characterized by three salient phenomena. First, the large-scale and continuing immigration inaugurated by the 1965 immigration law not only introduced significant populations of adherents of world religions hitherto little represented in the United States but also, and more significantly, changed the face of American Christianity. Perhaps the most striking impact has been on the ethnic and geographical rearrangement of American Catholicism. There have been steep declines in Catholic affiliation in the Northeast and rapid growth in the South and West, thanks in large part to an increase in the population of Latinos, who currently constitute roughly one-third of the

American Catholic population. California now has a higher proportion of Catholics than New England, which, since the middle of the nineteenth century, had been by far the most Catholic region of the country.

A second major phenomenon is the realignment of non-Catholic Christians. As recently as 1960, half of all Americans identified with mainline Protestant denominations—Congregationalist, Disciples of Christ, Episcopalian, Lutheran, Methodist, Northern Baptist. Since then, and especially since 1980, such identification has undergone a steep decline and by 2015 was approaching 10 percent of the population. The weakening of the mainline is further revealed by the shrinkage of those simply identifying as "Protestant" from 17.2 million in 1990 to 5.2 million in 2008, reflecting the movement of loosely tied mainline Protestants away from any institutional religious identification. By contrast, over the same period those who identify as just "Christian" or "non-denominational Christian" more than doubled their share of the population, from 5 to 10.7 percent. Based on current demographic trends, these people, who tend to be associated with megachurches and other nondenominational evangelical bodies, will soon equal the number of mainliners. In most parts of the country, adherents of evangelicalism now outnumber mainliners by at least two to one, making it the normative form of non-Catholic American Christianity. Simply put, American Protestantism is no longer the "two-party system" that the historian Martin Marty identified a generation ago.

The third phenomenon is the rise of the Nones. Their prevalence varies from region to region, with the Pacific Northwest and New England at the high end and the South and Midwest at the low. Americans of Asian, Jewish, and Irish background are particularly likely to identify as Nones. Likewise, Nones are disproportionately male and younger than those who claim a religious identity. But there is no region, no racial or ethnic group, no age or gender cohort that has not experienced a substantial increase in the proportion of those who say they have no religion. It is a truly national phenomenon and one that is at the same time more significant and less significant than it appears. It is less significant because it implies that religious belief and behavior in America have declined to the same extent as religious identification, and that is simply not the case. But that very fact makes it more significant because it indicates that the rise of the Nones has at least as much to do with a change in the way Americans understand

Series Editors' Introduction

religious identity as it does with a disengagement from religion. In a word, there has been a shift from understanding one's religious identity as inherited or "ascribed" and toward seeing it as something that individuals choose for themselves. This shift has huge implications for all religious groups in the country, as well as for American civil society as a whole. In order to make sense of it, some historical context is necessary.

During the colonial period, the state-church model dominated American religious life. There were growing pressures to accommodate religious dissent, especially in the Middle Atlantic region, a hotbed of sectarian diversity. But there wasn't much of a free market for religion in the colonial period because religious identity was closely connected to particular ethnic or immigrant identities: the Presbyterianism of the Scots Irish; the Lutheranism, Calvinism, and Anabaptism of various groups of Pennsylvania Germans; the Judaism of the Sephardic communities in Eastern seaboard cities; the Roman Catholicism of Maryland's English founding families. The emergence of revivalism in the late eighteenth century and the movement to terminate state establishments after the Revolution cut across this tradition of inherited religious identity. Different as they were, evangelical Protestants and Enlightenment deists—the coalition that elected Thomas Jefferson president—could together embrace disestablishment, toleration, and the primacy of individual religious conscience and choice. This introduced amazing diversity and religious change in the early nineteenth century, in what came to be known as the Second Great Awakening. Within a few decades, however, ascribed religious identity was back in the ascendancy. By the 1830s, Baptists, Methodists, Presbyterians, Congregationalists, Disciples, and Episcopalians were establishing cultural networks—including denominational schools and colleges, mission organizations, and voluntary societies—within which committed families intermarried and built multigenerational religious identities.

The onset of massive migration from Europe in the 1840s strengthened the salience of ascribed religious identity, creating new, inward-looking communities as well as a deep and contentious division between the largely Roman Catholic immigrants and the Protestant "natives." Moderate and liberal Protestant denominations moved away from revivalism and sought self-perpetuation by "growing their own" members in families, Sunday Schools, and other denominational institutions. And religion as a dimension of relatively stable group identities persisted into the middle of the twentieth century; indeed, after World War II, sociologists saw it as a key foundation of the American way. Will Herberg famously argued that the American people were divided into permanent pools of Protestants, Catholics, and Jews, with little intermarriage. Yet by the end of the 1960s, it was clear that the century-long dominance of ascribed religious identity was under challenge. Interfaith marriage had become more common as barriers of prejudice and discrimination fell; secularization made religion seem optional to many people; and internal migration shook up established communities and living patterns.

In addition, conversion-oriented evangelical Protestantism was dramatically reviving, with an appeal based on individuals making personal decisions to follow Jesus. At the same time, a new generation of spiritual seekers was exploring religious frontiers beyond Judaism and Christianity. As at the end of the eighteenth century, evangelicals and post-Judeo-Christians together pushed Americans to reconceptualize religion as a matter of individual choice. By the 1990s, survey research indicated that religious bodies that staked their claims on ascribed identity—mainline Protestants and Roman Catholics above all, but also such ethnoreligious groupings as Lutherans, Jews, and Eastern Orthodox—were suffering far greater loss of membership than communities committed to the view that religion is something you choose for yourself (evangelicals, religious liberals, and the "spiritual but not religious" folk we call metaphysicals). Within the religious communities that have depended on ascription, that news has been slow to penetrate.

The bottom line for the future of religion in America is that all religious groups are under pressure to adapt to a society where religious identity is increasingly seen as a matter of personal choice. Ascription won't disappear, but there is little doubt that it will play a significantly smaller role in the formation of Americans' religious identity. This is important information, not least because it affects various religious groups in profoundly different ways. It poses a particular challenge for those groups that have depended upon ascribed identity to guarantee their numbers, challenging them to develop not only new means of keeping and attracting members but also new ways of conceptualizing and communicating who and what they are. Preeminent among such groups are the Jews, whose conception

Series Editors' Introduction

of religious identity has always been linked to parentage; it is only converts who are known as "Jews by choice." To a lesser degree, Catholics and Mormons have historically been able to depend on ascriptive identity to keep their flocks in the fold. But in a world of choice, American Catholicism has increasingly had to depend on new Latino immigrants to keep its numbers up, while the LDS Church, focused more and more on converts from beyond the Mountain West, has had to change its ways to accommodate "Mormons by choice."

In the wide perspective, what choice has done is to substantially weaken the middle ground between the extremes of religious commitment and indifference. With the option of "None" before them as an available category of identity, many Americans no longer feel the need to keep up the moderate degree of commitment that once assured that pews would be occupied on Sunday mornings. American society has become religiously bifurcated—a bifurcation signaled by political partisanship. Since the 1970s, the Republican Party has increasingly become the party of the more religious; the Democratic Party, the party of the less religious. In order to take account of this growing divide between the religious and the secular, the narrative of religion in America must thus go beyond both the Protestant hegemony story and the multiplicity story. The new understanding of religious identity as chosen, in a society where "None" is increasingly accepted as a legitimate choice, stands at the center of the narrative this series will construct.

ACKNOWLEDGMENTS

The Greenberg Center wishes to acknowledge several people and institutions that have provided critical support for the Future of Religion in America project. Lilly Endowment, Inc., funded the American Religious identification Survey of 2008 (ARIS), which provided data that shaped both the overall project and its volumes. Lilly also generously underwrote the first four volumes of the series, on evangelical Protestants, mainline Protestants, Roman Catholics, and African American religion, as well as the companion surveys designed by each of those volume teams.

Our distinguished Trinity College colleagues at the Institute for the Study of Secularism in Society and Culture, Barry Kosmin and Ariela

Keysar, enabled the project by conducting the ARIS 2008 survey and its smaller companions.

The center, which is now approaching its twentieth anniversary, also owes a great deal to Trinity College and to Leonard E. Greenberg, Trinity class of 1948, for their generous and continuing support of the center's work.

The Future of Evangelicalism in America

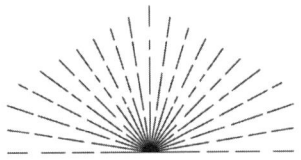

Introduction

Candy Gunther Brown

Since the middle of the twentieth century evangelicalism has reemerged as the normative form of non-Catholic American Christianity, supplanting what is usually referred to as mainline Protestantism. In the 1970s few people predicted the current state of affairs. Although evangelicals had dominated the American religious landscape until the 1870s, by the early twentieth century American Protestantism consisted of two, roughly equal parties—theologically liberal "mainliners" and theologically conservative "evangelicals." Gradually and relatively inconspicuously at first, "neo-evangelicals" grew in numbers and influence beginning in the 1940s. Today, "big tent" evangelicalism is three times the size of the mainline—encompassing eighty million American adults.

The center of the evangelical tent is predominantly occupied by white evangelicals whose theology, language, and worship practices have broad appeal to those standing on the peripheries—members of mainline, African American, or Roman Catholic churches who identify as "born again" or "evangelical" and take more theologically and politically conservative positions and attend church more frequently than other members of their congregations. Yet evangelicalism is anything but univocal or static. Many Americans identify as born again or evangelical without embracing the full slate of beliefs and practices associated with the evangelical center. There are signs of change on the horizon as younger evangelicals exhibit different priorities compared with the generation that founded the neo-evangelical movement; as evangelicalism, like America as a whole, becomes more ethnically and racially diverse; and as choice plays more of a role in religious and political affiliations. It seems possible that expansion of the

Introduction

evangelical big tent may be approaching its limits. Given evangelicalism's prominence and rapidly changing contours in today's religious, cultural, and political landscape, this book asks: How can American evangelicalism best be characterized? What are current trends and future trajectories?

The Future of Evangelicalism in America fits within a Columbia University Press series of multiauthor books on the current state and prospects of the principal religious groupings in the United States: The Future of Religion in America. Other volumes assess mainline Protestantism, Catholicism, African American religion, Judaism, Mormonism, Islam, Eastern Orthodoxy, Asian religions (Buddhism, Hinduism, Sikhism), metaphysical religion, and secularism. This series is designed to provide scholars, students, and general readers with an integrated portrait of religious change in America today. The series is also suited to fostering self-examination and discussion within each of the religious traditions examined.

This project emerged from the Leonard E. Greenberg Center for the Study of Religion in Public Life at Trinity College, with funding from the Lilly Endowment and the Posen Foundation. The Greenberg Center's director and associate director, Mark Silk and Andrew Walsh, are the general editors. Books in the series take as their starting point survey data generated by the Trinity American Religious Identification Survey (ARIS). The principal investigators, Barry Kosmin and Ariela Keysar, are the director and associate director of the Institute for the Study of Secularism in Society and Culture (ISSSC), which is affiliated with the Greenberg Center through the Trinity College Program on Public Values.[1]

AMERICAN RELIGIOUS IDENTIFICATION SURVEY

ARIS consists of three large, nationally representative random digit dialed telephone surveys conducted in 1990, 2001, and 2008 that track changes in religious loyalties of the U.S. adult population. The ARIS sequence provides the most extensive longitudinal data available on religious identification in contemporary America.[2]

Methods

The survey team in 2008 asked 54,461 American adults, "What is your religion, if any?" The survey included an option of conducting an inter-

Introduction

view in English or in Spanish. Pollsters asked additional questions of five subgroups, or "silos," of 1,000 respondents each: religious "Nones" who identified no religion, African Americans who identified some religion, nonblack evangelical Protestants, mainline Protestants, and Catholics. All except the Nones were asked, "Are you an evangelical or born again Christian?," allowing comparisons between those evangelicals who do and do not belong to denominations usually classified as evangelical.

Determining who to count as "evangelical" is an enormously complex issue, discussed at length throughout this volume. The evangelical silo consists of a statistically representative sample of the first 1,008 respondents who answered the religious identification question by saying they were (a) a member of one of the denominations listed as evangelical Protestant on the ARIS roster (see appendix C), (b) a born-again or evangelical Christian, and (c) nonblack. The survey also reported demographic data on a larger group of 13,085 nonblack "evangelicals" who reported membership in a denomination on the evangelical Protestant roster but were not asked if they are born again or evangelical.

Social scientists working with survey data generally treat whites and blacks separately because of statistical problems of analyzing data with small sample sizes. There are, moreover, historical and cultural reasons that black and white Christians who share much in common theologically have different experiences and priorities—which lead many theologically conservative African Americans to reject the label "evangelical." Analyzing data from African Americans in a dedicated silo—and series volume—allows for more, rather than less, attention to be paid to their distinctive concerns.

Findings

The ARIS survey sequence identifies three major, interrelated trends that are analyzed in detail throughout the series volumes: the paired growth of evangelical Christians and Nones, and the decline of mainline Protestants.

ARIS 2008 reveals that 34 percent of all American adults and 45 percent of American Christians self-identify as "born again or evangelical Christians." At the end of World War II only a third of American Protestants identified as born again or evangelical; now more than half do. What is more, self-identified evangelicals can be found by the millions in mainline

Protestant, Roman Catholic, and "nondenominational" congregations, as well as in denominations historically associated with the evangelical movement. There are regional variations, with nearly half—49 percent—of evangelicals concentrated in the South, compared with 21 percent in the North Central region, 20 percent in the West, and just 10 percent in the Northeast. Demographically, evangelicals do not look dramatically different from other Americans. Compared with national averages, evangelicals are slightly more female and younger and have somewhat lower educational and income attainments. Just over half (53 percent) are women. Evangelicals can be found in every age-group: 21 percent are ages 18–29, 38 percent are 30–49, 30 percent are 50–69, and 12 percent are at least 70 years old. Over 75 percent of evangelicals have at least a high school education, and 19 percent are college graduates. More than half (57 percent) of evangelical adults are married, 10 percent are divorced, 8 percent are widowed, and 18 percent have never been married. Nearly half (46 percent) work full time, 11 percent work half time, and 17 percent are retired. Evangelicals can be found in every income bracket—with the largest segment (14 percent) earning a total household gross income between $50,000 and $75,000. Most evangelicals own their own homes (76 percent) and are registered to vote (77 percent). What these numbers suggest is that evangelicals can be found across the American social landscape, and American Christianity as a whole is becoming more evangelical in outlook.[3]

At the same time, there is unprecedented growth in the number of Americans who are answering "none" when asked what their religion is, if any. Americans increasingly regard "religion" as a chosen rather than an ascribed identity. Between 1990 and 2001 the ranks of the Nones grew from 8 percent to 14 percent of the population, rising more modestly to 15 percent in 2008, and hiking up to 20 percent by 2012 (according to a 61,412-respondent poll conducted by Social Science Research Solutions, the same research firm, adopting a similar methodology, as used for ARIS). In 1990 one in ten adults did not identify with a religion of any kind compared with one in five by 2012; notably, however, 68 percent of the religiously unaffiliated say they believe in God, and 37 percent describe themselves as "spiritual, but not religious," making it problematic to view Nones and "seculars" as equivalent categories. Although 86 percent of American adults identified as Christians in 1990, only 77 percent did so in 2012.

Introduction

More recent surveys confirm the patterns noted by ARIS. The largest of these is the Pew Research Center's Religious Landscape Studies, which surveyed 35,000 Americans in 2007 and again in 2014. Nones grew from 16 percent in 2007 up to 23 percent in 2014, while the Christian share of the U.S. population dropped from 78 percent to 71 percent during this same interval. Notwithstanding the overall trajectory of Christian decline, evangelicals—a category that Pew defines in terms of identification with particular churches—lost less than a percentage point of their share of the total U.S. population (dropping from 26.3 percent to 25.4 percent), while gaining market share among Protestants (rising from 51 percent to 55 percent). Consistent with ARIS, Pew 2014 found that more adults have chosen an evangelical identity, having grown up in other traditions (10 percent), than those raised evangelical who no longer identify as such (8 percent). Given that the U.S. population as a whole grew between 2007 and 2014, Pew estimates that the absolute numbers of evangelicals may have climbed from 60 million to 62 million adults.[4]

The challenge to Christianity in American society does not come from the expansion of other world religions, which still attract only 5 to 6 percent of American adherents, but rather from a growing rejection of all organized religions (though not necessarily a rejection of "spirituality"). Trends suggest a polarization in American society, in which one-third of the population attests to enjoying a personal relationship with God, while a quarter of the population eschews identifying with any religion.[5]

The Protestant mainline has been receding since the 1960s, but the rate of decline has accelerated in the twenty-first century. Membership in mainline denominations dropped from 19 percent to 17 percent between 1990 and 2001 but plummeted to 13 percent by 2008. Methodists—the powerhouse of nineteenth-century evangelicalism—lost American members every year between 1964 and 2012, with an overall decline of 4.5 million members. The Presbyterian Church USA lost 20 percent of its overall membership between 2000 and 2012. Pew's Religious Landscape Studies, using different criteria from ARIS, reported a drop-off in mainline Protestants from 18 percent of the total U.S. population in 2007 down to 15 percent in 2014. The data suggest that the steady growth of evangelicalism has occurred at the expense of mainline denominations.[6]

Introduction

WHAT IS EVANGELICALISM?

Defining "evangelicalism" is remarkably complicated. In recent decades the media have equated evangelicalism with the religious Right, Republican politics, and social conservatism. Nevertheless, self-described evangelicals are a diverse group of individuals, congregations, denominations, and nondenominational ministries that express a range of theological, political, and social convictions. There are evangelicals who defend the doctrine that God predestined some people for salvation and others for damnation (Calvinists—named for John Calvin, 1509–1564), and there are evangelicals who affirm that God gave humans free will (Arminians—named for Jacobus Arminius, 1560–1609). Although most evangelicals avow the veracity of miracles described in the Bible, some believe that miraculous gifts of the Holy Spirit ceased with the apostles (cessationists, many of whom are Calvinists), whereas others believe that spiritual gifts continue to the present day (continuationists, notably Pentecostals and Charismatics). Evangelicals have adopted a variety of political positions in different historical eras, and even today different constituencies of evangelicals support Republican, Democratic, and Independent candidates and policy agendas or refrain from involvement in politics. Whereas some evangelicals are particularly concerned about legislating personal morality, others consider the pursuit of social justice more pressing. Certain evangelicals speak of taking God-ordained dominion over the earth, while others call Christians to follow Jesus's example as a humble, suffering servant.

Evangelicalism can be viewed as a movement, an affinity group, or an ethos. The evangelical impulse leaks through religious and social boundaries. The ARIS 2008 survey silos reveal that 39 percent of mainline Protestants, 58 percent of African American religious believers, and—perhaps of greatest surprise to some readers—18 percent of Catholics self-identify as born again or evangelical. Yet less than half (49 percent) of nonblack respondents who belong to a historically evangelical denomination and consider themselves born again or evangelical accept the label "evangelical" as a self-description. Only 19 percent of African American religious believers describe themselves as evangelical, though 21 percent accept the label "Pentecostal" and 38 percent identify as Charismatic.[7]

Evangelical self-identity can be correlated with certain theological beliefs and values. The historian David Bebbington influentially articulated,

Introduction

in 1989, a four-part definition of evangelicalism as characterized by conversionism, biblicism, crucicentrism, and activism. In other words, evangelicals believe that Christianity involves conversion to Christ; the Bible is the inspired word of God; the Bible reveals that conversion is possible because God provided forgiveness from sin through the sinless life, atoning death, and miraculous resurrection of Jesus, the Christ, or anointed one; and Christians should encourage non-Christians to become Christians.[8]

ARIS 2008 supports Bebbington's analysis. Of evangelicals who identify as "born again or evangelical" (conversionism) and belong to an evangelical denomination, 85 percent (compared with 42 percent of mainline Protestants) "strongly agree" that the Bible is the "actual word of God";[9] 93 percent (versus 70 percent mainline) strongly agree the Bible is a reliable guide for faith; 90 percent (versus 67 percent mainline) strongly agree the Bible is a reliable guide for morality; and 73 percent (versus 40 percent mainline) claim to read the Bible outside worship at least weekly, all of which indicate strong biblicism. Reflecting crucicentrism, 92 percent of evangelicals (versus 58 percent mainline) strongly agree that Jesus Christ is the only way to salvation. Indicative of activism, 76 percent of evangelicals strongly agree that it is very important to share one's faith with nonbelievers, and 69 percent (versus 38 percent mainline) say they actually do share their faith at least monthly. Nevertheless, ARIS also indicates that the segment of the evangelical tent that is expanding most rapidly (notably including the growing ranks of "nondenominational" Christians) stands along the peripheries where individuals tend to be less committed to core evangelical beliefs and practices. Consequently, as evangelicalism expands numerically, it may become less distinctively "evangelical" in the sense that this term has historically been used.

The historian Mark Noll has both popularized Bebbington's "quadrilateral" and forwarded a complementary definition of evangelicals as "culturally adaptive biblical experientialists." Thus evangelicals are Christians who seek a transformative presence in culture by appropriating non-Christian resources to evangelize outsiders and edify believers. At the same time, evangelicals strive to use the Bible as a safeguard against cultural contamination and to conserve doctrinal orthodoxy. A related way of framing the evangelical project is to say that evangelicals are those who share with one another the goal of using the word of God to transform the world, which demands balancing purity from and presence in the world. Toward these ends, evangelicals envision themselves as contending for the faith once delivered to the saints, ministering as the priesthood of all believers, sanctifying the surrounding world, and uniting as the church universal.[10]

HISTORICAL BACKDROP

The terms *evangelical* and *born again*, as well as *Pentecostal* and *Charismatic*, can be traced back to the New Testament. The Greek *euaggelion* and the Anglo-Saxon *godspel*, or "good news," refer to preaching a message of salvation from sin and death through Jesus Christ. Before his ascension Jesus gave his disciples what evangelicals call the "Great Commission": "go and make disciples of all nations." When asked how to attain salvation, Jesus replied that one must be "born again" through the Holy Spirit. Jesus's disciples reputedly received the Holy Spirit on Pentecost, a Jewish holiday fifty days after Passover, shortly after Jesus's crucifixion. Early Christian writers, such as the apostle Paul, used the Greek word *charismata* to refer to gifts of the Holy Spirit, such as healing, miracles, prophecy, and speaking in unknown tongues.[11]

The Protestant Reformation began when Martin Luther (1483–1546), a German monk, posted ninety-five "Theses of Contention" on a church door at Wittenberg on October 31, 1517. The Reformers protested against what they viewed as extrabiblical church traditions and affirmed the principles of *sola gratia, sola fides, solus Christus, sola scriptura, soli Deo gloria*: salvation by grace alone, through faith alone, in Christ alone, as revealed in the Bible alone, glory to God alone. Luther's followers in Germany first adopted the name Evangelische Kirche, or Evangelical Church.[12]

Since the Reformation, evangelicals have sought to balance the goals of Christian unity and doctrinal purity, resulting in an uneasy tension between denominational and nondenominational identities and institutions. The same zeal for purity that led the sixteenth-century reformers to break from the Roman Catholic Church fueled repeated splits within evangelicalism. The four major branches of the Reformation—Lutheran, Reformed (Congregational, Presbyterian), Tudor (Anglican), and Radical (Mennonite, Amish)—birthed an ever-lengthening list of denominations. By the eighteenth century evangelical leaders articulated a denominational theory that there is one Christian church divided into multiple branches, each legitimate and vital to the growth of the whole. In America, denominations developed not as dissenting parties from an established church but as the dominant form of church organization. Rather than suffer from lack of government support, denominations thrived in a context of church-state separation as they relied on voluntarist, entrepreneurial, democratic strategies for growth and sustenance.[13]

The term *evangelical* began as a synonym for Protestant but narrowed in meaning over time. During pietistic revivals in Europe and America in the 1670s, evangelicals protested against ecclesiastical formalism and appealed for a living religion of the heart. Amid the transatlantic religious revivals of the 1720s–1740s, known as the Great Awakening, evangelicals formed transatlantic networks of people, voluntary associations, print, and song. By the eighteenth century, self-proclaimed evangelicals reserved the label for Protestants of whom they approved. Evangelicals could be distinguished from sacramentalist High Churchmen, whom evangelicals accused of relying on sacraments and tradition instead of the Bible. Evangelicals also saw themselves as different from rationalist liberals, whom they accused of denying the Gospel's power by privileging reason over the Bible. By the same token, opponents of revivals used the term *evangelical* as a label of reproach to denote presumed fanaticism. During the Second Great Awakening of the 1790s–1840s, evangelical churches, organized into denominations, spread rapidly across the American frontier. Congregationalist, Presbyterian, and Episcopal churches grew modestly, while Methodist and Baptist memberships exploded, accounting for two-thirds of U.S. Protestants by 1870. Between 1790 and 1870 the U.S. population grew 1,000 percent while the evangelical population grew 7,500 percent.[14]

Until the 1870s most Protestant denominations—whether Calvinist or Arminian, cessationist or continuationist—espoused conservative theological views and belonged to the evangelical movement. Churches of every denomination promoted revivals—protracted religious meetings that featured emotionally intense preaching and singing that heightened the apparent urgency of personally experiencing conversion to Christ and growth in holiness. Evangelicalism with its hallmark characteristic of revivalism was the normative form of American non-Catholic Christianity. By the early twentieth century American Protestantism had divided into two major theological parties—modernists and fundamentalists. Modernists reinterpreted the Bible in light of modern scholarship and embraced historical-critical methods and evolutionary biology. Fundamentalists sought to preserve historic Christian doctrines they considered fundamental to the Christian faith. The Federal Council of Churches, founded in 1908 (and reorganized as the National Council of Churches in 1950), endorsed theological modernism, the Social Gospel, and the Progressive movement in politics. Although antebellum evangelicals had spearheaded social reform movements, fundamentalists backed away from social activism because of its connections with theological liberalism. The Scopes "Monkey" Trial of 1925—during which fundamentalists fought a losing battle against teaching evolution in public schools—proved a breaking point after which many Americans associated fundamentalism with intellectual backwardness. As modernists secured control of mainline Protestant denominations, fundamentalists withdrew to establish separate institutions in order to protect religious purity.[15]

The National Association of Evangelicals (NAE) was formed in 1942 to promote conservative theology and social engagement, as opposed to theological modernism or fundamentalist separatism. The NAE brought together Calvinists, Arminians, and Pentecostals, despite their significant theological differences. Its founding marks the birth of the "neo-evangelical" movement, which soon came to be identified with the whole of twentieth-century evangelicalism. By 1976 evangelicals had made it onto the national media radar, with a *Newsweek* story, "Born Again!," pronouncing "The Year of the Evangelicals." In 2005 *Time* magazine ran a cover story identifying "The 25 Most Influential Evangelicals in America." Such media notice came after a rising tide of evangelical influence had been building for decades.[16]

The reasons for evangelical growth are multifaceted. There are sociological factors such as the higher fertility rates of evangelical Protestants relative to mainliners. Furthermore, as the social status of evangelical churches improved over time, fewer upwardly mobile members fled to socially respectable liberal congregations. There are, moreover, theological and cultural aspects of evangelicalism that suited the movement to benefit from the trajectory of American cultural change. Evangelicalism has from the start emphasized the importance of individuals making a personal decision to follow Christ—and publicly acknowledging that decision by testifying about one's conversion experience, getting baptized—or rebaptized—often after reaching an age of personal accountability, and encouraging others to become Christians. By requiring individuals to choose their religious identity and articulate reasons for their choice to others, evangelicalism intensified individuals' commitment to their decisions. By the late twentieth century evangelicalism's emphasis on personal choice resonated with a broader cultural ethos of choice, including choosing rather than being born into one's religious identity.[17]

As a backdrop to evangelical resurgence, the quest of post–World War II Americans for deeper spirituality created hunger for a "counterculture." As the Vietnam War aggravated building frustrations, people expressed dissatisfaction with American "institutions," including religious institutions, while demanding immediately satisfying religious experiences. Evangelicals—who had long been media-savvy innovators—deployed new music, sound, lighting, artistic, canvassing, and mass-media technologies to create aesthetically rich worship experiences and to publicize the availability of these experiences to broadening audiences.[18]

The 1960s marked a watershed in the revitalization of American evangelicalism. The significance of the Second Vatican Council (1962–1965) can scarcely be overestimated. Vatican II accepted Protestants as "separated brethren" and authorized Charismatic renewal. The ecumenical Charismatic renewal and "Jesus people" movements of the 1960s–1970s ushered the practice of spiritual gifts, notably divine healing, and participatory worship styles into mainstream Protestant and Catholic churches and gave Charismatic Protestants and Catholics a shared spirituality. The United States had been mostly closed to immigration between 1924 and 1965. The Immigration Act of 1965, an outgrowth of the civil rights movement, removed restrictions based on national origins, leading to a dramatic increase in immigration from Latin America and Asia and a growing stream of new arrivals from Africa and the Middle East. Two-thirds of the new immigrants were Christians, and most of the Protestants could also be described as evangelical and/or pentecostal.[19]

Over the course of the twentieth century, the Pentecostal and Charismatic movements (grouped under the umbrella term *pentecostals*) within evangelicalism grew exponentially, both within the United States and globally, from a handful of adherents to more than a quarter of the world's two billion Christians. Pentecostalism attracts adherents primarily through its characteristic practice of praying for divine healing coupled with the widespread perception that pentecostal prayers are effective. A survey by the Pew Forum for Religion and Public Life in 2006 singles out divine healing—above other factors, such as glossolalia and financial prosperity—as uniting pentecostals with one another and distinguishing them from other Christians.[20]

By the 1960s the centuries-old rift between Catholics and Protestants—which gave birth to evangelicalism—had begun to mend, while the evangelical movement became increasingly fragmented as old animosities between Calvinists and Arminians resurfaced and a chasm widened between cessationists and pentecostals. Debates about divine healing that started in the sixteenth century as a division between Catholics and Protestants came to divide Protestants from one another. One of the most influential Protestant reformers, John Calvin, developed the doctrine of "cessationism" to argue (against Catholic miracle claims) that miracles had ceased with the biblical era because they were no longer needed to confirm the Gospel. God might still heal in response to prayer, but such healing was not miraculous, and most healing should be expected through medical means. Clergy influenced by Calvin taught that God sends sickness to sanctify the souls of his children, so the proper response is passive resignation.[21]

Beginning in the mid-nineteenth century, a growing number of Americans rejected Calvinism's view of the body as enemy of the soul in favor of the Wesleyan (named after Methodist founder John Wesley, 1703–1791) view that purification of the soul and the body are complementary. These Christians began to reason that if it was possible for sanctified Christians to escape the spiritual consequences of sin, it should similarly be possible to escape the physical consequences that led to bodily sickness. The resultant "divine healing" movement grew out of the transnational Holiness and Higher Christian Life revivals within evangelicalism, then caught fire with the birth of Pentecostalism in the twentieth century. A nationwide telephone survey by the Barna Group in 2008 reported that 36 percent of U.S. adults self-identify as pentecostal. The two largest groups of evangelicals who specified an identity more specific than "Christian" for ARIS 2008 were Baptists (many of whom are cessationist Calvinists) and Pentecostals. Despite sharp disagreements among evangelicals (a state of affairs that is scarcely new), the overall picture, as of 2016, is that evangelicalism has reemerged as the normative form of American Protestant Christianity.[22]

CHAPTER PREVIEW

This book is organized thematically into five chapters. Each chapter tells a story of how American evangelicalism has developed between the 1970s and the present, notes current trends, and forecasts where evangelicalism may be headed. The contributors to this volume were selected for their expertise in particular aspects of evangelical thought and practice and represent a range of disciplinary methods and theological perspectives.

The first chapter, written by Michael Hamilton, associate professor of history at Seattle Pacific University, identifies cultural characteristics of American evangelicalism. Hamilton describes evangelicalism as an affinity group that expresses a common-denominator Bible faith that is entrepreneurial, populist, cosmopolitan, voluntarist, pragmatic, responsive to popular culture, and most visibly represented by megachurch pastors and nondenominational parachurch ministries. He points toward a future marked by experimentation with ways of doing church and growing social awareness as American evangelicals become increasingly attentive to their global context.

Chapter 2, written by Chris Armstrong, professor of theology at Wheaton College in Illinois, considers evangelical spirituality. Armstrong identifies a youth-oriented, democratic, populist ethos and the rise of emotionally transformative pentecostal praise and worship styles that emphasize immediate access to a personal experience of God and the meeting of individual needs. He suggests that the rising generation of this increasingly global, pentecostalized movement will continue to embrace new devotional forms and borrow resources from older Christian traditions and diverse branches of the church as they pursue the long-standing evangelical goal of expressing heart religion.

Chapter 3, by Roger Olson, the Foy Valentine Professor of Christian Theology and Ethics at Baylor University, examines evangelical theology. The key features Olson notes are ongoing biblicism and growing theological sophistication yet lack of consensus on what the Bible means or who can set doctrinal boundaries, building toward a crisis of theological authority. Olson's prognostications for evangelicalism's future are more pessimistic than those of his fellow contributors: further fragmentation and absence of definitive leadership, possibly depleting the label "evangelical theology" of any distinctive meaning.

Chapter 4, contributed by Amy Black, professor of political science at Wheaton College, asks what the evolution of evangelical politics means for the future of both evangelicalism and American politics. Black notes that despite the widespread tendency to associate evangelicalism with the religious Right, Republican politics, and social conservatism, evangelicals have historically taken a range of political and social positions. She depicts a future in which evangelical policy agendas are broadening and shifting, and ties to party politics may be weakening.

Chapter 5, by Timothy Tseng, former director of the Institute for the Study of Asian American Christianity and current pastor of English ministries at Canaan Taiwanese Christian Church in San Jose, California, draws attention to the shifting racial and ethnic composition of American evangelicalism as Hispanic and Asian memberships grow. Although observing failures of evangelical institutions to reckon with demographic change, Tseng remains optimistic that American evangelicalism can adapt to its new ethno-racial diversity.

The conclusion draws together insights of the contributed chapters to paint a portrait of the present state and future prospects of evangelicalism in America. The conclusion highlights nine interrelated themes that emerge from this book: biblicism, nondenominationalism, magnetic leadership, popular culture, pentecostalization, globalization, ethnic diversification, political realignment, and generational change. As of 2016 the evangelical movement faces a number of critical challenges, and it remains an open question how the current and rising generations will respond. There is reason for hope and concern, whether one is a self-identified evangelical or an observer of this culturally influential movement. One thing is certain: that, for better or for worse, evangelicals are here to stay, and their story and the American story will remain intertwined for the foreseeable future.

NOTES

1. Barry A. Kosmin and Ariela Keysar, *The American Religious Identification Survey (ARIS 2008): Summary Report* (Hartford, Conn.: Trinity College, 2009), http://

Introduction

commons.trincoll.edu/aris/files/2011/08/ARIS_Report_2008.pdf, accessed August 3, 2015.

2. ARIS is not the only source of survey data that sheds light on American religious identification. For example, the General Social Survey has been conducted every one to two years since 1972, with sample sizes ranging between 1,372 and 2,992 respondents; General Society Survey, "FAQs," http://publicdata.norc.org:41000/gssbeta/faqs.html. The National Congregations Study is based on interviews conducted in 1998, 2006–2007, and 2012 with leaders of a combined total of 4,000 religious congregations; "National Congregations Study," http://www.soc.duke.edu/natcong/. The Baylor Religion Survey, conducted in 2005, 2007, and 2010, provides data from a combined total of 5,000 respondents; Association of Religion Data Archives, "Baylor Religion Surveys," http://www.thearda.com/Archive/NatBaylor.asp. All accessed August 6, 2015.

The Pew Research Center's Forum on Religion & Public Life has conducted a number of illuminating, large-scale surveys, including the Religious Landscape Studies in 2007 and 2014, based on interviews with 35,000 Americans, as well as surveys specific to Latinos, Asian Americans, and Nones. Contributors to this volume are conversant with a breadth of survey data and draw on other surveys in addition to ARIS where relevant.

3. ARIS figures for evangelicals can be compared with data from 2008 in the U.S. Census Bureau Statistical Abstract, http://www.census.gov/compendia/statab/2010/2010edition.html, accessed August 6, 2015.

4. Pew Research Center, "America's Changing Religious Landscape," May 12, 2015, http://www.pewforum.org/2015/05/12/americas-changing-religious-landscape/, accessed August 3, 2015.

5. Cary Funk and Greg Smith, et al., "'Nones' on the Rise: One-in-Five Adults Have No Religious Affiliation" (Washington, D.C.: Pew Research Center, February 2012), 9, http://www.pewforum.org/files/2012/10/NonesOnTheRise-full.pdf, accessed August 6, 2015. ARIS 2008 found that 76 percent of Americans identify as Christian; this percentage remained relatively stable as of 2012 when a Gallup poll of 326,271 adults reported that 77 percent identify as Christians, and 18 percent as Nones; Frank Newport, "In U.S., 77% Identify as Christian; Eighteen Percent Have No Explicit Religious Identity," *Gallup Politics*, December 24, 2012, http://www.gallup.com/poll/159548/identify-christian.aspx, accessed August 6, 2015.

6. Michael Gryboski, "United Methodist Church Continues to Decline in America, but Gains in Africa," *CP Church & Ministries*, August 3, 2012, http://www.christianpost.com/news/united-methodist-church-continues-to-decline-in-america-but-gains-in-africa-79384/, accessed August 3, 2015.

7. In presenting data from respondents screened into thousand-person silos, reported percentages reflect weighted results: a valid projection of results up to the projected national sample size. In all, 87 percent of African Americans identify with some religion, and 92 percent of the religious identify as Protestant.

Introduction

In ARIS 2008, 6 percent of African Americans identified as Catholic, 1 percent as Muslim, and 1 percent as New Religious Movement or Other; 13 percent answered None or Didn't Know/Refused.

8. David W. Bebbington, *Evangelicalism in Modern Britain: A History from the 1730s to the 1980s* (London: Unwin Hyman, 1989), 2–17; Mark A. Noll, D. W. Bebbington, and George A. Rawlyk, eds., *Evangelicalism: Comparative Studies of Popular Protestantism in North America, the British Isles, and Beyond, 1700-1990* (New York: Oxford University Press, 1994), 6. Bebbington originally listed the elements of the evangelical "quadrilateral" in the order conversionism, activism, biblicism, and crucicentrism, but over time scholars (including Bebbington and Noll) have reordered the list in a variety of ways, generally without distorting Bebbington's basic analysis.

9. The wording of the questions asked of the evangelical and mainline Protestant silos differed for this particular question because the two research teams were interested in slightly different information. Both groups were asked whether the Bible is the "actual word of God," but the mainline question added "and is to be taken literally." If the two groups had been asked the same question, the response gap might have been narrower.

10. Mark A. Noll, *American Evangelical Christianity: An Introduction* (Malden, Mass.: Blackwell, 2000), 2; Candy Gunther Brown, *The Word in the World: Evangelical Writing, Publishing, and Reading in America, 1789–1880* (Chapel Hill: University of North Carolina Press, 2004), 1–7.

11. Matthew 28:19; John 3:3; Acts 2:1–4; 1 Corinthians 12:1–10. This volume uses lowercase letters for the terms *evangelical* and *pentecostal* as umbrella categories, but capital letters for certain subgroups (including *Pentecostals* and *Charismatics*) and other groups (for instance, *Nones*) in order to reduce confusion with other meanings of such terms. Scholars often refer to three "waves" of modern emphasis on the Holy Spirit: the first at the turn of the twentieth century with the Azusa Street revivals in Los Angeles, California; the second with the ecumenical Charismatic movement of the 1960s–1970s; and the third with the "signs and wonders" movements of the 1980s–1990s. Throughout this volume we capitalize the term *Pentecostal* when referring to classical Pentecostal denominations, such as the Assemblies of God, that trace their origins to Azusa Street. The lowercase term *pentecostal* functions as a shorthand way of referencing both Pentecostals and second- and third-wave Charismatics (both Protestant and Catholic) who emphasize the ongoing activity of the Holy Spirit in bestowing gifts (or *charismata*) similar to those (e.g., healing, glossolalia) described in Acts. The lowercase term *charismatic* is used where authors have in mind the sociologist Max Weber's influential theory of leadership; Weber, "The Sociology of Charismatic Authority," in *Max Weber: Essays in Sociology*, ed. and trans. H. H. Gerth and C. Wright Mills (New York: Oxford University Press, 1946).

12. Brown, *Word in the World*, 2–3.

13. Ibid., 34.

14. Ibid., 34–36.

15. Martin Marty, *Righteous Empire Revisited* (Worcester, Mass.: American Antiquarian Society, 2007); George M. Marsden, *Fundamentalism and American Culture: The Shaping of Twentieth-Century Evangelicalism, 1870–1925*, 2nd. ed. (New York: Oxford University Press, 2006), 6, 91.

16. Noll, *American Evangelical Christianity*, 19; Kenneth L. Woodward et al., "Born Again! The Year of the Evangelicals," *Newsweek*, October 25, 1976, 68–78; David Van Biema et al., "The 25 Most Influential Evangelicals in America," *Time*, February 7, 2005, cover story.

17. Dean M. Kelley, *Why Conservative Churches Are Growing: A Study in Sociology of Religion*, reprint ed. (Macon, Ga: Mercer University Press, 1996), xxv; Robert Wuthnow, *After Heaven: Spirituality in America Since the 1950s* (Berkeley: University of California Press, 1998), 59; Mark Chaves, *American Religion: Contemporary Trends* (Princeton, N.J.: Princeton University Press, 2011), 55–68.

18. Brown, *Word in the World*, 245–46.

19. Candy Gunther Brown, *The Healing Gods: Complementary and Alternative Medicine in Christian America* (New York: Oxford University Press, 2013), 10; Philip Jenkins, *The Next Christendom: The Coming of Global Christianity*, 3rd ed. (New York: Oxford University Press, 2011), 133.

20. Candy Gunther Brown, ed., *Global Pentecostal and Charismatic Healing* (New York: Oxford University Press), 3–8; Luis Lugo et al., *Spirit and Power: A 10-Country Survey of Pentecostals* (Washington, D.C.: Pew Forum on Religion & Public Life, October 2006), http://www.pewforum.org/Christian/Evangelical-Protestant-Churches/Spirit-and-Power.aspx, accessed August 3, 2015.

21. Robert Bruce Mullin, *Miracles and the Modern Religious Imagination* (New Haven, Conn.: Yale University Press, 1996), 13; Candy Gunther Brown, *Testing Prayer: Science and Healing* (Cambridge, Mass.: Harvard University Press, 2012), 65–66.

22. Brown, *Testing Prayer*, 29; Barna Group, "Is American Christianity Turning Charismatic?" January 7, 2008, http://www.barna.org/barna-update/article/18-congregations/52-is-american-christianity-turning-charismatic, accessed August 3, 2015. Critics have charged that the Barna survey overestimates the prevalence of pentecostals, and a lower (though still noticeably high) ratio of pentecostals, 23 percent of the U.S. population (who share "pentecostal markers" and/or self-identify as pentecostals), was reported by an older, national survey in 1992, analyzed by Corwin E. Smidt et al., "The Spirit-Filled Movements in Contemporary America: A Survey Perspective," in *Pentecostal Currents in American Protestantism*, ed. Edith L. Blumhofer, Russell P. Spittler, and Grant A. Wacker (Urbana: University of Illinois Press, 1999), 120.

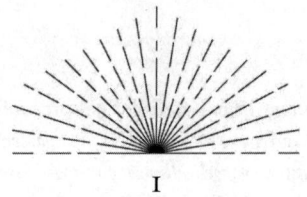

I

American Evangelicalism

CHARACTER, FUNCTION, AND TRAJECTORIES OF CHANGE

Michael S. Hamilton

The biggest surprise of the U.S. presidential election in 2008 was that Americans voted an African American into the White House. The second-biggest surprise was orchestrated by an evangelical minister. Before the official presidential debates between Barack Obama and John McCain, Pastor Rick Warren upstaged the national media and establishment power brokers by bringing both candidates to his Saddleback Church for a nationally televised question-and-answer session. This was the first time the two candidates had appeared onstage together since becoming their parties' presumptive nominees. There were no other politicians on the stage, no journalists asking questions, and no university presidents playing host. It was just Rick Warren choosing the topics and asking the questions, with Obama and McCain doing their best to give sincere answers—while the entire nation looked on. Nothing like this had ever before happened in a presidential campaign.[1]

The event was extraordinary, but the pastor and his church were not. Rick Warren (b. 1954) and Saddleback Church are not so much singular and unique as they are representative of American evangelicalism generally. Like the tip of an iceberg they are the highly visible portion of a much larger phenomenon. A close look at the visible portion tells us much about the rest of American evangelicalism—its demographic makeup, religious signatures, populist character, dual-mindedness, voluntary structure, and location in a global movement. Its chief organizational innovation—the parachurch agency—infused traditional evangelical Protestantism with American entrepreneurial energy and values.

American Evangelicalism

Put all the pieces together and it is clear that American evangelicalism is a synthesis of traditional evangelical Protestantism and American popular culture. As American culture changes, so does American evangelicalism. This helps account for the movement's newest trajectories—a humanitarian emphasis, a focus on personal well-being, the rapprochement with Roman Catholics, a flowering cosmopolitanism, and increasing traffic with a fast-changing global Christianity.

DEMOGRAPHICS

What brought McCain and Obama to Saddleback was the fact that tens of millions of Americans count themselves as evangelicals, and Warren is one of their most popular leaders. Between 2004 and 2006 several national news magazines declared that Warren was one of the most influential living Americans.[2] It makes sense that in 2008 both candidates felt that coming to Saddleback was an opportunity to win the votes of evangelicals and not to come was to risk losing them.

How many Americans are evangelicals? In an extensive survey in 2008, 34 percent of all American adults identified themselves as "born again or evangelical Christians." This added up to over 77 million people, not counting their children. Restrict the focus to the three-quarters of Americans who identify themselves as Christians and the percentages are substantially higher—45 percent of all American Christians are evangelicals, and 55 percent of all non-Catholic Christians are evangelicals. This was not always the case. In 1945 perhaps a third of Protestants were evangelicals, but by about 1990 half of all Protestants were evangelicals. Most evangelicals attend churches that are either independent or part of evangelical denominations, but the survey found unexpectedly large numbers in other denominational locations. Nearly two in five members of so-called mainline Protestant denominations identify themselves as evangelicals. Even more unexpected is that nearly one in five Catholics also call themselves evangelicals.[3] Since evangelicalism throughout history has been exclusively Protestant, this finding will be discussed more fully later in this chapter.

Given the large percentages of Americans who identify as evangelicals, it is not surprising that they are a diverse lot—as diverse, in fact, as America itself. In several categories evangelicals mirror national demographic averages more closely than does any other religious tradition. Evangelicals are slightly younger, and only very slightly more female, than the rest of the nation. All other Christian traditions in the United States are composed of larger percentages of women, while all non-Christian traditions are majority male. The levels of marriage, cohabitation, divorce, and childbearing among evangelicals are very close to national averages, and income and educational levels are only slightly lower than average. In racial and ethnic composition, evangelicals are less black, Asian, and Hispanic than America as a whole but are still closer to national averages than any other religious grouping except for the unaffiliated. This ability of evangelicalism to reach across lines of denomination, ethnicity, and social class has led many to call it America's "folk religion."[4]

RELIGIOUS SIGNATURES

When historian David Bebbington reconstructed the eighteenth-century origins of evangelicalism he identified four signatures of the faith: individual conversion and a personal relationship with Christ, biblical authority, the atoning work of Christ on the cross, and activism to spread the Gospel to unbelievers and strengthen the faith of believers. Nearly three hundred years later all four emphases are prominent at Saddleback Church. Warren made conversion the centerpiece of the church from the beginning, and in the first twenty years it logged twenty thousand conversions. The church has a ten-point statement of faith, one of which specifies that the Bible "is the supreme source of truth for Christian beliefs and living." Multiple Bible verses buttress all ten points. Six of the ten points have Jesus Christ at their center, emphasizing his divinity, his atonement for sin, and the need for a personal relationship with him as a prelude to eternal life. And finally, the activist nature of Saddleback's evangelicalism is evident across its website. The church advertises that it has "something for everyone," and its website offers members a cornucopia of church-sponsored activities through which to put their faith into action. As Warren once told his congregation, "If we can figure out a way to turn an audience into an army . . . it will change the world. It's time to stop debating and start doing."[5]

These primary signatures of evangelicalism are all religious—Saddleback's faith statement has not a whiff of politics or culture wars, even though its pastor has cultivated a political presence. Since 1970 evangelicals have received much attention for their political activities, and for good reason. But it is important to keep in mind that evangelicalism is primarily a religious movement. Its core religious values remain constant over time while its modes of relating to society and politics fluctuate with changes in American culture, a point that Amy Black elaborates in chapter 4 of this book.

Evangelical religious signatures have a strong hold on the religious thinking of ordinary Americans, and this does not seem to have diminished since the 1970s. This is when pollsters first became aware of evangelicalism and began exploring its dimensions in their surveys. In 1976 Gallup began asking Americans if they thought the Bible was the literal word of God, the inspired word of God, or a book of fables. The surveys found that 38 percent of Americans held the literalist view, with another 45 percent saying they believed the Bible was inspired by God. Both positions are common in evangelicalism and consistent with its theology. Since the 1970s there has been a slight decline in the literalist position among the general population, but this has been balanced by an increase in the inspiration position. The fable position remained stable at about 15 percent. Among young adults who attended churches in evangelical denominations between 1984 and 2002, a steady 54 percent believed that the Bible is literally God's word.[6]

In 1976 pollsters also began asking two other questions about the evangelical religious signatures—was there "a turning point in your life when you committed yourself to Jesus Christ?" and "have you ever tried to encourage someone to believe in Jesus Christ?" In 2005 a remarkable 48 percent of Americans answered yes to the first question (up from 35 percent in 1976), and an equally remarkable 52 percent said yes to the second question (up from 47 percent). Taken together, these figures suggest that evangelicals' core religious commitments have remained unchanged.[7]

Yet if the core commitments of evangelical belief remain the same, cultural shifts have prompted changes at the periphery. Since 1945 evangelicals have become much better educated and America has grown far more culturally diverse, and this appears to have had an impact on evangelical religious views. A 2003 survey found that 64 percent of biblical literalists believe that "all major religions contain some truth about God," and 58 percent of literalists believe that "God can only be known as people empty their minds and look inside themselves." The former view, if carefully nuanced, *can* be consistent with evangelical theology. But the latter view is not at all consistent with evangelical teachings, which stress that individuals can know God through his revelation in the Bible and through the work of the Holy Spirit in their lives. What these findings seem to show is that while core evangelical beliefs remain stable, individuals often interpret them in ways that permit them to adjust to the realities of American diversity and the complexities of modern culture.[8]

POPULISM

American evangelicalism has a populist character, meaning that it is oriented toward the ordinary people rather than social elites. This was on full display at the Saddleback Forum. Rick Warren came onto the stage dressed casually and so did Obama and McCain—not a necktie among them. Warren delivered his opening remarks in his usual folksy manner without teleprompter or notes, visibly more relaxed and less formal than the journalists who chair presidential debates. In the interviews Warren jumped straight to matters of a highly personal character, asking both senators to discuss their religious faith and their moral failings. Elites usually regard these matters as private and consider it bad form to ask about them. But Warren tacked to the values of ordinary evangelicals who care deeply about these questions. Passage from sin through repentance to salvation is the central evangelical narrative, and evangelicals expect every Christian to be able to talk publicly about this passage in his or her own life. Evangelicals also believe that genuine religious faith should make a difference in every aspect of one's life. When the Gallup Poll asks Americans how important religion is in their lives, both white and black evangelicals are far more likely than any other group to say "very important." Warren understood that his audience wanted the candidates to explain how their faith and moral values were important to them, so he came right out and asked.[9]

One feature of evangelical populism is that a leader's authority is conferred by the size of his or her audience. Warren was only twenty-six years old when he started Saddleback in a rented high school building. His success in attracting large numbers to his church led to invitations from Fuller Theological Seminary's Church Growth Institute to speak at their pastor training workshops. Warren's talks generated positive response from this new audience, so in 1988 he launched his own church growth workshops in California and around the nation. He used these to build a network of thousands of pastors and churches who looked to him for leadership. Then in 1995 Warren published *The Purpose Driven Church*, which distilled his church growth principles into five simple "purposes" of a healthy church. What he was now calling his "Purpose Driven Network" of churches bought tens of thousands of copies, and they spread the word to churches all over the country. The book eventually sold over a million copies—unprecedented for a book aimed at pastors. With his publisher pleading for a sequel, Warren adapted his church growth ideas into a set of spiritual growth principles for individuals, published in 2002 as *The Purpose Driven Life*. Warren marketed the book brilliantly by persuading some 1,500 churches in the network to sponsor congregation-wide "40 Days of Purpose" campaigns. This gave the book launch sales of a quarter million copies. Favorable publicity and word-of-mouth promotion made the book one of the best-selling nonfiction books of all time with well over 30 million copies in print. None of this had a thing to do with theological insight, politics, or culture wars. It was Warren's ability to articulate how to live the Christian life in a way that appealed to ordinary Americans that made him a leader in evangelicalism.[10]

Evangelical populism got its start back in the era of the early republic, when a generalized revolt against social elites democratized American Christianity and transformed the evangelical Methodists and Baptists into the nation's most popular religious traditions. Since that time populism has been a recurring impulse, helping shape several movements—Holiness, Pentecostal, fundamentalist—that are the antecedents of contemporary evangelicalism.[11]

A consequence of evangelical populism is that the movement takes its cues from popular culture. This means that evangelicalism is constantly being updated. Its leaders are those who can speak the language of the American people and develop ministry approaches that meet their needs. It also means that shifts in the general culture tend to produce parallel shifts in evangelicalism. A telling example is the most famous evangelical missionary hymn, *So Send I You*, written by Margaret Clarkson in 1936:

So send I you—to leave your life's ambitions,
To die to dear desire, self-will resign,

To labor long and love where men revile you,
So send I you—to lose your life in mine.

By 1963 the hymn's theme of suffering and self-denial—fitting for the depths of the Great Depression—was starting to seem out of step with an increasingly prosperous society. So Clarkson reworked it for an evangelicalism that found itself in a changed culture:

So send I you—by grace made strong; to triumph
O'er hosts of hell, o'er darkness, death and sin;
My name to bear, and in that name to conquer,
So send I you, my victory to win.[12]

Such examples could be multiplied indefinitely. Once rock and roll was here to stay, evangelical churches began to replace their organs with guitars and drums. Once Americans started to see the pursuit of personal happiness as the purpose of life, evangelicals began to think that Christianity ought to meet a believer's emotional and psychic needs. Beginning in the 1970s American evangelicals spoke less of self-denial and more of self-fulfillment. In the final analysis this close contact with popular culture has a dual effect. As evangelicalism adjusts to cultural changes it both incorporates those changes into its thinking and keeps itself relevant to new generations of ordinary Americans.[13]

DUAL-MINDEDNESS

Evangelicalism has a dual mentality—it is both heavenly minded and down-to-earth; it is both otherworldly and worldly wise. One of Rick Warren's central teachings was that a purpose-driven life is aimed at eternity but focused on the here and now. He also gave voice to the tensions of this dual-mindedness by attributing the popularity of his books to God's favor rather than to his carefully planned marketing strategy, which was specifically designed to maximize sales. When his books gave him a high profile he intentionally sought to capitalize on that to gain influence outside of evangelical circles. He did so by quietly cultivating relationships with nonevangelical elites in government, business, philanthropy, media, and entertainment. His outreach was effective, and his popularity made him a magnet for politicians. But here again his reflex was to explain his passage into elite circles as God's doing, not his own.[14]

This dual-mindedness allows evangelicals to think of themselves as a beleaguered minority living in a hostile culture despite the fact that they orient themselves toward many of the values of that culture. This way of thinking draws on biblical language that often portrays sharp contrasts between the evils of this world and the glories of the next. It also draws on a long-standing American tradition—religious groups often position themselves as outsiders as a way of distinguishing themselves from other groups for the purpose of building loyalty within. Dual-mindedness also helped foster the creation of a distinctive evangelical subculture. What began in the late nineteenth century as a few special organizations designed to spread the Gospel has become a web of schools, publishers, broadcasters, retreat centers, and merchandisers that cater to the already converted. It is a parallel institutional world that helps reinforce evangelicals' faith and also partially insulates them from the elements of American culture that might threaten their faith.[15]

VOLUNTARISM

American evangelicalism is a voluntary form of religion so it thrives where church and state are separated—a tradition Rick Warren affirmed in his opening remarks at the Saddleback Forum. When the state cut its ties to churches in the period of the early republic, the American people became sovereign in matters of religion. By choosing which churches and religious organizations to support, Americans select their own religious leaders. Therefore the religions that are most skilled at attracting popular support are the ones that flourish. In the early nineteenth century Congregationalists and Presbyterians still clung to the ideals of government-supported religion, but they were quickly surpassed in size by the more voluntary Baptists and Methodists. And by the middle of the twentieth century the evangelicals' reliance on their purely voluntary parachurch network helped them out-compete the more bureaucratically run mainline denominations. While the percentage of Americans connected to churches has remained about the same since 1950, the majority now choose to participate in evangelical churches that have perfected the art of voluntary popular appeal.[16]

The voluntary principle in America not only means choosing one's own religion, it also means one can choose to ignore religious boundaries between religions. A big reason for evangelicalism's popularity is its transdenominational appeal to the Bible as the only trustworthy religious authority. Although Saddleback Church is nominally affiliated with the Southern Baptist Convention, there is no mention of this anywhere on the church's website. Hardly any of its members would describe themselves as Southern Baptists. In 2009 Warren's website left open the question of denomination when giving advice to new converts about how to choose a church. But it did advise people to "avoid any church that does not accept the Bible as God's *complete* word. It's not the Bible plus our little book. It's not the Bible plus denominational traditions. It's not the Bible plus what some leader in the past said. It's just the Bible. The Bible is God's word!"[17]

This lines up with popular attitudes in two ways. First, Americans have long revered the Bible as "the inspired word of God"; and second, Americans' attachments to denominations have steadily weakened since 1950. Evangelicalism, with its Bible-oriented theology and its institutional networks of nondenominational megachurches and transdenominational parachurch organizations, has been well positioned to benefit from this shift.[18]

EVANGELICALISM AND ITS PARACHURCH ORGANIZATIONS

Evangelicalism harnesses popular support through entrepreneurial leadership. Warren—an irrepressibly self-confident protégé of management guru Peter Drucker—would have been an entrepreneur in whatever field he chose. His intense Christian faith steered him into religion, and in short order he grew his church of 150 people to over 22,000. It now has more than 200 separate ministry programs, some of which are worldwide in reach. Traditional religious denominations, like governments, typically rely on bureaucratic leadership, which favors stability, continuity, and institutionalized processes of decision making. By contrast, evangelical entrepreneurs like Warren are charismatic innovators skilled at marshaling human and economic resources to advance a vision for something new.

Once a new program strikes a vein of popular success, evangelical leaders expand operations and mine it as fast as they can. If the vein plays out, they drop that program and launch something bigger and better.[19]

The public face of evangelical entrepreneurialism is the megachurch (churches with weekly attendance of at least 2,000) led by a high-profile, charismatic, indefatigable "senior pastor" whose burning desire is to start new programs and grow them. As of 2011 there were some 1,600 megachurches in the United States, the largest of which has attendance topping 45,000. Like Saddleback, they often occupy multiple campuses, sponsor scores of ministry programs, employ dozens of full-time paid staff, and enlist hundreds of unpaid volunteers.[20]

Despite the high profile of megachurches, evangelicalism's most characteristic and important institution is the parachurch organization. These are independent, nondenominational not-for-profit organizations set up for specific religious purposes. Compared to the 1,600 megachurches there are perhaps 30,000 parachurch organizations in the United States, although nobody really knows how many there are. These are the main conduits of evangelical entrepreneurialism and activism. Many have been around for over a century, and some—for example, Cru (until 2011 called Campus Crusade for Christ) and World Vision—are among America's largest charitable organizations.[21]

HISTORICAL DEVELOPMENT OF THE EVANGELICAL PARACHURCH NETWORK

In the nineteenth century evangelicalism's institutional center of gravity was located in denominations, primarily the larger Baptist, Methodist, Presbyterian, Churches of Christ, and Congregationalist groups. But change was on the horizon. In 1844 one of the first modern parachurch organizations, the interdenominational Young Men's Christian Association (YMCA), was founded in London. The Boston branch of the YMCA opened in 1855, and it played a crucial role in the evangelical conversion of Dwight L. Moody (1837–1899). He took up full-time religious work and by the 1870s was the single most important evangelical leader in the English-speaking world. He encouraged talented evangelicals, both men and women, to channel their energies into parachurch organizations. They responded with energy, quickly building an impressive network of independent evangelization societies, missionary agencies, Bible institutes, summer Bible conferences, and publishing houses.[22]

Evangelicals and theological liberals universally respected Moody, but a generation after his death in 1899 the two parties fought a series of bitter battles over theology and control of the large northern Protestant denominations. In the end the denominations opted to permit theological pluralism. This decisively shifted evangelicalism's center of gravity away from the denominations and into the Moody network of independent churches and parachurch organizations. At the time this seemed like a disaster—evangelicals felt they had been robbed of their ecclesiastical inheritance. But the shift actually left evangelicalism better prepared for the future. American loyalty to denominations was starting to diminish, so control of the denominations was less important than it seemed at the time. Also, Americans were at that very moment embarking on a love affair with not-for-profit corporations as their preferred vehicle for charitable activity. As denominational attachments weakened and support for not-for-profits swelled, evangelicalism and its parachurch organizations were perfectly positioned to ride the wave.[23]

Billy Graham (b. 1918) continued building the parachurch network that Moody had begun. Graham attended college at three of the network's schools, the last being Wheaton College in Illinois. There he learned that, despite denominational divisions and theological disagreements, at the grass-roots level of American Protestantism there was a common-denominator Bible faith to which an evangelist could appeal. He also saw talented Wheaton graduates from his era forming new parachurch organizations, such as Christian Service Brigade, InterVarsity Christian Fellowship, and Youth for Christ (YFC). In 1944 Graham eagerly accepted an offer to become YFC's first paid evangelist, and his success in preaching at its massive young people's rallies led him to resign four years later to head up his own parachurch organization, the Billy Graham Evangelistic Association (BGEA). In subsequent years Graham and the BGEA supported the founding of dozens of other important parachurch organizations, including *Christianity Today* magazine, Gordon-Conwell Theological Seminary, Fuller Theological Seminary, Tyndale House publishers, Campus Crusade for Christ, Young Life, and Fellowship of Christian Athletes. Whether they know it or not, the founder

American Evangelicalism

of every present-day parachurch organization, from Medical Teams International to Christian Broadcasting Network, owes a direct debt to Moody and Graham.

THE PARACHURCH NETWORK AND THE DENOMINATIONS

Although this is a simplification, for some purposes it is helpful to think of most Protestant denominations as either *conservative* (some use the term *orthodox*) or *pluralist* (many use the term *mainline*). Conservative denominations typically hold to traditional understandings of the Bible, the classic orthodoxy of historic creeds (for example, the Apostles' Creed and Nicene Creed), and the belief that salvation is available only by God's grace through faith in Jesus Christ. Pluralist denominations permit more theological diversity on these matters. For example, a leader who publicly denied the physical resurrection of Jesus and interpreted the story as purely symbolic could retain his or her position in a pluralist denomination but probably not in a conservative denomination.

The pluralist denominations belong to the National Council of Churches and tend to dominate it. These include the American Baptist Church, Episcopal Church, Evangelical Lutheran Church in America, Presbyterian Church (USA), United Church of Christ, and United Methodist Church. The conservative denominations, by contrast, are a much larger and more diverse group. One category includes the denominations that dissent from the pluralism of their mainline cousins. Examples are the Southern Baptist Convention, Reformed Episcopal Church, Lutheran Church—Missouri Synod, Presbyterian Church in America, Churches of Christ, and Free Methodist Church. Other important categories, each with many denominations, are the Pentecostals (for instance, Assemblies of God, Church of God in Christ), Holiness denominations (Church of the Nazarene, Salvation Army), immigrant denominations (older arrivals such as the Christian Reformed Church and more recent arrivals such as the Korean Presbyterian Church in America), descendants of the 1960s Jesus movement (Calvary Chapel, Vineyard USA), other uniquely American-origin denominations (Seventh-Day Adventists), and various loose "fellowships" of independent churches (Independent Fundamental Churches of America, Independent Baptists).[24]

Evangelical parachurch organizations have the great advantage of being able to speak directly to people no matter what kind of church they attend, or if they attend none at all. They are like an offshore radio broadcaster that transmits across all state and national borders. Parachurch organizations have workers from many denominations, and the message they transmit is nondenominational. If you're a Presbyterian, they never ask you to give up your Presbyterianism. Instead, following the pattern of the YMCA, they ask you to focus on a generic form of evangelical Christianity and to join forces with other types of evangelicals to cooperate on various kinds of religious projects. Denominational particularities—for example, whether to baptize infants or believers—are treated as personal preferences that are secondary to the larger tasks of converting people to Christianity, enlivening the spiritually dormant, and drawing the already-persuaded into deeper commitments of service.

This direct connection between parachurch and individual is an important reason why many evangelicals can be found in churches affiliated with pluralist mainline denominations. An evangelical family in any church might subscribe to *Christianity Today* magazine; own copies of the International Bible Society's New International Version of the Bible; occasionally listen to James Dobson's (b. 1936) *Focus on the Family* broadcast on a local not-for-profit evangelical radio station; attend a weekly study group organized by Bible Study Fellowship; volunteer once a week at a Mothers of Pre-Schoolers (MOPS) International meeting; sponsor an orphan in Africa through World Vision; support a missionary in the Philippines working with Wycliffe Bible Translators; and spend two weeks of their summer vacation in Mexico helping build a house or church through Youth with a Mission (YWAM). Out of four children the oldest might attend evangelical Wheaton College; the second might be active in Inter-Varsity Christian Fellowship at her public university; the third might be active in his public high school's chapter of Young Life, and the youngest might attend a parent-directed elementary school affiliated with Christian Schools International.

In other words, the evangelical parachurch offers a dizzying array of specialized religious services and ministry opportunities that no single denomination can come close to providing. No surprise, then, that relations between evangelical denominations and the parachurch are often uneasy. Parachurch organizations promote a common-denominator evangelicalism that stresses the Bible, conversion, and active service on behalf of others. Evangelicals who are invested in a denomination's theology and programs often see the parachurch as a threat to draw away support and reshape the theology of its members. This is why most evangelical denominations have a history of struggling to a find a healthy balance between cooperating with the parachurch and fending off its encroachments.[25]

Because parachurch organizations undertake the kind of activities that formerly denominations alone conducted—for example, overseas church-building and development activities—they have for many churches supplanted denominations. This has made possible what appears to be the fastest-growing major sector of American Christianity—independent evangelical nondenominational churches. The first sophisticated attempt to count these was the U.S. Religious Census of the Religious Congregations and Membership Study in 2010, which found an extraordinary 35,496 independent congregations. Nondenominational churches are now the second-largest group of congregations in America (behind only the 50,816 of the Southern Baptist Convention) and the third largest in terms of numbers of people (after the Southern Baptists and the Roman Catholics). Together the Southern Baptist churches and the nondenominational churches constitute 25 percent of all American congregations (Christian and non-Christian) and 45 percent of all congregations affiliated with a conservative Christian tradition. Of all Americans who are connected to any kind of congregation (Christian or non-Christian), one in ten have chosen an evangelical nondenominational church.[26]

PARACHURCH FIELDS OF ACTIVITY

One good window into the parachurch world is the Evangelical Council for Financial Accountability (ECFA). This is a voluntary, member-run accrediting organization founded in 1979 to function as an evangelical "Better Business Bureau." To ensure compliance with its seven standards, the ECFA's central office audits members regularly. Almost all ECFA members are parachurch organizations and their subsidiaries. In 2015 the ECFA membership numbered 1,960 organizations.[27]

The ECFA membership is just a small sample of the parachurch world, but it includes nearly all the largest organizations. In terms of budgets, five of America's thirty largest charities are evangelical parachurch agencies, all of them ECFA members: the Salvation Army, World Vision, Cru, the National Christian Foundation, and Compassion International. In 2014 donors gave ECFA members $16 billion cash and several billion more of in-kind donations.[28]

At the more local end of the scale, however, only a small percentage of parachurch organizations belong to the ECFA. Nearly 7,000 evangelical elementary and secondary schools belong to the three largest national umbrella organizations, but only about 1 percent of these are ECFA members. Over a thousand pregnancy resource centers are members of the Care Net group, but only about 10 percent are members of ECFA. There are nearly a thousand members of the Christian Camp and Conference Association, but only 15 percent belong to the ECFA. There are some 300 local members of the Association of Gospel Rescue Missions, less than half of which are ECFA members. Also, some very large organizations are so decentralized that they have no national headquarters, and only a fraction of their individual units have joined the ECFA. For instance, of the more than two hundred Teen Challenge addiction treatment centers in the United States, less than 20 percent belong to the ECFA. And of the approximately 150 North American units of YWAM (noted for its short-term foreign mission projects), fewer than 5 are ECFA members. Taking into account both large and small organizations, a responsible guess would be that maybe 10 percent of evangelical parachurch organizations belong to the ECFA. Based on the total number of ECFA members and subsidiaries, this suggests that there are at least 30,000 parachurch agencies in the United States.[29]

The evangelical parachurch world thrives in large part because when it comes to donating money, American evangelicals are relatively generous. Americans in general donate more money than people in other developed countries, perhaps because the other advanced economies depend less on charity and more on taxation to fund social welfare programs. One study found that American evangelicals tend to give away 1 percent more of their annual income than Canadian evangelicals. Also, virtually all major studies of charitable giving have found that evangelicals are more generous than Americans in most other religious and nonreligious groupings—mainline Protestants, Catholics, non-Christians, and the nonreligious. Only sectarian groups with a strong communal identity—Mormons, for example—show higher rates of giving. The average evangelical reports giving away perhaps 6 to 8 percent of annual income. A large portion of this goes to local churches, some of which is passed on to parachurch organizations. Evangelicals also give substantial amounts directly to parachurch organizations as well as to nonreligious charities. The studies also show that the amount of giving correlates directly with three variables: Those who attend churches in the broad evangelical tradition tend to give more than those who attend mainline or Catholic churches. Those who hold typical evangelical religious beliefs tend to give more than those who do not. And finally, those who show high levels of church activity tend to give more than those who do not. The upshot of all this is that giving is a function of religious commitment. The stronger one's religious commitment, the greater one's giving, and evangelicals tend to show relatively high commitment levels.[30]

TRAJECTORIES OF CHANGE

The New Humanitarianism in Evangelical Mission

In the 1930s the evangelical parachurch network concentrated on religious activities—evangelism, Bible distribution, church planting, discipleship, and training of religious workers. This set evangelicals apart in the American not-for-profit world. But evangelical concerns broadened considerably after World War II to include all manner of humanitarian and social service work, and in the process parachurch organizations started to look more like mainstream American charities. Domestically this can be seen in the thousands of evangelical human services agencies that now dot the American landscape. But the shift is especially noticeable internationally—in 2011 seven of the eleven largest evangelical organizations specialized in global relief and development. The largest of the seven is World Vision, begun by Robert Pierce (1914–1978), an evangelist with Youth for Christ (the parachurch organization that launched the career of Billy Graham). An evangelistic tour of Asia in 1947 aroused Pierce's compassion for orphaned children, and he returned to the United States pleading with evangelicals to sponsor children abroad. Today World Vision is a multinational nonprofit with 40,000 workers that raises $2.79 billion worldwide for disaster relief and economic development work in nearly one hundred nations around the world. By 1978 there were so many evangelical relief organizations that they formed their own umbrella organization, Accord, which now has over sixty members.[31]

Since parachurch organizations are structured like businesses they tend to follow American business trends. Just as America's largest corporations are growing ever larger through diversification and internationalization, so too are parachurch organizations. In 1951 Bill and Vonette Bright started Campus Crusade for Christ (now Cru) to evangelize students at UCLA. The Brights always intended to expand to other campuses as quickly as possible, but soon Bill Bright (1921–2003)—another consummate entrepreneur—had his eyes on the entire world. Today Cru's multinational 25,000-person staff runs programs for evangelism, discipleship, education, relief, and development in just about every nation of the world. Its single most famous outreach project is the *Jesus Film*, a retelling of the Gospel of Luke that has been translated into over 1,000 languages and viewed billions of times around the globe. In 2014 U.S. revenues for all Cru programs totaled half a billion dollars, with another $150 million in international revenues.[32]

Just as small businesses produce half of America's jobs and gross domestic product, small parachurch organizations harness and direct much of evangelicalism's energy. New organizations are continually launched to seize newly discovered ministry opportunities and to meet neglected human needs. In 1995 Chris Clark, a staff worker with Youth for Christ, returned from a trip to Africa troubled by the continent's enormous orphan crisis. Despite all the evangelical secular agencies working with homeless children, Clark saw too many orphans still without help and hope. So like any good evangelical entrepreneur, he and his wife Debbie started their own organization, Children of the Nations (COTN). His home church in Washington state supplied all his initial staff and a substantial portion of the early finances. Today COTN has a budget of more than $7 million. Its 400 staff and thousands of volunteers provide services to 35,000 children in the Dominican Republic, Haiti, Liberia, Malawi, Sierra Leone, and Uganda.[33]

Together these three trends—the turn to human services, the rise of multinational mega-ministries, and the continual creation of new organizations—are producing a new convergence between the evangelical parachurch and mainstream American philanthropy. The impact of this convergence runs in both directions. The turn to this-worldly humanitarian service shows evangelicals operating much like other American charities. Older organizations are often changing their names to sound less evangelical and broaden their support base. But less obviously, the convergence is helping reshape American philanthropy. At home and abroad evangelicals are winning a new respect for the power of humanitarian service that is driven by religious concerns and that incorporates attention to people's spiritual longings. And Americans, by broadly supporting parachurch charities, are saying that they value both the entrepreneurial responsiveness and spiritual motivation that evangelical activists bring to humanitarian work.[34]

Meeting Personal Needs in Communal Settings

Before World War II Sunday morning in an evangelical church usually meant one of two worship styles: three hymns and a sermon of traditional churches or the ecstatic emotionalism of Pentecostal and Holiness churches. The former highlighted evangelism and instruction; the latter mediated the experience of the Holy Spirit. Evangelical churches with formal liturgy were few and far between. But in the 1960s the Pentecostal spirit began to leak out of Pentecostal churches. When this mingled with a new popular religious music descended from rock and roll, a new evangelical worship style was born—"praise and worship" (also known as "contemporary worship")—as Chris Armstrong details in chapter 2 of this volume. The central element is that amid a large group the worshipper has an experience of direct connection with God, an experience that is personal and joyful and meets the emotional needs of the worshipper. This is the baby boom generation's way of doing church, and it has spread well beyond evangelicalism. As sociologist Alan Wolfe once observed, this kind of personal, emotional, needs-centered approach to religion is now so ubiquitous in America that "we are all evangelicals now."[35]

This personal approach to religion also shows up in the proliferation of evangelical small groups in the late twentieth century. Layperson-led small groups for prayer, Bible study, and discipleship appear throughout evangelical history. New England Puritans had house meetings for adults and sometimes for young people. Early American Methodists made "class meetings" and "bands," often led by women, the cornerstone of their local assemblies. "Holiness bands," also often led by women, were central in the Holiness movement of the middle and late nineteenth century. Despite those antecedents, the twentieth-century spread of evangelical small groups had more immediate origins, both domestic and imported. Background influences included Plymouth Brethren house churches that originated in England in 1829; a mainline Protestant conversation in the 1940s and 1950s about using "cell groups" to revitalize the church; and Dietrich Bonhoeffer's descriptions of the fellowships of Confessing Church Christians during the Nazi regime.[36]

The more direct influences came from the proliferating parachurch network. Four organizations were especially important—InterVarsity Christian Fellowship (IVCF), Young Life, the Billy Graham Evangelistic Association, and Bible Study Fellowship. Founded in England in 1877, IVCF spread to Canada in 1928 through the work of Howard Guinness (1903–1979). He helped Canadian university students set up campus organizations that featured daily prayer gatherings and weekly Bible studies. When Wheaton College graduate C. Stacey Woods took over the leadership of IVCF-Canada, he brought on to the staff Jane Hollingsworth, another Wheaton graduate, who had learned the "inductive Bible study method" at Biblical Seminary in New York. Beginning in 1940 she and other staff members helped organize Bible study groups at dozens of universities throughout the United States and Canada. About the same time Jim Rayburn (1909–1970), formerly a student at Dallas Theological Seminary, founded Young Life, which sponsored home-based fellowship clubs for high school students in hundreds of U.S. communities. From its earliest days in the late 1940s and early 1950s, Billy Graham's staff organized local groups that would begin praying for crusades months in advance. After the San Francisco crusade of 1958 they asked Audrey Wetherell Johnson (1907–1984), a former missionary with China Inland Mission, to bring her Southern California–based home Bible study program, begun in 1952, to the Bay Area as a follow-up to the crusade. With initial organizational help from BGEA she and her staff spread Bible study groups throughout the Bay Area. A year later she incorporated her own organization, Bible Study Fellowship, which by 2015 sponsored over a thousand local fellowship groups on six continents.[37]

The idea that evangelical churches ought to make small groups integral to their program took hold in the 1970s. Larry Richards of Wheaton College, prominent in the field of Christian education, argued in a landmark 1970 book that "the small group" is "the basic building block of the life of the gathered church." Members of the countercultural Jesus Movement, who had long favored home-based fellowships, began moving into churches like Calvary Chapel and brought their preference for informality and decentralization with them. Then a few years later the Charismatic movement took the idea and ran with it. At the Graham-sponsored International Congress of World Evangelization in Lausanne in 1974, the Argentine Assemblies of God pastor Juan Carlos Ortiz reported on phenomenal church growth in Buenos Aires after setting up a "small cell group" structure. His address received so much attention that Ortiz quickly wrote two books for American audiences that became immediate best-sellers. Later promoters of using "cell groups" who influenced evangelicals included Korean Assemblies of God pastor David Yonggi Cho (b. 1936) and Ralph W. Neighbour (b. 1929), a Southern Baptist missionary to Singapore.[38]

Prompted by these influences, evangelical churches in the 1980s began to sponsor Bible study and prayer groups as vehicles for spiritual growth and congregational revitalization, and their numbers exploded. By the 1990s 40 percent of American adults belonged to a small group, and another 12 percent either had recently belonged or were planning to join one in the near future. These percentages translate into 115 million people, two-thirds of whom reported that their groups are religious in nature. This small-group religion is overwhelmingly evangelical regardless of the denomination of the participants. Religious small groups are one of the main engines spreading the belief that the Bible is literally true. Small groups also support the idea that everyone can have a personal relationship with God and that God cares so deeply about every individual that he will answer their prayers in supernatural ways. Small-group members said that they joined small groups searching for community and deeper spirituality, but the main thing they reported gaining was an improved sense of emotional well-being. Like praise and worship church services, religious small groups are valued most for the way they meet participants' spiritual and emotional needs.[39]

Evangelical megachurches are also intentionally organized around meeting individuals' felt needs. Back in the 1950s aspiring pastor Robert Schuller (b. 1926) surveyed neighborhoods in Orange County, California, to learn who was not attending church and why. He then designed his

Crystal Cathedral to attract those people by addressing the needs they had expressed. Bill Hybels (b. 1951) used the same technique in 1975 in launching Willow Creek Community Church in the Chicago-area suburbs, and Rick Warren followed suit five years later. Schuller led his church down a road pioneered by Norman Vincent Peale (1898–1993), preaching a thin-broth Christianity that promised happiness through positive thinking; however, the ministry declared bankruptcy in 2010, selling its elaborate edifice to a Roman Catholic diocese in 2011. Hybels took a different path, retaining the full evangelical theological framework that stressed sin, repentance, and conversion. His goal was to take that framework and make it newly relevant for suburban nonchurchgoers. The result was Willow Creek's pioneering dual structure. The Sunday "Seeker Service" introduced Christianity in a comfortable setting by showing how it applies to problems suburbanites face. Then on every other day of the week the church offered an enormous range of services, activities, and small groups designed to deepen people's faith and teach them how to put it into action. The formula bred success, quickly transforming Willow Creek into one of America's largest and most influential churches. True to its origins, Willow Creek continued to keep its finger on the pulse of what its people say they need. When congregational surveys in 2004 and 2007 showed that a substantial number of faithful members reported that they were not growing spiritually, the leadership responded by reconceiving the church as "personal trainer" for spiritual improvement. The new goal is to teach people how to take responsibility for their own spiritual growth so they can become better disciples of Jesus Christ.[40]

Rapprochement Between Evangelicals and Roman Catholics

Wycliffe Bible Translators is one of the largest evangelical parachurch organizations, founded by William Cameron Townsend (1896–1982). He began his missionary career in 1917 in Guatemala, where, like every other evangelical, he thought of Catholicism as an enemy of the faith. Missionary work in Latin America was based on the assumption that people in those "priest-ridden, Rome-blighted lands" were "as much in the need of the Gospel as any heathen in the world." But by 1948 Townsend required his missionaries in Latin America to support the work of Catholic priests whenever possible, and in 1966 he fought long and hard to get his mission directors to accept a Catholic seminarian as a Wycliffe missionary. Billy Graham made a similar shift. In 1950 his organization insisted it would never refer a crusade convert to a Catholic church, but seven years later Graham reversed that policy. In 1962 his organization denied that priests would ever participate in a crusade, but by the 1980s priests regularly served on crusade planning committees, helped train counselors, and appeared on the platform. The change was undoubtedly helped along in 1964 when, during the Boston crusade, Cardinal Richard Cushing (1895–1970) invited Graham to appear with him on local television. Cushing praised Graham and his crusades, assured him that Catholics would be praying for him, and urged Catholic young people to attend the crusade. "I'm one hundred percent for Dr. Graham," said Cushing. "The hand of God must be upon him." Graham returned the sentiments, lavishing compliments on Cushing, Pope John XXIII, Pope Paul VI, and the Second Vatican Council, which was then under way.[41]

The ecumenical journeys of these three men paralleled the journeys of many ordinary Catholics and evangelicals. By the mid-1950s most Protestants had ceased to see Catholicism as un-American, and most Catholics had ceased to see America as an environment hostile to their faith. Vatican II (1962–1965) knocked down many of the final barriers guarding the border. It acknowledged Protestants as Christian brothers, committed itself to separation of church and state, stressed the role of Christ as mediator between God and humanity, defined the "church" as its people, not its hierarchy, and urged Catholics to be more active in private devotions, Bible study, and evangelization.[42]

Other cultural changes accelerated the traffic across the border. Christianity expanded rapidly in Africa and Asia, distant from the sites of historic Catholic-Protestant conflict. Catholics and Protestants in Africa and Asia were less inclined to perpetuate that conflict, and cooperation in those regions modeled new possibilities. The Charismatic movement of the 1960s and 1970s, in which Pentecostalism spilled out of its denominational confines, gave many Christians in evangelical, mainline, and Catholic churches a common spirituality and worship style. The concurrent rise of the counterculture, with its informality and anti-institutionalism, further diminished all types of denominational divisions. And from the Catholic side, John Paul II, pope from 1978 to 2005, put a strong priority on interfaith cooperation.[43]

The emergence of the religious Right and the onset of the culture wars in the 1980s gave the Catholic-evangelical rapprochement its most public expression—the *Evangelicals and Catholics Together* (ECT) document of 1995. The major premises of the religious Right are that abortion and sexual immorality are on the rise while absolute moral values and the nuclear family are in decline; that these trends are due to ongoing governmental suppression of religion in education and public life; and that these trends can be reversed by organizing religious coalitions into democratic majorities that can bring about change in governmental policies. The evangelical writer Francis Schaeffer (1912–1984) popularized the idea of organizing evangelicals, Catholics, and others for common political action in the 1970s and early 1980s. He called this the principle of "cobelligerence," and it was first embodied in the Moral Majority, an action organization founded in 1979 by the evangelical minister Jerry Falwell (1933–2007).[44]

The instigators of ECT were Richard John Neuhaus (1936–2009) and Charles Colson (1931–2012). Neuhaus was a former Lutheran minister who had become a Catholic priest and a neoconservative intellectual. Colson, a former Nixon White House aide who converted to evangelicalism, spent time in prison for Watergate crimes, founded the parachurch agency Prison Fellowship Ministries, and then helped spread the ideas of Francis Schaeffer. It was primarily the cause of cobelligerence in the culture wars that led them to initiate the ECT project. But many of the ECT's other thirteen authors and twenty-five original endorsers were more interested in shifting the focus of evangelical-Catholic relations away from differences toward shared beliefs, historical roots, and mutual enrichment. This produced a furious backlash by a minority group of all-male evangelical leaders whose bread and butter had always been doctrinal purity. Their protests rehearsed traditional anti-Catholic arguments and led to a drop-off in donations to Prison Fellowship Ministries and to Campus Crusade for Christ, whose founder, Bill Bright, had endorsed ECT.[45]

The drop in donations was only temporary, however, for it represented the views of a shrinking minority. At the grassroots level evangelicals and Catholics had been interacting and cooperating for many years before ECT. The transdenominational logic of evangelical parachurch organizations meant that once Catholicism came to be considered just another denomination, evangelicals would start appealing to and incorporating Roman Catholics. At least since the 1960s Catholics and evangelicals—especially women—have participated together in thousands of neighborhood Bible study groups. Catholic bookstores began carrying many evangelical titles, and evangelical bookstores began carrying a few Catholic books. Simplified versions of the Bible popular with evangelicals—the Good News Bible (1966; with deuterocanonicals, 1979) and the Living Bible (1971; with deuterocanonicals, 1976), and *The Message* (2002; with deuterocanonicals, 2013)—proved popular with Catholics. Many evangelical parachurch agencies—InterVarsity, Young Life—and a few colleges, such as Seattle Pacific University, treated Catholics just the same as Christians from any other denomination. As of 2016 there were still a few evangelical holdouts. Wheaton College, for example, dug in on the side of the doctrinal purists. In 2004 it fired a faculty member for converting to Catholicism, and in 2010 it chose a leader of the Alliance of Confessing Evangelicals, a leading opponent of ECT, as its new president. But on this question Wheaton's leadership was out of step with most of evangelicalism. The wider Catholic-evangelical cooperation kept spreading and proved mutually beneficial. Catholics valued the vitality of evangelical personal faith and its multidimensional tradition of active lay ministry, and evangelicals valued Catholicism's historical depth, liturgical richness, and aesthetic engagement.[46]

The New Evangelical Cosmopolitanism

For all the populist characteristics of evangelicalism, a contrary trend emerged after the 1970s—a new cosmopolitanism. Substantial numbers of evangelicals began moving into the elite levels of society by virtue of their education at prestige institutions and their high positions in major corporations, government, education, media, entertainment, and the military. Although their religious beliefs are similar to those of their populist cousins, their educational background and social position put them ill at ease with evangelical anti-elitism. Rick Warren, for instance, is by nature and background a populist, but his expanding contacts with more cosmopolitan elites have modulated this. Shortly after becoming famous he started a weekly, by-invitation-only conference call Bible study with over a hundred influential business, government, and cultural leaders. Whatever impact Warren had on them, it is clear that they also had an impact on him. He toned down his concerns about gay marriage and, urged on by his wife

Kay, began urging Christians to concern themselves with poverty, HIV/AIDS, and global warming. He went back to the Bible and, as he tells it, "found those 2,000 verses on the poor. How did I miss that? I went to Bible college, two seminaries, and I got a doctorate. How did I miss God's compassion for the poor?" The answer, of course, is that before Warren started moving in elite circles, the populist evangelicals he spent time with focused on different parts of Scripture. But after he became a national figure his new relationships with cosmopolitan evangelicals taught him new ways of reading the Bible.[47]

Populists see themselves as outside the power structure of society, while elites see themselves as insiders. Evangelicals with an outsider mentality are more likely to launch mass crusades protesting something they dislike, while elites are more likely to use their institutional positions and personal connections to influence change. For example, the modus operandi of the American Family Association is to employ mass boycotts to oppose sex and violence in the media. By contrast, when a group of evangelicals among senior White House and congressional staffers decided to do something about sex and violence in the media, they arranged meetings between high-ranking government officials and media and business executives. Rather than go public and whip up a crowd, they preferred to informally persuade media leaders to be more sensitive on the subject. These meetings also produced new initiatives, including a Harvard study of the media's effect on children.[48]

The key characteristic of evangelical cosmopolitanism—a noncombative stance toward mainstream society—had become well entrenched among evangelical young adults by the twenty-first century. This can be seen in the agenda of the so-called Emergent Church and wider emerging church movement, which is driven by two impulses. The first is a desire to opt out of old conservative-liberal polarities. Emerging Christians have little interest in fighting battles against theological error, nor in focusing Christianity on the next life rather than this one, nor in maintaining moral purity by separating from mainstream culture, nor in politicizing Christianity to fight culture wars. The second impulse is a desire for a Christianity that is engaged with the world in a way that encounters contemporary ideas, art, literature, and music. Those who identify with the movement tend to prefer dialogue over confrontation. They care about the environment, poverty, and violence. They affirm the authority of the Bible but want new ways of reading it, often emphasizing stories that engage the emotions and are adaptable to individual application. They experiment with new ways of doing church, often borrowing from liturgical traditions to incorporate arts, literature, and music in ways designed to meet what the congregation feels it needs. In this regard the emerging church movement is an expression of evangelicalism's general reorientation to the protean demands of the self. This shows clearly in the title of a book by the movement's most celebrated spokesperson, Brian McLaren (b. 1956): *A Generous Orthodoxy: Why I Am a Missional, Evangelical, Post/Protestant, Liberal/Conservative, Mystical/Poetic, Biblical, Charismatic/Contemplative, Fundamentalist/Calvinist, Anabaptist/Anglican, Methodist, Catholic, Green, Incarnational, Depressed-Yet-Hopeful, Emergent, Unfinished Christian* (2006).[49]

The transition toward the values of social elites helped precipitate changes in evangelical moral views. Evangelicals firmly believe that to be a "Christian" is to be different from everyone else, especially in morals—Christian morality is superior to "worldly" morality, and Christian moral living ought to distinguish Christians from non-Christians. In the abstract, evangelicals tend to believe that God sets and the Bible reveals moral values, and that they are therefore universal and unchanging. Yet evangelical moral values have always been subject to change over time. Dancing, drinking, moviegoing, and card-playing were widely forbidden before World War II, but since then those prohibitions have largely been abandoned. More recently, some studies are finding that young evangelicals are more permissive than their elders on same-sex marriage, premarital sex, cohabitation, and pornography, and more apt to regard environmental and economic justice issues as part of the biblical moral mandate.

Whenever such changes are under way, it is common for some evangelicals to worry that the "erosion" of older "moral boundaries" threatens evangelicals' "identity as a distinctive moral and religious community." But the reality is not so simple. The moral values of the general society also change over time, so even a changing evangelicalism can remain distinctive from the rest of society. On recent sexual issues, young evangelicals are still less permissive than their nonevangelical peers. Moreover, changes within evangelicalism do not always move in a more permissive direction. In the mid-1960s evangelicals were fairly permissive on abortion, but ten years later they had become quite restrictive. And even the young evangelicals who are liberalizing on sexual issues remain as conservative as their elders on abortion. Although evangelicals think that their moral values ought to remain constant, in fact they are always renegotiating them in light of the changing moral values of the culture. This is possible because the Bible is not an unambiguous moral guidebook but rather an adaptable source of principles. The two evangelical constants are that moral positions must have biblical support and must be distinctive from the values of the broader society.[50]

Evangelicalism and the Global Church

Evangelicals get their name from their emphasis on evangelism, so why did they begin supporting parachurch-sponsored humanitarianism? The new cosmopolitanism is part of the answer, but there were deeper forces at work. As evangelicals ramped up their religious work in the 1940s and 1950s, they encountered pressing human needs among those they hoped to convert. It took them longer to learn that cross-cultural evangelism usually produces only limited results. Evangelism is most successful when the evangelist is from the same people group as those being evangelized. Consider the case of Prison Fellowship Ministries. Its original purpose was simple—to evangelize prisoners and guide them toward Christian living. But as the ministry confronted prisoners' complex this-worldly needs, it began to expand its activities, providing education, family support, postrelease mentoring, family reconciliation, guidance for churches on how to help former prisoners, and advocacy for legal reforms. It also has learned that the most effective prison evangelists are prisoners and former prisoners, so it now has programs to train prisoners for Christian leadership. And it works to overcome ethnic barriers through special programs to recruit and train Hispanic leaders and mentors to work with Hispanic prisoners and ex-convicts.[51]

The same realities have shaped evangelical organizations that work abroad. They have stepped up relief and development work because they cannot, in Christian conscience, stand idle while disease and destitution exact a heavy toll from those they came to serve. But it also became clear that the only truly effective evangelists were indigenous evangelists. Cross-cultural missionaries will win a few initial converts, but then, writes historian Mark Noll, the movement from Christian beachhead to functioning Christian community is almost always the work of local Christians. Korean revivalists; African prophets, catechists and Bible women; Indian preachers and bishops; Latin American priests; Pentecostal preachers and cell group leaders; South Sea Islander chiefs and teachers; imprisoned Chinese apostles—these are the human agents that over the last century and a half have transformed Christianity from a Western to a genuinely world religion.

Thanks to the effectiveness of indigenous preachers, 75 percent of the world's evangelicals now live in Africa, Asia, and Latin America. Global evangelicalism exhibits many of the same basic characteristics as North American evangelicalism—it is a collection of grassroots mass movements that are conversionist, voluntarist, entrepreneurial, and transdenominational. This is not primarily because America has exported its religion but because the conditions that favor evangelical-style Christianity now prevail in Africa, Asia, and Latin America.[52]

As evangelical Christianity became a global religion, evangelical organizations themselves internationalized. World Concern, the relief-and-development arm of Crista Ministries, operates in twenty-four countries with over 1,000 full-time employees—95 percent of them nationals. Children of the Nations, mentioned earlier, established a national governing board and hired national staff for each of its projects, limiting the American role to consulting.[53]

Another new evangelical direction is the advent of short-term missions. Sociologist Robert Wuthnow estimates that 20 to 25 percent of American churchgoers will, at least once in their lives, travel abroad for a religious service project lasting a few days to a few months. In the old days becoming a missionary was a lifetime calling reserved to the most dedicated. Then in the 1960s evangelical college students began going on summer mission projects, and soon some entrepreneurs organized new parachurch organizations such as YWAM around the idea. By the 1980s ordinary churchgoers wanted to have a personal involvement in missions, and soon all ages were getting into the act. What professional missionaries at first objected to as "sanctified tourism" has proven to be an effective way to assemble a team of workers to complete a finite project like construction or mass inoculation in a short period of time. It has, moreover, turned into a great fund-raising strategy. People who go on short-term mission projects develop a personal connection to the organization's work and often become long-term financial supporters. But the deepest impact of short-term missions is that they give ordinary American believers an on-the-ground experience with the lives of believers in the non-Western world. They learn that though Christians in Malawi may be poor, they are defined not by their poverty but by their personalities, their families, and their faith. The thousands of Americans who have spent their two-week vacations not touring the art museums of Florence but building orphan homes in the Dominican Republic have returned to America with a new awareness that evangelical Christianity is not an American but a global religion.[54]

One does not, however, need to travel to Korea to learn that evangelicalism is global. The Korean evangelicals are coming to the United States—as are Christians from Mexico, China, Iran, India, and dozens of other nations. The United States was mostly closed to immigration between 1924 and 1965, but since then large numbers of immigrants have arrived, especially from Latin America and Asia but also from Africa and the Middle East. Fully two-thirds of these new immigrants are Christians, and the overwhelming majority of Protestants are evangelicals. As ordinary Christians migrate from, say, Brazil to Boston, Brazilian missionaries, evangelists, and pastors accompany them. The United States may still send out more missionaries than any other nation (though South Korea and India are close behind), but more missionaries also *come* to the United States than to any other country. There is no doubt that immigration is introducing a new diversity into American evangelicalism; it seems likely that immigration will also reinvigorate American evangelicalism.[55]

CONCLUSION

American evangelicalism is so tightly interlocked with American culture that cultural change will always stimulate religious change, and vice versa. Some developments are quite recent—for example, the evangelicalism of emotional well-being is obviously tracking the sharp rise in self-concern among Americans that pollsters have documented since the 1970s. Other characteristics entered evangelicalism generations ago. Evangelicals got their populism just after the American Revolution when people were besotted with the idea of liberty, and evangelicals were turning talented preachers into national celebrities as far back as the colonial era. As for politics, its importance in evangelicalism has ebbed and flowed over the years. As recently as the 1930s many evangelicals were thoroughly apolitical, interested only in religion. And when politics has been important, evangelical views have fluctuated wildly between the radical progressivism of abolitionism and the tenacious conservatism of the pro-life movement. But the many changes notwithstanding, some elements of evangelicalism have remained immutable since the movement took shape in eighteenth-century Europe. These are the elements at its religious core. Evangelicalism in all times and places has been about the truth of the incarnation, crucifixion, and bodily resurrection of Jesus Christ. It has been about the Bible that preserves and explains these truths and applies them to the human condition. It has been about the spiritual rebirth necessary for living as a disciple of Jesus. And it has been about doing whatever is necessary to bring people of all races, places, and times into fellowship as Christian believers. The centrality and persistence of this religious core ensures that evangelicalism's relationship to American society will always be something of a paradox—at one moment uncritically adopting American ways but at the next moment standing apart, holding out an alternative vision for how Americans ought to live.

NOTES

1. The Saddleback Civic Forum on the Presidency took place on August 17, 2008. A transcript is at http://transcripts.cnn.com/TRANSCRIPTS/0808/17/se.01.html; the full broadcast can be viewed in seventeen segments beginning at http://www.youtube.com/watch?v=6YbmiZpJkPU; both accessed August 3, 2015.

2. Jefferey L. Sheler, "Preacher with a Purpose," *U.S. News & World Report*, October 31, 2005; Sonja Steptoe, "Rick Warren: A Pastor with a Purpose," in "The Time 100: The Lives and Ideas of the World's Most Influential People," *Time*, April 18, 2005; Jerry Adler et al., "The Giving Back Awards: 15 People Who Make America Great," *Newsweek*, July 3, 2006.

3. Barry A. Kosmin and Ariela Keysar, *The American Religious Identification Survey (ARIS 2008): Summary Report* (Hartford, Conn.: Trinity College, 2009), http://commons.trincoll.edu/aris/files/2011/08/ARIS_Report_2008.pdf, 2, 5, 9, accessed August 3, 2015. For changes since 1945, see Michael S. Hamilton, "More Money, More Ministry: The Financing of American Evangelicalism Since 1945," in *More Money, More*

Ministry: Money and Evangelicals in Recent North American History, ed. Larry Eskridge and Mark A. Noll (Grand Rapids, Mich.: Eerdmans, 2000), 109–10; for trends among young adults since the 1970s, see Robert Wuthnow, *After the Baby Boomers: How Twenty- and Thirty-Somethings are Shaping the Future of American Religion* (Princeton, N.J.: Princeton University Press, 2007), 77–84.

4. Luis Lugo, et al., *U.S. Religious Landscape Survey* (Washington, D.C.: Pew Research Center, February 2008), 36–71, http://www.pewforum.org/files/2013/05/report-religious-landscape-study-full.pdf, accessed August 3, 2015. In this report, "evangelicals" are people who attached to denominations that the Pew researchers have classified as evangelical, whereas in the ARIS report "evangelicals" are people who self-identify as such. The Pew researchers classified all "historically black Protestant churches" into a separate category, so none of these people are classified as evangelicals—despite the fact that many of them show up as evangelicals in the ARIS report. This means that the racial and ethnic makeup of self-identified evangelicals is surely closer to the national average than is shown in the Pew report. For a vivid example of the diversity of self-identifications *within* each denomination, see Christian Smith et al., *American Evangelicalism: Embattled and Thriving* (Chicago: University of Chicago Press, 1998), 241. On American "folk religion," see Randall Balmer, *Mine Eyes Have Seen the Glory: A Journey into the Evangelical Subculture in America*, 4th ed. (New York: Oxford University Press, 2006), 7.

5. David W. Bebbington, *Evangelicalism in Modern Britain: A History from the 1730s to the 1980s* (London: Unwin Hyman, 1989), 2–17; "What We Believe," https://saddleback.com/visit/about/what-we-believe, accessed August 3, 2015; Jeffery L. Sheler, *Prophet of Purpose: The Life of Rick Warren* (New York: Doubleday, 2009), 173; Rick Warren, "The Church Must Take Action," http://ministrytodaymag.com/index.php/features/19793-our-global-mission-peace-on-earth, accessed August 3, 2015.

6. Albert L. Winseman, "U.S. Evangelicals: How Many Walk the Walk?" May 31, 2005, http://www.gallup.com/poll/16519/US-Evangelicals-How-Many-Walk-Walk.aspx, accessed August 3, 2015; Wuthnow, *After the Baby Boomers*, 96–101, 110–211.

7. Winseman, "U.S. Evangelicals."

8. Wuthnow, *After the Baby Boomers*, 103–7.

9. Virginia Lieson Brereton, *From Sin to Salvation: Stories of Women's Conversions, 1800 to the Present* (Bloomington: Indiana University Press, 1991), 43–60; Frank Newport, "Who Are the Evangelicals?" June 24, 2005, http://www.gallup.com/poll/17041/who-evangelicals.aspx, accessed August 3, 2015.

10. Nathan O. Hatch, "Evangelicalism as a Democratic Movement," in *Evangelicalism and Modern America*, ed. George Marsden (Grand Rapids, Mich.: Eerdmans, 1984), 71–82; Sheler, *Prophet of Purpose*, 100–120, 140–41, 156–91; Lea Goldman, "By the Numbers: Top-Earning Authors," *Forbes*, December 8, 2006, http://www.forbes.com/2006/12/08/top-earning-authors-tech-media_cz_lg_books06_1208authors_slide_5.html?thisSpeed=29000, accessed August 3, 2015.

11. Nathan O. Hatch, *The Democratization of American Christianity* (New Haven, Conn.: Yale University Press, 1989), esp. 210–19.

12. Hatch, "Evangelicalism as a Democratic Movement," 78–80; "So Send I You: Margaret Clarkson's Life of Triumphant Praise," Wheaton [College] Archives and Special Collections Exhibit Gallery, http://www2.wheaton.edu/learnres/ARCSC/exhibits/clarkson/, accessed August 3, 2015.

13. Michael S. Hamilton, "The Triumph of the Praise Songs: How Guitars Beat Out the Organ in the Worship Wars," in *Worship at the Next Level: Insight from Contemporary Voices*, ed. Tim A. Dearborn and Scott Coil (Grand Rapids, Mich.: Baker Books, 2004), 74–85; Nathan O. Hatch and Michael S. Hamilton, "Taking the Measure of the Evangelical Resurgence, 1942–1992," in *Reckoning with the Past: Historical Essays on American Evangelicalism from the Institute for the Study of American Evangelicals*, ed. D. G. Hart (Grand Rapids, Mich.: Baker Books, 1995), 401–4, 410–12. On the general ascendency of self-fulfillment and self-expression, see Ronald Inglehart and Pippa Norris, *Rising Tide: Gender Equality and Cultural Change Around the World* (Cambridge: Cambridge University Press, 2003), 149–59; and Jean M. Twenge, *Generation Me: Why Today's Young Americans Are More Confident, Assertive, Entitled—and More Miserable than Ever Before* (New York: Free Press, 2006). On the impact of these values on American religion and especially evangelicalism, see Alan Wolfe, *The Transformation of American Religion: How We Actually Live Our Faith* (New York: Free Press, 2003), 1–36.

14. Grant Wacker, *Heaven Below: Early Pentecostals and American Culture* (Cambridge, Mass.: Harvard University Press, 2001), 8–17; Sheler, *Prophet of Purpose*, 212–24; D. Michael Lindsay, *Faith in the Halls of Power: How Evangelicals Joined the American Elite* (New York: Oxford University Press, 2007), 1–2, 12.

15. R. Laurence Moore, *Religious Outsiders and the Making of Americans* (New York: Oxford University Press, 1986), 150–72; 201–10; Balmer, *Mine Eyes Have Seen the Glory*, 3–11; Randall Balmer, *The Making of Evangelicalism: From Revivalism to Politics and Beyond* (Waco, Tex.: Baylor University Press, 2010), 43–58.

16. Roger Finke and Rodney Stark, *The Churching of America 1776–2005: Winners and Losers in Our Religious Economy*, rev. and exp. ed. (New Brunswick, N.J.: Rutgers University Press, 2005).

17. Saddleback Community Church, "How to Find a Church," 2009, http://docs.google.com/document/d/1IRJTc68EWws202Ha6ElOFWthfuvTySX-Th7qJmXaJh8/edit?pli=1, accessed August 3, 2015. Emphasis in the original.

18. Frank Newport, "One-Third of Americans Believe the Bible Is Literally True," May 25, 2007, http://www.gallup.com/poll/27682/onethird-americans-believe-bible-literally-true.aspx, accessed August 3, 2015; Robert Wuthnow, *The Restructuring of American Religion: Society and Faith Since World War I* (Princeton, N.J.: Princeton University Press, 1988), 71–172; Michael S. Hamilton, "Willow Creek's Place in History," *Christianity Today* 13, no. 44 (November 13, 2000): 62–68.

19. Julia Boorstin, "The Best Advice I Ever Got," *Fortune* 151, no. 6 (March 21, 2005).

20. Scott Thumma and Dave Travis, *Beyond Megachurch Myths: What We Can Learn from America's Largest Churches* (San Francisco: Jossey-Bass, 2007), 1–20; Hartford Institute for Religion Research, "Megachurch Definition," http://hirr.hartsem.edu/megachurch/definition.html, accessed August 3, 2015.

21. Wesley Kenneth Willmer, J. David Schmidt, and Martyn Smith, *The Prospering Parachurch: Enlarging the Boundaries of God's Kingdom* (San Francisco: Jossey-Bass, 1998), xi–xiv, 3–60; Hamilton, "More Money, More Ministry," 110–13, 118–30.

22. For a history of antebellum not-for-profit religious organizations, see David Paul Nord, *Faith in Reading: Religious Publishing and the Birth of Mass Media in America* (New York: Oxford University Press, 2004).

23. Robin Klay and John Lunn, with Michael S. Hamilton, "American Evangelicalism and the National Economy, 1870–1997," in Eskridge and Noll, *More Money*, 33–34; Peter Dobkin Hall, *Inventing the Nonprofit Sector and Other Essays on Philanthropy, Voluntarism, and Nonprofit Organizations* (Baltimore: Johns Hopkins University Press, 1992), 58–80.

24. Clifford Grammich et al., *Religious Congregations and Membership Study: 2010 U.S. Religious Census* (Kansas City, Mo.: Association of Statisticians of American Religious Bodies, 2012), http://www.thearda.com/rcms2010/r/u/rcms2010_99_us_tradition_2010.asp, accessed August 3, 2015.

25. Jerry E. White, *The Church and the Parachurch: An Uneasy Marriage* (Portland, Ore.: Multnomah, 1983).

26. Grammich et al., *Religious Congregations . . . 2010 U.S. Religious Census*, May 1, 2012, 10, 12, 17, http://www.rcms2010.org/images/ACP%2020120501.pdf, accessed August 3, 2015.

27. "About ECFA," http://www.ecfa.org/Content/About, accessed August 3, 2015. The nearly 2,000 members also have nearly as many separately incorporated subsidiaries, which are also ECFA members.

28. "The Philanthropy 400," *Chronicle of Philanthropy*, October 14, 2011, http://philanthropy.com/article/Biggest-Charities-Expect-Flat/135006/; "2014 ECFA Annual State of Giving Report," http://www.ecfa.org/Content/2014-ECFA-Annual-State-of-Giving-Report; ECFA, "NonprofitPulse" (June 2015), http://www.ecfa.org/Pulse/Nonprofit/2015/NonprofitPulse_M06_2015.pdf; all accessed August 3, 2015.

29. The figures in this paragraph come from "ECFA Member Search" website (http://www.ecfa.org/MemberSearch.aspx) and from the websites of the various umbrella organizations: Association of Christian Schools International (http://www.acsiglobal.org/); American Association of Christian Schools (http://www.aacs.org/); Christian Schools International (http://www.csionline.org/); Care Net (http://www.care-net.org/); Christian Camp and Conference Association (http://www.ccca.org/); Association of Gospel Rescue Missions (http://www.agrm.org/); Teen Challenge (http://teenchallengeusa.com/); Youth with a Mission (http://www.ywam.org/); all accessed August 3, 2015.

30. Dean R. Hoge and Mark A. Noll, "Levels of Contributions and Attitudes Toward Money Among Evangelicals and Non-Evangelicals in Canada and the U.S.," in Eskridge and Noll, *More Money*, 351–73; Christian Smith and Michael O. Emerson, with Patricia Snell, *Passing the Plate: Why American Christians Don't Give Away More Money* (New York: Oxford University Press, 2008), 30. See also Hamilton, "More Money, More Ministry," 114–17. Self-reporting is the basis for much of the data on charitable giving, but all researchers recognize that the percentages reported tend to be higher than the actual percentages.

31. Tim Stafford, "Imperfect Instrument," *Christianity Today*, February 24, 2005, http://www.christianitytoday.com/ct/2005/march/19.56.html; World Vision International, Annual Review 2011, http://www.wvi.org/nepal/publication/annual-review-2011; Accord (formerly the Association of Evangelical Relief and Development Organizations), http://www.accordnetwork.org; all accessed August 3, 2015.

32. Cru, "2014 Annual Report," http://www.cru.org/content/dam/cru/about/2014-cru-annual-report.pdf, accessed August 3, 2015.

33. *The Small Business Economy 2008: A Report to the President* (Washington, D.C.: U.S. Government Printing Office, 2009), 7; "About COTN: History," http://cotni.org/about-cotn/history, and "Partners," http://cotni.org/about-cotn/partners, both accessed August 3, 2015.

34. Robert Wuthnow, *Boundless Faith: The Global Outreach of American Churches* (Berkeley: University of California Press, 2009).

35. Hamilton, "Triumph of the Praise Songs"; Wolfe, *Transformation of American Religion*, 36.

36. Richard Shaull, "Toward the Conversion of the Church," *Theology Today* 3, no. 4 (January 1947): 502–11; "Conference on the Intentional Cell Group" (Lane Hall, University of Michigan, November 1, 1947), reprinted in *The Friend* 118, no. 2 (February 1, 1948): 22, 30; John A. T. Robinson, *On Being the Church in the World* (Philadelphia: Westminster, 1960), 85; John L. Casteel, *Spiritual Renewal Through Personal Groups* (New York: Association Press, 1965); Elton Trueblood, *While It Is Day: An Autobiography* (New York: Harper and Row, 1974), 107; and Dietrich Bonhoeffer, *Life Together* (New York: Harper, 1954).

37. Keith and Gladys M. Hunt, *For Christ and the University: The Story of InterVarsity Christian Fellowship—USA* (Downers Grove, Ill.: InterVarsity Press, 1992), 64, 96–99; Char Meredith, *It's a Sin to Bore a Kid: The Story of Young Life* (Waco, Tex.: Word, 1978); William C. Martin, *A Prophet with Honor: The Billy Graham Story* (New York: William Morrow, 1991), 113, 165, 226; "Our History," https://www.bsfinternational.org/bsf-history, accessed August 3, 2015.

38. Larry Richards, *A New Face for the Church* (Grand Rapids, Mich.: Zondervan, 1970), 152; Juan Carlos Ortiz, *Call to Discipleship* (Plainfield, N.J.: Logos, 1975), and *Disciple* (Carol Stream, Ill.: Creation House, 1975); David Yonggi Cho, with Harold Hostetler, *Successful Home Cell Groups* (Plainfield, N.J.: Logos, 1981); Ralph Webster Neighbour and Lorna Jenkins, *Where Do We Go from Here? A Guidebook for*

Cell Group Churches (Houston: Touch Publications, 1990). An early, uneven, but occasionally helpful attempt at scholarly assessment of the small-group phenomenon is C. Kirk Hadaway, Stuart A. Wright, and Francis M. DuBose, *Home Cell Groups and House Churches* (Nashville: Broadman, 1987), esp. 11–37.

39. Robert Wuthnow, *Sharing the Journey: Support Groups and America's New Quest for Community* (New York: Free Press, 1994), 3–4, 31, 44, 47–49, 76, 91–92, 188, 215, 219–55, 277–82. See also Robert Wuthnow, ed., *"I Came Away Stronger:" How Small Groups Are Shaping American Religion* (Grand Rapids, Mich.: Eerdmans, 1994).

40. Greg L. Hawkins and Cally Parkingson, with Eric Arnson, *Reveal: Where Are You?* (Barrington, Ill.: Willow Creek Resources, 2007); Sheler, *Prophet of Purpose*, 105–7.

41. William Lawrence Svelmoe, *A New Vision for Missions: William Cameron Townsend, the Wycliffe Bible Translators, and the Culture of Early Evangelical Faith Missions, 1896–1945* (Tuscaloosa: University of Alabama Press, 2008), 25, 308–14; Martin, *Prophet with Honor*, 222–23, 309–10; Mark A. Noll and Carolyn Nystrom, *Is the Reformation Over? An Evangelical Assessment of Roman Catholicism* (Grand Rapids, Mich.: Baker Academic, 2005), 18.

42. Will Herberg, *Protestant Catholic Jew: An Essay in American Religious Sociology* (New York: Doubleday, 1956); Noll and Nystrom, *Is the Reformation Over?*, 60–62.

43. Noll and Nystrom, *Is the Reformation Over?*, 62–66.

44. Charles Colson and Richard John Neuhaus, eds., *Evangelicals and Catholics Together: Toward a Common Mission* (Nashville: Thomas Nelson, 1995), ix–xxxv; William M. Martin, *With God on Our Side: The Rise of the Religious Right in America* (New York: Broadway, 1996), 197–200.

45. Colson and Neuhaus, eds., *Evangelicals and Catholics Together*, 1, 29–30; Noll and Nystrom, *Is the Reformation Over?*, 151–58, 181–82, 192–207.

46. Noll and Nystrom, *Is the Reformation Over?*, 25, 67, 151–2, 197–99, 207–8; Alan Jacobs, "To Be a Christian College," *First Things* (April 2006), http://www.firstthings.com/article/2007/01/to-be-a-christian-college, accessed August 3, 2015. Publishers have sought to attract Catholic readers by issuing Bible editions that include the Deuterocanonical writings, in some cases gaining Catholic imprimaturs; American Bible Society, *Good News for Modern Man: The New Testament in Today's English Version* (New York: American Bible Society, 1966); *Good News Bible with Deuterocanonicals/Apocrypha: Today's English Version* (New York: American Bible Society, 1979); Kenneth N. Taylor, *The Living Bible* (Wheaton, Ill.: Tyndale, 1971); *The Catholic Living Bible* (Wheaton, Ill.: Tyndale, 1976); Eugene H. Peterson, *The Message: The Bible in Contemporary Language* (Colorado Springs, Colo.: Navpress, 2002); *The Message: Catholic/Ecumenical Edition, with Deuterocanonical Writings Translated by William Griffin* (Chicago, Ill.: ACTA, 2013).

47. Lindsay, *Faith in the Halls of Power*, 1–12; Dan Gilgoff, "Rick Warren: Stopping Gay Marriage 'Very Low' on Priority List," *U.S. News & World Report*, April 23, 2009; quotation in Timothy C. Morgan, "Purpose Driven in Rwanda," *Christianity Today*,

September 23, 2005, http://www.christianitytoday.com/ct/2005/october/17.32.html, accessed August 3, 2015.

48. For a typical AFA action see, Bill Carter, "Police Drama Under Fire for Sex and Violence," *New York Times*, June 22, 1993; Lindsay, *Faith in the Halls of Power*, 212–13.

49. Brian McLaren, *A Generous Orthodoxy* (Grand Rapids, Mich.: Zondervan, 2006). McLaren's many books on the subject began with *Reinventing Your Church* (Grand Rapids, Mich.: Zondervan, 1998), and the first to get him a lot of attention was *A New Kind of Christian: A Tale of Two Friends on a Spiritual Journey* (San Francisco: Jossey-Bass, 2001). For points of commonality and diversity within the movement, see Scot McKnight, "Five Streams of the Emerging Church, *Christianity Today* (February 2007), http://www.christianitytoday.com/ct/2007/february/11.35.html, accessed December 12, 2013.

50. Christian Smith, et al., *American Evangelicalism: Embattled and Thriving* (Chicago: University of Chicago Press, 1998), 126–32; Justin Farrell, "The Young and the Restless? The Liberalization of Young Evangelicals," *Journal for the Scientific Study of Religion* 50, no. 3 (September 2011): 517–32; Jeremy N. Thomas and Daniel V. A. Olson, "Evangelical Elites' Changing Responses to Homosexuality 1960–2009," *Sociology of Religion* 73, no. 3 (Autumn 2012): 239–72; National Association of Evangelicals, "For the Health of the Nation: An Evangelical Call to Civic Responsibility" (2004), http://www.nae.net/government-relations/for-the-health-of-the-nation, accessed August 3, 2015; James Davison Hunter, *Evangelicalism: The Coming Generation* (Chicago: University of Chicago Press, 1987), 64; Allan C. Carlson, *Godly Seed: Evangelicals Confront Birth Control 1873–1973* (New Brunswick, N.J.: Transaction, 2012), 134–43, 150–52.

51. *PFM Annual Report 2007–2008*, http://www.prisonfellowship.org/images/pdfs/legal_statements/2007_2008_annual_report.pdf, accessed August 3, 2015.

52. Mark A. Noll, *The New Shape of World Christianity: How American Experience Reflects Global Faith* (Downers Grove, Ill.: IVP Academic, 2009), 195–96.

53. "World Concern," http://www.worldconcern.org/; "Children of the Nations," http://cotni.org/; both accessed August 3, 2015.

54. Wuthnow, *Boundless Faith*, 171–85; Brian M. Howell, *Short-Term Mission: An Ethnography of Christian Travel Narrative and Experience* (Downers Grove, Ill.: IVP Academic, 2012).

55. R. Stephen Warner, "Coming to America: Immigrants and the Faith They Bring," *The Christian Century* 121, no. 3 (February 10, 2004): 20–23; Joel A. Carpenter, "The Christian Scholar in an Age of World Christianity," in *Christianity and the Soul of the University: Faith as a Foundation for Intellectual Community*, ed. Douglas V. Henry and Michael D. Beaty (Grand Rapids, Mich.: Baker Academic, 2006), 65–84.

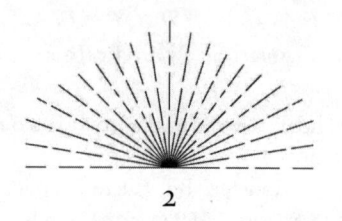

Sound, Style, Substance

NEW DIRECTIONS IN EVANGELICAL SPIRITUALITY

Chris R. Armstrong

Readers pulling the June 21, 1971, edition of *Time* magazine out of their mailboxes or grabbing it from newsstands were greeted by a psychedelic cover featuring a portrait of a purple Christ, under the words "The Jesus Revolution." Within the issue, *Time* writers attempted to explain one of the more colorful modern manifestations of the modern evangelical movement: the "Jesus freaks":

> There is an uncommon morning freshness to this movement, a buoyant atmosphere of hope and love. . . . Their love seems more sincere than a slogan, deeper than the fast-fading sentiments of the flower children; what startles the outsider is the extraordinary sense of joy that they are able to communicate. . . . If any one mark clearly identifies them it is their total belief in an awesome, supernatural Jesus Christ, not just a marvelous man who lived 2,000 years ago but a living God who is both Savior and Judge, the ruler of their destinies. Their lives revolve around the necessity for an intense personal relationship with that Jesus, and the belief that such a relationship should condition every human life. They act as if divine intervention guides their every movement and can be counted on to solve every problem.

Of course, the "man bites dog" zinger in this news was that nobody expected such a revival of Old Time Religion among the youth of the late 1960s and early 1970s. Many had repudiated traditional religion and dropped out of church. The era promised seemingly boundless "personal freedom," including "sexual liberation" and "mind expansion" from recreational drugs. Yet here many of them were, claiming a "born again" conversion experience, forming churches, and evangelizing far and wide. Evangelicalism would never be the same again.[1]

Having begun in the late 1960s with a flurry of mass baptisms on Southern California beaches, by 1971 the Jesus movement was already spreading across the nation, bringing Bible studies and folk-rock gospel choruses to "the streets, coffee houses, rescue missions, communes, [and] rock festivals." These "animated young Christians came from Haight-Ashbury (San Francisco's hotbed of hippiedom); 'Surf City,' California; small towns in Ohio; and New York's Hell's Kitchen." Bible studies and newly composed songs provided the language of the movement, and the laid-back, anti-establishment culture of the hippies provided its style and ethos.[2]

Old-style evangelicalism was not slow to respond. One year after the *Time* issue, Bill Bright's (1921–2003) Campus Crusade for Christ, working with Billy Graham (b. 1918) as honorary chairman, put on Explo '72—the Jesus movement's "Woodstock." The festival, held at Dallas's Cotton Bowl, featured an all-star lineup including Graham, Johnny Cash (1932–2003), original Christian rocker Larry Norman (1947–2008), and many musical groups and soloists who gained national prominence from their appearance there. In those early years, sociologist Donald Miller explains,

> "Jesus freaks," as they were sometimes called, began Bible studies in parks and started churches in homes, which soon pushed their way into recreation centers and rented school auditoriums as hundreds and then thousands of people responded . . . people getting high on Jesus rather than drugs and embracing gifts of the spirit, such as speaking in tongues, that were normal in the early Christian church. . . . Fervent Bible study had a remarkable democratizing effect on these Jesus people, who felt no need for an official seminary-trained clergy to interpret this sacred text.

During the decades that followed, thousands of new local churches and parachurch organizations sprang up under the leadership of those converted in the Jesus movement. New denominations and quasi-denominational networks emerging from the movement included the Calvary Chapel churches (birthed out of the Costa Mesa ministry of Chuck Smith, 1927–2013),

Hope Chapel churches, Horizon Christian Ministries, John Wimber's (1934–1997) Association of Vineyard Churches, and Jews for Jesus.[3]

The movement also transformed existing evangelical churches forever. First, the Jesus revolution solidified "youth ministry" as a job category as congregations hired full-time "youth pastors" for their enlarging youth constituencies. Second, it radically relandscaped evangelical worship and music. Third, the tide of converted young baby boomers floated all evangelical boats, contributing significantly to the rise of evangelicalism as a national phenomenon. Not to be outdone by *Time*, when in 1976 Jimmy Carter, outspoken in his identity as an evangelical (of, admittedly, an older, more established southern style), won the presidency, *Newsweek* declared the "Year of the Evangelicals." The following year, Watergate fixer Charles Colson (1931–2012) told his story of evangelical conversion in *Born Again* (a half million copies sold in that year alone), and televangelist Pat Robertson (b. 1930) founded his CBN University, now Regent University. A Gallup poll in 1979 revealed that America's evangelical population had jumped from 40 million to 70 million in the previous three decades, and in the election of 1980 Ronald Reagan rode into office on the shoulders of voting evangelicals.[4]

MUSIC TO YOUNG EARS

No social movement emerges out of nowhere, and the sudden flourishing of evangelical hippiedom that created this late-century shot in the arm of evangelicalism was no exception. The stage had been set decades before, during the Second World War, as "youth culture" first became an American reality. During that time not only had baby boomers come on the scene in vast numbers, they had also come equipped with pocket cash and leisure time. Naturally, Madison Avenue had noticed, promoting youth music, youth clothes, and youth crazes. Jukeboxes had blared the latest tunes as teens jitterbugged their Saturday nights away. Boys had donned their flashy, broad-shouldered zoot suits (a mark of defiant and extravagant freedom in that era of austerity) and girls their baggy sweaters and bobby sox. The end of the decade brought the advent of television, further feeding youth culture (think the early 1960s world of the musical and movie *Hairspray*).

Sound, Style, Substance

As the culture moved, so moved evangelicalism. Youth leaders who had begun to emerge in the 1930s, such as Philadelphia's Percy Crawford (1902–1960) and New York's Jack Wyrtzen (1913–1996), picked up on these trends. In evangelical wartime ministries, clothes became brighter, music more energetic and sophisticated, and the pacing of evangelistic meetings more split-second. And youth-conscious ministries reaped the rewards, their rallies soon outgrowing all but the largest halls and stadiums. The biggest and most influential network of such evangelical youth ministries in the 1940s and beyond was Youth for Christ (YFC), whose motto was (and still is) "Geared to the Times, Anchored to the Rock." Their first full-time employee and most energetic promoter was the young Billy Graham. Wearing loud ties and bright suits, backed by girl trios and swing-band instrumentals, Graham joined other evangelists of the day in galvanizing teen-packed rallies with crackling talks delivered in the clipped, staccato manner of such radio personalities as Walter Winchell (1897–1972). Wyrtzen, Graham, and their colleagues were savvy leaders. They knew religion was competing for "airtime" with all the new amenities and entertainments of an increasingly affluent America. Young people had many options. "Dare to offer something shoddy," warned the authors of *Reaching Youth for Christ* (1944), "and they'll shun your meeting." Evangelical youth leaders took note and sought to cater to young people's already more sophisticated tastes with attention-grabbing music and fast-paced, polished presentations with a current-events feel.[5]

Thousands of young people responded, pouring into rallies, Bible clubs, boat tours, and other innovative events. William Randolph Hearst and President Truman praised these efforts as effective tools against the day's newest social problem—juvenile delinquency. Soon even such venues as Madison Square Garden could not hold all the young people who came. Nearly three decades before 80,000 youth attended Explo '72, the Memorial Day 1945 youth rally at Soldier Field in Chicago drew 70,000.[6]

As the decades marched from wartime theaters in Europe, to Korea, to Vietnam, and the "Jesus people" began emerging out of the peaceniks and flower children of the 1960s, the lessons of those earlier youth revivals were not forgotten—especially in the area of church music. Whereas the music of the 1940s youth movement had reached churches through well-organized national evangelistic organizations and their packed stadium events, the worship revolution of the 1960s grew up more organically, from beaches, coffeehouses, and living rooms.

In the late 1960s, while Chuck Smith doffed his suit and tie and donned khaki shorts and flip-flops to preach, baptize, and sing on Huntington Beach in California, a nationwide Charismatic movement (which was to overlap significantly with the Jesus people movement) was springing up in mainline churches across the country. Charismatic laypeople meeting for small groups and healing services began to write their own songs: brief, simple—often dispensing with verses altogether and focusing on a single, repeated chorus (a practice common in the Youth for Christ movement of the 1940s). Often Scripture-based, though mostly written in first-person singular to better communicate personal, affective commitment to God, the songs of this new "praise and worship" style gained their power from their "brevity and simplicity."[7]

The Jesus freaks picked up these Charismatic-influenced "choruses" in a worship style newly free-flowing, participatory, and impassioned, supplanting the stage-focused, tightly arranged evangelistic songs of radio-era crusade music. This was not their daddy's churches—neither the sedate and classical style of the mainline nor the respectable if energetic Graham-era crusade clones.[8]

Befitting a people's movement, the new music reached for its inspiration into the folkways of rock, jazz, folk, gospel, pop, and country. Contributing to this mix were the new genre of "youth musicals" such as *Good News* (1967) and *Tell It Like It Is* (1969). These were written to be sung by youth choirs accompanied by pop bands. They thus validated what the "kids" were already listening to, paving the way for the Jesus music of the 1960s and 1970s.[9]

The most popular of the early praise and worship songs—released on LPs and in sheet music—came from Maranatha! Music, a Jesus-people company birthed at Calvary Chapel and run by (among others) Chuck Smith's nephew Chuck Fromm. Many of these songs are sung today in a wide array of evangelical as well as Charismatic churches: "Father, I Adore You," "Seek Ye First," "Glorify Thy Name," "I Love You, Lord." Although record companies have typically produced and distributed such music, as Fromm tells it, "the most powerful and enduring songs were written by nonprofessionals from the depths of their own experience. They were truckers, former strippers, and housewives who wanted to share their love of God." And their direct, personal message resonated with wide swaths of the American public.[10]

At the same time as the praise and worship trend began to sweep through evangelical churches, a parallel industry focused on "message music" written for performance rather than congregational singing: Contemporary Christian Music (CCM). This style emerged from such Christian artists as Larry Norman (whose disc *Upon This Rock* from 1969 is considered one of the first of the genre), Mylon LeFevre (b. 1944), and Keith Green (1953–1982), as well as groups such as 2nd Chapter of Acts, Petra, and Andrae Crouch and the Disciples. By the 1980s CCM had become a multimillion-dollar industry, represented by labels such as Word and Sparrow. Crossover artists such as Amy Grant (b. 1960), Michael W. Smith (b. 1957), and Jars of Clay played on secular as well as Christian stations.

Away from the stages and radio control rooms, in sanctuaries across the nation, a related but distinctive Christian Worship Music (CWM) developed. As Vineyard Fellowship leader Kevin Springer put it: "You don't understand the Vineyard if you don't understand the worship music. . . . That is probably the greatest contributor to the growth and advancement of the Vineyard movement. More than healing, more than books, more than tapes." The Jesus movement churches that evolved in the last few decades of the twentieth century did not set aside traditional hymns entirely (though giving them updated arrangements). This was appropriate enough, as those hymns had themselves been the culturally adaptive, new music of the eighteenth and nineteenth centuries. But in the twentieth century the new worship music quickly became the Jesus movement's most powerful legacy to future generations as private Christian schools cranked out worship leaders adept in the new musical styles.[11]

As a bellwether of this music's popularity, when Maranatha! Music and CCM Communications started *Worship Leader* magazine in 1986, it took only eight years to attract more than 40,000 paid subscribers. Praise and worship music reached new heights by the 1990s, when Christian Copyright Licensing, Inc. (CCLI) emerged in 1991 as a way to pay artists for all those songs projected on sanctuary screens. Musical composition and selection became market transactions (though it is questionable whether individual musicians profited nearly as much as big companies), just as low production costs democratized the recording process, and the low cost of Internet marketing and sales did the same for the marketing and distribution of worship music. As of 2015 product sales were still climbing, with both evangelical and mainline churches using CWM to "close the gap" dividing church from culture. The Charismatic link to this new worship style deserves a moment more: Most of the emerging Jesus movement churches were open to Charismatic gifts: Donald Miller claims that a "high percentage" of movement worshipers spoke in tongues, and most saw "no reason why they should exclude visions and ecstatic experiences from the realm of religious knowledge." Some, like the Vineyard churches, may be considered to fall squarely within the Charismatic movement itself.[12]

The worship music of the new movement thus brought to the national evangelical scene the exuberance and expressiveness that had been typical of Pentecostal worship since that movement's birth in the early 1900s. In historic Pentecostal and modern Charismatic worship, hands are clapped, raised, and waved; tears are shed; dances are danced; and "Hallelujahs" are shouted to encourage the preacher after the manner of the African American "call and response" tradition. Robert Duvall's film *The Apostle* (1997) reflects the tradition well, and in many ways it has been continued in the Jesus movement and the worship music it created. Since the 1970s these pentecostal characteristics have increasingly emerged in churches with no formal ties to the Charismatic movement: hand raising, laying on of hands in prayer, exuberant choruses, and the like are just standard operating procedure in many if not most evangelical churches, across denominational, class, and ethnic boundaries.[13]

"HEART RELIGION" REDUX

This brings us to two key traits of worship and spirituality in the Jesus movement—and from that movement into evangelicalism as a whole: its democratic, populist ethos and its emotional power to transform the heart of the worshipper.

First, this new movement brought with it a "democratization of the sacred" that laypeople found inviting and empowering. Nothing looked like the stuffy, regimented worship of old-style Protestant churches. These congregations met in warehouses, school auditoriums, and strip malls. Consistent with the boomers' allergy to the trappings of "organized" religion, they kept their worship spaces free of the sober symbols of the older devotional arts. Folding chairs replaced pews. Sound equipment instead of an altar loomed at the front. Laypeople and ministers alike arrived in casual clothes, and pastors spoke informally, using lots of personal examples. Their style was familiar, informal, and conversational. Here were none of the polished, professional stylings of the midcentury evangelical youth circuit's stars (or the emerging televangelists of the 1980s). Everywhere in these new churches, laypeople led worship, counseled other members, and ran church programs. Clergy encouraged ordinary members to create programs and ministries rather than dictating these from above. This was an ethos of equipping the saints to do the work of the ministry, and for thousands it opened ministry arenas where they could exercise their own gifts and inclinations.[14]

Nowhere was this democratized structure more powerfully on display than in the "ministry time" common to many of these churches. As the band played softly, congregants formed small groups all over the sanctuary, praying for one another directly and naturally. Jesus seemed to be present to meet all needs, and healing power lay not in the official function of the priest but in the human touch and intimate prayer of the people.[15]

In that newly opened populist space, the Jesus people treated conversion as something much more than a single experience of walking up an aisle at a big event and saying a single "sinner's prayer." For this tired, battered generation, the born-again experience proved only a beginning. Eschewing the buttoned-down style of older evangelical churches, the Jesus revolution churches of the Calvary/Vineyard ilk ushered worshipers into an ongoing experience of "deep and highly complex emotions" resulting in long-term personal transformation. Movement members identified the worship experience as the nexus of this process of affective and moral change: there, as they sang and swayed, they reported feeling both "joy, peace, love, gratitude, intimacy, happiness" and "brokenness, pain, sorrow, repentance." A typical testimony of a new attendee at these churches is that "when I first came, I would cry and cry, as if a dam was loosening." Many told of feeling their everyday "defenses and pretenses" vanish. The joy of knowing Jesus's restorative, unconditional love and grace "allowed them to acknowledge the underside of their lives, the ugliness that they usually attempted to hide from view." The result was a "reordering" of "the worshiper's unconscious life." In other words, the emotions did not end with themselves: the point was not the emotion but rather the change in people's hearts.[16]

SOMETHING NEW UNDER THE SUN?

What are modern observers to make of all this? What does it tell us about the present state of evangelicalism, particularly in its worship and spiritual practices? Sociologist Donald E. Miller concluded from his study of three church movements birthed from the hippie Jesus people era that such new quasi-denominations had launched a "second Reformation" that was reinventing American Protestantism from the ground up for a new cultural reality, in the process creating a new paradigm on the American religious landscape.[17]

It is easy enough to see that contemporary evangelicalism indulges a sort of fetish for reinventing itself. *Christianity Today* editor Mark Galli describes a flier he received in the mail some years ago: "A new flavor of church is in town! Whether you prefer church with a more traditional blend or a robust contemporary flavor, at [church name], we have a style just for you! Casual atmosphere, relevant messages, great music, dynamic kids' programs, and yes, you can choose your own flavor!" The "flavors" the flier advertised were things like "'Real-life messages,' 'Safe and fun children's program,' 'Friendly people,' and the marketing coup de grace, 'Fresh coffee and doughnuts!' "[18]

Although this is a banal example, and easy to deride, it indicates a truth: evangelicalism has indeed injected something new into the world of religion. It may be considered a uniquely strong instance of what Lamin Sanneh has called the "translatability" of Christianity—a movement whose intense pragmatism could only have emerged on the Lockean blank slate of the New World sociocultural landscape.[19]

But this characteristic did not suddenly emerge in the 1960s and 1970s. In each of its generations since the Anglo-American evangelical revivals of the mid-1700s, evangelicalism has sought ecclesial, liturgical, and spiritual forms that will best serve (1) direct, unmediated, transformative encounter with God, (2) church reform, (3) social reform, and (4) missions/evangelism/church growth (note the relationship between this claim and two of David Bebbington's famous fourfold elements of historical evangelicalism: conversionism and activism). Whatever ecclesial forms have seemed to work for each new generation and subculture, evangelicals have eagerly taken them up.[20]

We have seen this plastic (in the sense of malleable, changing) pragmatism in the evangelical youth movement of the 1940s and 1950s. But we could also turn back the clock further, to find other striking antecedents. Given the Charismatic flavor of the Jesus movement, one important example may be found in the birth-culture of Pentecostalism. Here, seventy years before the Jesus people, were all the same sorts of lay participation, personal expression, and creative freedom. African American pastor William J. Seymour (1870–1922), the driving force behind the Azusa Street, Los Angeles, California, revivals of 1906–1907—among the earliest and most globally influential Pentecostal revivals—typified a new breed of church leader. Seymour allowed and encouraged worshipers to exercise their gifts during services, providing what the historian Cecil Robeck called "a forum for various members of his congregation to make their case or to demonstrate their charism in the context of the worshiping community, without fear of recrimination." Seymour also worked with a diverse team of volunteers and gave them a great deal of autonomy within certain boundaries. His leadership model was decentralized and open to what he perceived to be a genuine moving of the Spirit in his co-workers and in the entire congregation. Lay ministers were encouraged and empowered, because the Holy Spirit presumably blew wherever he wanted to—and God forbid anyone stand in the way. This is just the transparent personal style and nonhierarchical corporate structure that have predominated in the church movements spawned by the Jesus revolution.[21]

Even further back, we find the Moody revivals (led by Dwight L. Moody, 1837–1899) that began in the 1870s using popular music, the mid-nineteenth-century Finneyite revivals (led by Charles Grandison Finney, 1792–1875) using popular preaching styles and "new measures" to draw and convert people, and the eighteenth-century Methodist songs (many of them written by Charles Wesley, 1707–1788) that drafted popular music to express sacred themes. In short, evangelicalism *is and has always been* in its essence a reinventing movement. Since the heyday of John Wesley (1703–1791) and Jonathan Edwards (1703–1758), the movement has grown rapidly within and across all flavors of Protestantism, at every point subordinating ecclesial forms to the direct, unmediated experience of God. This plasticity met its perfect medium in nineteenth-century America, the Mecca of what historian Mark Noll calls "populism, individualism, democratization, and market-making," bequeathing an intensified "reinventing" mode to the twentieth century. Nineteenth-century evangelical worship and spirituality promoted a direct and personal relationship with God; fluid, pragmatic worship forms tailored to specific situations and purposes; democratic lay participation in worship; and importations from popular culture—as one nineteenth-century Methodist exclaimed: "Why should the Devil have all the good tunes!" In the 1970s Larry Norman—sometimes dubbed the "father of Christian Rock"—turned the century-old Methodist quip into a song title: "Why Should the Devil Have All the Good Music?" Thus it was in the beginning, is now, and (quite likely) ever shall be.[22]

As each new generation of evangelicals has forged its own culturally attuned mode of worship and spirituality, the movement has held "the church invisible"—the fellowship of saints across time, space, and denominational traditions—to be a sacred reality. And it has held the individual's relationship with God to be another sacred reality. But everything else between those two—all the doctrinal formulations, liturgies, polities, and other ecclesiological forms—became negotiable and plastic, modified and remodified to achieve pietistic ends. In the path of the evangelical pietist juggernaut, all ecclesiastical constructions were flattened to *adiaphora* (theologically inessential things).[23]

Not surprisingly, then, it is difficult to describe a "typical" evangelical church service today. Perhaps the best way to look at this is to see evangelical worship as taking place across a series of spectrums or continuums—one for each aspect or dimension of the service. The *sermon* is the main event in many churches—from evangelical Anglican, to Baptist, to Presbyterian, to Wesleyan, to Pentecostal. Perhaps oddly (to outsiders), often the more Pentecostal you get, the longer the sermon. Probably the shortest would be the most liturgical churches—Congregational, Anglican, Presbyterian.

As for *music*, there is a traditional-to-contemporary spectrum. In congregations of medium or larger size it is quite usual to have two different styles of service—one that is more traditional and one more contemporary, with traditional and contemporary being defined by how many songs written before the 1960s are in play. Of course these services tend to be generationally divided, so one will usually find older people in the more traditional service, younger people in the more contemporary. In smaller churches, there may be an attempt to blend the two styles, with some hymns and some modern praise songs and choruses. In many contemporary services, worship displaces the sermon as the primary attraction.

As for *the structure of the service*, on the continuum from spontaneity to locked-in liturgy there is great variation, with Anglican and Presbyterian churches tending to lean toward liturgy, and Charismatic churches leaning toward spontaneity. However, in those latter churches, there is often an unspoken liturgy of how the music ramps up and at what time (even) prophecies take place during the service. There is variance among Charismatic churches as to whether prophecies are approved beforehand, or spoken by people approved beforehand, following I Corinthians 14, that everything be done decently and in order, even in the exercise of the Charismatic gifts.

Prayer often features prominently in evangelical services. Across the spectrum of churches, there may be a designated moment for corporate prayer, in which needs are announced—usually by a designated layperson who leads the congregation in prayer from the front of the church, and sometimes also from those throughout the congregation. There may also be a moment during the service when people can go and receive prayer confidentially by prayer teams or designated prayer leaders, at one side or the back of the church. In churches where there is some form of regular "altar call" to the front of the church, borrowed from revivalistic practice dating back to the nineteenth century, congregants who are struggling in some way, wish to rededicate their lives, or want prayer for issues in their lives may come to the front to receive prayer from pastoral staff and/or designated lay "pray-ers."

All this describes worship services held Sunday morning (and sometimes Sunday evening, and even Saturday evening). But since the 1980s, especially in larger churches where people can easily feel alienated and unnoticed if all they attend is a large Sunday service (of course some who are "seekers" and with certain personalities welcome the anonymity), the "small group" has become an essential part of church experience. Even in smaller churches, such groups have become the place where the bulk of a congregant's spiritual development presumably occurs—especially in those traditions where there is a strong focus on visible Christianity: Christianity that makes itself seen in the discipleship of the people and growth in spiritual maturity, for instance Baptist, Mennonite, Holiness. Even in more modestly sized churches, the generalized American antipathy toward institutions of all sorts—certainly including churches—may lead people to be more comfortable with seeking spiritual nourishment and teaching in a freer, more democratic small-group setting.

Small groups vary along a spectrum from intellectual, inductive Bible study to prayer gatherings where people relate their struggles from the week and in some version of a therapeutic group dynamic receive prayer and encouragement from the group. Of course there may be a mixture of these elements as well as other sorts of study and elements of worship in the group, as songs and choruses are led either by a single group leader or on suggestion by the group as a whole. Even the leadership structure of small groups ranges from one leader who always leads a Bible or other book study and takes people through it step by step, week by week, to a rotating democratic cadre of volunteer leaders, depending on the sense of the group of who is both willing and able to lead.[24]

The *end* to which evangelicalism has perpetually reinvented itself has always been *immediate access to God*. But this pietism has often been pursued in ways that have made evangelicalism, a theologically conservative movement to be sure, culturally liberal to the point (at times) of multiple personality disorder. One might almost say that evangelicalism has served as a useful bellwether of popular culture in every era. Want to know which way the cultural wind is blowing? Look to the innovative, pragmatic, malleable evangelicals. Born in the newly democratizing climates of eighteenth-century England and nurtured in the free air of America, this movement became a new thing on the religious landscape: a chameleon that shows no signs of becoming any less chameleonic in the twenty-first century than it was in the eighteenth, nineteenth, and twentieth.

Post–Jesus revolution evangelicalism—innovative, democratic, diverse, youthful, and energetic; some have said consumeristic, overemotional, superficial, human-centered rather than God-centered—is not only quintessentially evangelical but also quintessentially American. If this is true, then it explains the ARIS 2008 survey's conclusion that evangelicalism is not flagging in America—indeed, is still increasing its dominance. Despite the usual headline derived from the study—the increase of the religious "Nones"—the ARIS-published summary of the study identified a "rise in the preference to self-identify as 'born again' or 'evangelical' rather than with any Christian tradition, church or denomination."[25]

CONVERSIONISM AS HEART RELIGION

Now we need to turn from this key evangelical trait of cultural currency/reinvention—what I take to be the movement's distinctive contribution in world Christianity—to what I have said is the reality that has driven this distinctive: evangelicalism's thirst for direct, experiential access to God. Unlike its plasticity, I do not call this a "distinctive": evangelicalism shares its "heart religion" with many other historic Christian churches and movements. But it is still strongly characteristic of the movement and holds great explanatory power for modern evangelical worship and spirituality, as for other aspects of evangelical culture.

David Bebbington famously defined evangelicalism with a fourfold typology: conversionist, biblicist, crucicentrist, and activist. I suppose that in raising "matters of the heart," we are here beginning to talk about conversionism, but that term by itself is inadequate to describe what might be called the *habitus* of affective devotion so central to this movement. In short, evangelical conversionism entails a focus on personal relationship with God in Christ, accessed through a crisis conversion experience and experienced in a continuing way through a series of affectively powerful, transforming encounters with God.[26]

I have insisted at several points that this affectively toned conversionism, flourishing in the modern Anglo-American petri dish, has spawned the evangelical willingness to reinvent all ecclesial forms. What is it about heart religion that works this particular organic transformation?

Since the Reformation, Protestants have always distrusted tradition as potentially leading people away from God and back into what Martin Luther (1483–1546), the original evangelical, had called the "Babylonian Captivity of the Church." Evangelicals have strengthened and universalized this distrust into a suspicion of all sacramentalism, all mediation of God to humanity. Any time ecclesiasts have claimed that in order to meet God people must use *mediated* forms such as statues, images, rituals, gestures, positions, and indeed the offices of the ecclesiasts themselves, evangelical Protestants have demurred. The proto-evangelical "free church" Protestants—first the Anabaptists, then later the varieties of Reformed Christianity stemming from Huldrych Zwingli (1484–1531) and John Calvin (1509–1564), then the nonconformist varieties of Puritans

(Baptists, Congregationalists, etc.), then all their heirs up to the modern Pentecostal denominations and Charismatic movements—had a desire to be "free" not only from state control and all the elaborate hierarchy of the Roman Catholic Church but also from the perceived tyranny of material or "merely human" mediation of God's grace: "priestcraft," as they called it. How dare any human tell other people that they must do this or that to reach God: each person stands before God on one's own two feet, and God, in turn, stands ready to meet each person in every time and situation of life, without the poor helps of human tradition.[27]

This allergy to mediation in worship has given evangelical Protestantism a decided lean toward the sort of democratic, participatory forms of worship and leadership that the sociologist Donald Miller observed in the churches emerging out of the Jesus people movement. Congregationalism has been the movement's favored (though not exclusive) ecclesiological form, and worship styles have tended to follow whatever seems to relate most naturally and directly to the worshiper. This has meant preaching in plain language and singing in popular styles (famously, even tavern tunes); if God meets people where they are, then people should use in worship whatever popular-culture material already feels natural and "homey" to them. The driver, in every case, is the desire to meet God—directly, affectively—for oneself. Let us turn, then, to a closer examination of that desire.[28]

While this has been part of the evangelical DNA all along, I think it is fair to speak of the Pentecostal and Charismatic movements, and by association the Jesus revolution begun in the 1970s, as a particularly potent revival of heart religion. Along with the praise choruses and freedoms that by the turn of the twenty-first century had spilled over from Charismatics and Jesus people to almost all evangelical churches has come a rising acceptance of Christian immediatist desire and fulfillment. In the glow of worship, in tender moments of prayer within the warm community of saints, the many evangelicals who have been influenced by the Christian eudaemonist tradition can experience the bliss of intimacy with Christ as a valid and nourishing part of their faith lives. Evangelicals today can rejoice, along with Augustine of Hippo (354–430), signatories of the Westminster Confession (1646), and John Wesley, that the human desire for a transcendent experience of intimacy with God is itself God-given—a blessing to be enjoyed both in heaven and here on earth.

To some modern critics (among them many evangelicals), such "divine love" seems mawkish or self-indulgent—an illegitimate borrowing from an individualistic age. They complain that many of the songs sung in Charismatic congregations seem to be all about "me" and "I." However, although there is certainly room for self-indulgence in the modern praise and worship movement, its emphasis on encounter puts God, not humanity, at the center. In an encounter with God, the believer cannot help but gasp in amazement at the condescension of the holy God who comes and meets still-sinful people where they live. Although this may look like a sort of "Jesus-as-buddy" syndrome to some—and surely at times it does degenerate into such an irreverent stance—it flows from deeper wells. The critics forget that many of the thousands of still-venerable hymns written by the poet Charles Wesley (1707–1788, one of the grandfathers of evangelicalism) were also written in the first person. The "me" language is designed, now as then, not to indulge self-absorption but to express appropriate awe and amazement that God would condescend to save and work in the lives of individuals. The historian Grant Wacker calls this approach to God "submissiveness" and argues that it stems from "a deep-seated awareness that humans do not create themselves and therefore owe their lives to another source."[29]

It is worth pointing out that most of today's cultural backlash against evangelicalism's more emotion-affirming forms is based on a misunderstanding. Critics (again, including some evangelicals) see nothing but raw "feelings" involved in heart religion. They see the religion of the heart as irrational or even antirational. And of course in the twentieth and twenty-first centuries reason trumps all. In this scientific age, whatever the postmodern malcontents say, reason is still patently power, because of the tremendous power of technology, grounded as that is in scientific rationality. Therefore critics tend to believe that emotion—which after all (they think) has nothing to do with reason, unless it clouds it and befuddles decision making—should have no role in the important things of life, including religion. It is OK to get excited at a football game or to weep at a movie, but it is not OK to get excited about Jesus or weep in one's prayers. That is to rely on emotion too much for safety.[30]

What these critics do not see is that Christian groups in the pietistic tradition of evangelicalism have understood the "heart" not just as some organ of raw feeling but in biblical terms, as the center of emotion, thinking, and willing. Remember the description of the newly elongated and affective process of conversion in the Jesus revolution churches: its emotions are scripted cognitively by orthodox Christian theology and push toward full salvation: transformation of the entire personality and transformation of whole communities, not just individuals. These contemporary Christians have recognized that it is impossible for people to behave as Christians unless their whole being, including their emotional being, has become transformed or "converted."

All very well, one might say, but surely this is still the special preserve of the Charismatics, or at least just the more "excitable" sorts of evangelicals. One case should prove that this eudaemonist affective immediatism continues to characterize American evangelicals far from the Pentecostal or Charismatic folds. If even the most buttoned-down Reformed evangelicals today have one "patron saint" aside from Billy Graham, it is undoubtedly C. S. Lewis (1898–1963). Significantly, in his apologetic writings, Lewis frames the movement of the person toward faith as an Augustinian quest of desire. Augustine's dictum "Our hearts are restless until they rest in God" is transmuted in Lewis to the romantic experience of *sehnsucht*—longing for the divine—and thence, in modern evangelical lore, to "the hole in our hearts" or even, for evangelical kids, "the hole in the donut." For a particularly clear and direct statement of his eudaemonist philosophy of Christian happiness or joy, see Lewis's essay "The Weight of Glory."[31]

In post–Jesus revolution evangelical circles, across the wide variety of denominational and (increasingly) nondenominational church experiences, conversion has followed the script of desire-and-fulfillment: crisis-and-coming-home, with the tears and embraces of the prodigal son (or daughter) nestling suddenly and unexpectedly in the arms of an unexpectedly gracious and welcoming Father. These are converts whose hearts, in the words of John Wesley, have been "strangely warmed." They have been, in C. S. Lewis's phrase, "surprised by joy." And out of that powerful heart experience, they have moved out to tell the world the story of how their desire for something beyond what the world could offer has now been fulfilled in Jesus Christ.

WHITHER EVANGELICAL WORSHIP AND SPIRITUALITY?

Having told the story to this point, I now need to look forward into the future. What are some new movements, motions, gestures in evangelical worship and spirituality, and what do they portend for the movement's future?

I started this chapter with a vibrant youth movement and pointed to Christian youth movements of the past as examples of evangelicalism's skill at cultural adaptation. However, the young do not always set the table in culture (in church or in society). What will happen in evangelicalism as the boomer generation ages?

One answer, and a significant trend in evangelical worship and spirituality in the 2010s, is the mainstreaming of such formerly radical groups as the Pentecostals and indeed Donald Miller's "new paradigm" churches. Miller recognizes that "it is a mistake to think that today's ["new paradigm"] churches represent socially marginal countercultural values," though they do have their roots in the postwar counterculture. "As cultural norms have shifted to reflect the revolutions of the sixties—and as the movements of that period have moderated some of their ecstatic enthusiasms—these groups resonate with baby boomer and 'baby buster' values." In other words, the Jesus people movement has *already* moved significantly toward the mainstream in values, ethos, and tone in the few decades of its existence.[32]

What is true of the Jesus revolution is true of the older Pentecostal churches: as they have grown in size and influence, they have also become enculturated, losing some of the characteristics that once set them apart as a "radical" movement. For example, in many congregations, overt Charismatic practices have receded from public worship into private devotion, leaving only raised hands and "praise and worship music" in the public sphere of church worship. Often enough, only the *expectation* of Charismatic gifts such as healing and prophecy remains, without much of the *demonstration*.

It may be that the spectacular fall of prominent Charismatic televangelists in the 1980s and beyond contributed to this privatization of Charismatic spirituality among Pentecostals and Charismatics in the late twentieth and early twenty-first centuries. Or perhaps it is the upward sociological climb of the Pentecostals that has removed it from its radicalism of yore. But this "mainstreaming" of Pentecostalism should not surprise us.[33]

Think of the largest of the white Pentecostal denominations, the Assemblies of God (AG). Since the late twentieth century the denomination has continued in Latin America its lively heritage of public practice of spiritual gifts (such as tongues, prophecy, healing) and growth by evangelism, with Christian commitment perceived as leading new converts to evangelism and activism. In North America, by contrast, evangelical religion's old nemesis, nominalism, seems to some AG leaders to have settled over the church's converts all too quickly.[34]

Changes in spiritual "tone" are of course notoriously difficult to measure, but for many longtime AG adherents lively commitment to evangelism represents a key part of the denomination's spiritual character—a heritage without which the very identity of the Assemblies of God comes into question. One place this question of commitment comes to the fore is in the discrepancy between the recorded number of new converts (for example, over 500,000 in 1996) and the numbers of new adherents (79,606 in 1996) and new members (30,621 in 1996). Even allowing for skewed reporting and duplication in counting decisions to convert, these North American numbers seem to point to a certain flaccidity compared, for example, with the decidedly growth-oriented, "fiery" Latin American Pentecostals.[35]

Late twentieth-century revivals such as the "Toronto Blessing" (1994–2006) at the Toronto Airport Vineyard (later Toronto Airport Christian Fellowship, then Catch the Fire Toronto!) in Ontario, Canada, and the "Pensacola Outpouring" (1995–2000) at Brownsville Assembly of God in Pensacola, Florida, seemed to promise a renewal of spiritual commitment among evangelicals, including those within the AG, but they elicited mixed responses from denominational leaders. For instance, AG districts lined up pro- and anti-Brownsville. As several million people visited the rousing worship services, and many reported conversion and healing experiences, critics worried that the services distorted "biblical Christianity." The sticking point was typically the bodily and emotional "manifestations" that once characterized the camp-meeting Holiness heritage out of which Pentecostalism arose. Such deep responses as trembling, crying out, and being "slain in the Spirit" (not to mention the more extreme but rarer manifestations of animal noises, ecstatic dancing, and the host of apparently uncontrolled automatic behaviors long characteristic of heated revivals) have become unwelcome in many comfortable middle-class sanctuaries of the modern AG. In what some see as the age-old tension between charisma and institution, AG pastors and denominational leaders have often been reticent to valorize such "immature" or "extreme" emotional responses, seeing them as threats to the order enjoined by Paul in I Corinthians 14—not to mention the order represented by denominational bureaucracies, hierarchies, and district offices housed in multimillion-dollar facilities.[36]

Others in AG leadership, however, have publicly worried that denominational churches are in danger of becoming barely distinguishable from any other evangelical churches in the nation. Thomas Trask, AG general superintendent from 1993 to 2007, was not hesitant to call for revival as the key both to church growth and to the strengthening of denominational identity. But in so doing, he and the denomination wrestled with their place on the continuum between the biblical rationalism, respectable reserve, and powerful denominational machines of the older evangelicals and the freedom of worship, tolerance for emotional and physical manifestations, and loose, prophetic organization of many independent Charismatic groups. Far more than at their contested induction into the National Association of Evangelicals in the 1940s, AG leaders at the end of the millennium found themselves naturally taking on the "evangelical identities" of the interdenominational evangelicalism at whose seminaries many of them have trained (for instance, Fuller Seminary in California and Gordon-Conwell in Massachusetts). Today the AG, holding a comfortable and influential plurality within the NAE, has at last begun to look over its shoulder and wonder whether it has lost by the alliance as much as it has gained.

Facing survey data suggesting that nearly half of AG members had not received Spirit baptism, Trask stated after his election as general superintendent that "we may be Pentecostal in doctrine, but not in experience." Whether this trend has turned or will turn the corner back toward reclaiming historic Pentecostal experience and practice remains to be seen. Between the modern independent Charismatic megachurches and the older evangelical traditions (for example, certain Baptist and Presbyterian groups), the Assemblies of God must define its theological and spiritual borders and rehearse its history if it is to thrive.[37]

THE NEW SOCIAL-JUSTICE CONSCIOUSNESS: ITS DISCONTENTS AND DANGERS

A political realignment of younger evangelicals is in progress, away from their parents' fundamentalist-tinged affinity for conservatism in politics. Evangelical leaders such as Ronald Sider (b. 1939), founder of Evangelicals for Social Action and author of the much reprinted *Rich Christians in an Age of Hunger* (1977), and Tony Campolo (b. 1935), popular speaker and author of books such as *Red Letter Christians: A Citizen's Guide to Faith and Politics* (2008), have fostered among younger evangelicals a new social-justice consciousness. One manifestation of this impulse is the rise of a "New Monasticism" movement pioneered by evangelical activists such as Shane Claiborne (b. 1975) and Jonathan Wilson-Hartgrove. New Monastics emphasize prayerful contemplation, communal living and hospitality, and practical engagement with the poor. Some younger, better-educated evangelicals have likewise become fascinated with neo-Anabaptist thought (especially via Duke theologian Stanley Hauerwas, b. 1940, and his own inspiration, John Howard Yoder, 1927–1997). In this stream, younger evangelicals are espousing pacifism and an extreme distrust of the secular establishment (government, big business, etc.).[38]

These trends are encouraging—the older fundamentalist allergy to social action on any but a personal scale prevented the movement from having much impact on entrenched, socially oppressive systems in America. But they carry with them their own tradeoffs. The new social activism is at least momentarily shifting younger Christians' focus away from the experiential christocentrism that characterized and motivated previous generations of evangelicals in ways that may herald the secularization of the younger generation. Reflective New Monastic leaders such as Jon Stock of the Church of the Servant King in Oregon do admit that intense social activism can result in an underdeveloped ecclesiology and stunted spiritual practice—a far cry, indeed, from the beating heart of the "old monasticism," and leading many observers who know better to insist that the term "monasticism" is entirely misused in terms of this small but influential movement.

The late Jesuit ecclesiologist Avery Dulles (1918–2008) has said that the "servant" model of church, which sees Christianity's role as primarily one of ministering to social needs, has secularization as its Achilles' heel.

If Christians and non-Christians are working side-by-side on the same social problems (housing for the poor, disaster relief, sex trafficking, etc.), the Christians can easily forget the message of grace and the exclusivity of Christ as Savior: that all are *unable* to live in a fully moral way, either as individuals or as a society, which is why humans need God's grace in Christ.[39]

In fact, social-action ministries are only one kind of activist "renewal movement" that can end up downplaying the evangelical message of grace and losing awareness of the "Gospel," resulting in a slide into nominalism just as real as that arising from mere cultural inertia (as in the case of the Assemblies of God described above). *Christianity Today* editor Mark Galli summarizes the varied goals of recent renewal movements:

> Some of these movements focus on the lack of personal morality, and so champion accountability groups or the spiritual disciplines as the key to renewal. Others attack our individualism and strive to create a church life that is more meaningful, everything from "house church" to "simple church" to "deep church" to "missional church" to "ancient-future church." . . . Some say evangelicals are captive to white culture, and so advocate multiculturalism.

Each of these emphases, Galli observes, identifies a problem and then sets out an activist solution: Christians should *tell* people to *do things differently*. In the case of the (laudable) social justice emphasis, for example, proponents wage a kind of psychological guerilla warfare to get people to change their behavior, wielding guilt, fear, shame, and moralism in heavy-handed ways. Even in its less moralistic moments, the movement evinces a very unevangelical optimism about the human will.[40]

The multiculturalist movement within evangelicalism is heir to the same weakness: prophetic voices from activists such as the African American John Perkins and the Mexican American Rudy Carrasco have heightened evangelical awareness of Eurocentrism, white privilege, and the lingering racism that still mars evangelicalism, inspiring some evangelicals with a passion to overcome these problems.[41] Yet here too is the "horizontal temptation." Galli cites an unnamed Asian evangelical whose book seeks to "free the evangelical church from Western cultural captivity," and he takes issue with the author's assertion that "the more diverse we become, the more the church flourishes." This seems to Galli to put the human cart before the divine horse, arrogating to human ability what can only be experienced by God's grace.

And so it goes, case by case—the "spiritual disciplines" movement, the missional movement, movements in postmodern theology and emerging ecclesiology: when evangelicals put their finger on a problem within their own movement, "our practical and activist sensibility—one of our movement's stellar attributes—tends to undermine the vertical." And this, argues Galli, is ultimately fatal to the evangelical logic of conversion. The problem is that "we cannot simply harangue people to change their wills; our wills need divine attention first."

This is, perhaps, Bebbington's "activism" undermining his "conversionism."

LOSS OF THEOLOGICAL UNDERSTANDING IN YOUTH

Finally, before turning to a more encouraging trend in evangelicalism, we will look at one more retrograde phenomenon within the movement. This is a case in which youth can bring to the table not new energy and innovation but a slide into theological inanity. The diagnosis came in a book published in 2005 by sociologists Christian Smith and Melinda Lundquist Denton, *Soul Searching: The Religious and Spiritual Lives of American Teenagers*. A sobering book for mainliners and evangelicals alike, it heralds the complete enculturation and theological evisceration of the next generation.[42]

After interviewing 3,000 teenagers, the authors concluded that many youth raised in Christian homes today believe not the Gospel—in any form recognizable either to conservative evangelicals or to more liberal mainliners—but rather a distorted modern version of it that they call "moralistic therapeutic deism" (MTD). In this set of values that could belong to any number of world religions, God is a vague and impersonal deity who creates us, watches over us, and wants us to be good and nice to one another. Along the way, God also wants us to feel good about ourselves, but he rarely intervenes in our lives except to fix the occasional problem. And if we are good in this life, he rewards us by letting us into heaven when we die.

For a significant number of American youth, concluded Smith and Denton, "God is something like a combination Divine Butler and Cosmic Therapist: he is always on call, takes care of any problems that arise, professionally helps his people to feel better about themselves, and does not become too personally involved in the process." This description of youthful faith horrified evangelicals, triggering a wave of hand-wringing. Galli concluded that "while Smith and Denton intended to describe the state of teenage faith, they seem to have described large segments of evangelical faith." Among others, *Christianity Today* writer Collin Hansen pronounced a grim prognosis for an America ruled by MTD, characterizing it as a "vapid creed" that threatens to plunge church and nation alike into a "feel-good free-for-all." The study's coauthor, Smith, apparently agreed with this prognosis, as he fled his childhood evangelicalism to conservative Roman Catholicism and then wrote a "how-to" book encouraging other evangelicals to do likewise.[43]

"REROOTING": SELECTIVE RECOVERY OF TRADITION

What, then, can help evangelical churches stand and retain their relevance and usefulness in America? For a while megachurches seemed the answer. But their inherent inability to disciple people well (as confessed by Willow Creek leadership in 2007) seems to have put them in the rear-view mirror already, at least as far as many young people are concerned, despite the cell groups and other small-group formats that attempted to put a personal and warmly communal face on those churches.[44]

Nor have the mass formats that emerged in the 1940s youth movement and blossomed under Billy Graham shown much more longevity in the parachurch realm. For example, the heyday of the stadium parachurch ministries of Promise Keepers and their ilk has also now come and gone. One potential winner would seem to be the "Internet churches," usually extensions of multisite churches. One of these is Joel Hunter's (b. 1948) Northland Church, a 15,000-member "distributed congregation" whose main campus is in Longwood, Florida. This assembly beams out to its satellite churches a live feed not only of the pastor but of worshipers at each site, so as to emphasize unity. In 2009 it was also reaching around 2,000 worshipers who logged on from their home computers and accessed both the worship service and specially trained "web ministers" who would chat with them during the proceedings. Pastors in this church even introduce online viewers by name and ask their congregation to welcome them.[45]

Hunter does recognize that such virtual participation has its limitations, and he hopes to spark house churches started by viewers in geographic proximity to one another. He has also seen benefits in one-on-one counseling, as remote participants have felt "safer" talking from their home than in a church setting. But it is hard to say whether Internet churches are really catching on—they seem merely an extension of the existing megachurch and seeker-sensitive models. And they seem to focus participants on cognitive rather than holistic aspects of faith. Mennonite pastor Shane Hipps, author of *Flickering Pixels: How Technology Shapes Your Faith* (2009), remarks that online evangelism frames Christianity as "information you need, not a way that a community lives in the world." Without bodies present together, a community lacks "the capacity to hold someone's hand, feed the poor, and care for the sick."[46]

In the face of these continued pragmatic attempts to make church "relevant," many thoughtful twenty- and thirty-something evangelicals (those not much tempted to MTD but unsure of how best to avoid it) have become increasingly uneasy and alienated. Mall-like church environments; high-energy, entertainment-oriented worship; and boomer-era ministry strategies and structures modeled on the business world are not doing it for them. Increasingly, they are asking just how these culturally camouflaged churches can help them rise above the values of the consumerist world around them.

This generation is looking for authentic community and the personal touch (though that may not rule out media such as the Internet, as, for example, in this day of social networking, many young people have not hesitated to find life partners exclusively via Internet dating). But it is fair to say that today a new generation of evangelical Christians is questioning received forms, hungering for authenticity and community, yearning for a spiritual therapy that will heal their sin-sick souls, and above all, reaching out for that immediate, personal connection to the divine, which goes right back to Pietism and Puritanism and the "inner travels" of Augustine that lay, in turn, at the root of those movements.

In *Younger Evangelicals* (2002), Robert Webber (1933–2007) discerned three phases of evangelicalism since 1950, each dominated by a different paradigm of church life and discipleship: "traditional" (1950–1975), "pragmatic" (1975–2000), and "younger" (2000–). For Webber, each group continues in some form today, but the third has superseded the first two. *Traditionals* focus on doctrine—or as Webber grumps, on "being right." They pour their resources into Bible studies, Sunday school curricula, and apologetics materials. The *pragmatics* "do" church growth, spawning the culturally engaged (and hugely successful) seeker-sensitive trend, with full-service megachurches and countless outreach programs. Currently, the *younger evangelicals* seek a Christianity that is "embodied" and "authentic"—distinctively Christian. In this they follow Stanley Hauerwas and William H. Willimon's widely read manifesto, *Resident Aliens: Life in the Christian Colony* (1989), which calls the church to push back against the surrounding culture, rejecting individualism, consumerism, and a host of other modern malaises.[47]

For the younger evangelicals (Webber's tag refers to "emerging" if not "Emergent" evangelicalism), traditional churches are too centered on words and propositions, and pragmatic churches are compromising authentic Christianity by tailoring their ministries to the marketplace and pop culture. The younger evangelicals seek a renewed encounter with a God beyond both doctrinal definitions and super-successful ministry programs.[48]

ANCIENT-FUTURE CHURCH

One promising direction, though it stands in some tension with evangelicalism's history of antitraditionalism, is the spiritual *ressourcement* movement associated with authors such as Richard Foster (b. 1942), Dallas Willard (1935–2013), Eugene Peterson (b. 1932), and James Houston (b. 1922). Starting in the late 1940s, culture-engaging "new evangelicals" (represented by the NAE, *Christianity Today*, and Fuller and Gordon-Conwell theological seminaries) sought to recover spiritual traditions from past centuries, such as *lectio divina* (slow, meditative reading of Scripture) and contemplative prayer, attending retreats at monasteries, sitting under a spiritual director, and reading Catholic and Orthodox books. The movement "broke out" among a wider swath of evangelicals in 1978 with the publication of Richard Foster's *Celebration of Discipline*.[49]

Given the evangelical suspicion of tradition, this movement could never have happened without some radical change and barrier-crossing.

Discontent with church as usual paved the way for change. As we have seen in the Jesus people movement, the Age of Aquarius saw evangelicals hungering for genuine spiritual experience. For many, if this meant breaking out from the narrow biblicism and constrictive intellectual boundaries of their fundamentalist roots, then so be it. They sought a deeper Christian wisdom both about what makes disciples truly Christ-like and, simply, about what makes people tick, and some began to look for that wisdom in the church's own history.

The search for ressourcement developed in the wake of fundamentalism's spiritual legacy, which many found inadequate. The fundamentalist movement of the 1920s–1950s had dedicated itself to defending important doctrines such as the divinity and personal return of Christ against liberal modifications. In so doing, it had come to identify the Christian life with cognitive belief. Discipleship, or growth in spiritual things, took a back seat. This was one seed of a kind of "sanctification gap" in fundamentalism's evangelical progeny.[50]

Another seed was fundamentalism's fervid activism. The cry D. L. Moody raised in the late nineteenth century echoed down the decades: "This world is like a wrecked vessel. . . . God puts a life-boat in my hands and says 'Rescue every man you can.'" A rescue mission allows precious little time to engage in contemplation or protracted disciplines. This unreflective pragmatism was intensified by fundamentalism's inherited anti-intellectualism and its dispensational eschatology. If elite theology grounded in the traditions of the historic church served only to confound ordinary believers and lead them away from spiritual vitality, and if the world is not our home and is only getting worse and worse until the Rapture, then why delve into historical documents or work through arcane disciplines? In the words of the bumper sticker: "Jesus is coming! Look busy!"[51]

The intense, pragmatic activism of evangelicalism's history has taken its toll. For many, church has seemed little more than a dizzying round of activities and programs. Eugene Peterson, author of *The Message: The Bible in Contemporary Language* (2002), remembers his early years leading a Presbyterian church in suburban Maryland: "I can't tell you how many people came to me and said, 'Pastor, don't ask me to do anything.' And I'd say, 'Take as long as you'd like.' People were always being treated kind of as a recruit for a cause. . . . I think that burned out a lot of people." Compounding the tendency of pragmatism to wear Christians down, a theological misunderstanding about the nature of grace also contributed to the loss of healthy spiritual formation among evangelicals since the fundamentalist era. Fundamentalism became infected with a kind of "cheap grace" theology—a misunderstanding of Reformation teaching that tagged all moral effort as works-righteousness. By these lights, grace is *only* for forgiveness from guilt; it has nothing to do with spiritual growth.[52]

As early as 1947 NAE cofounder and future *Christianity Today* editor Carl F. H. Henry (1913–2003) sounded the alarm with his *Uneasy Conscience of Modern Fundamentalism*. Evangelicals could no longer deny the stark reality: the character of professing Christians was misshapen. Dallas Willard recalled that as far back as the 1950s younger Christians ransacked their fundamentalist heritage and found little there to satisfy their hunger for teachings and practices that would address not just salvation and the hereafter but spiritual depth, integrity, and personal growth in the here-and-now. The search took some to the religions of the East. Others stuck it out within Christianity but went beyond evangelicalism. The desire was to find "some kind of spiritual reality—not just some sort of performance from the church."[53]

As evangelicals searched for resources, printed material from the older traditions began trickling through. Willard remembered his own discovery of the Methodist-published *Upper Room* daily devotional guides during the 1960s, excerpting everyone from Augustine to the Church of England cleric Jeremy Taylor (1613–1667). These devotionals were printed in the millions. Another key disseminator of classical Christian spirituality was A. W. Tozer (1897–1963), a Christian and Missionary Alliance pastor and author who quoted freely from many great medieval and early church "saints." Peterson discovered Tozer as a teenager in the late 1940s and early 1950s and says, "I got my taste for the nature of the holy life from him."[54]

For all but a few evangelicals, such writings would have been off-limits if not for the breakdown of traditional denominational barriers. It is hard for most people to remember now how radical a change this "opening" was, because few people recollect today how unyielding denominational boundaries once were. Willard told the story of a teenage couple who lived not long before this loosening of boundaries. She kept getting pregnant, but every time, she had an abortion, as their parents prevented them from getting married because they were of different denominations. But by the late 1950s "people were beginning to understand," Willard recalled, "that what the particular denomination prescribed for their members was not necessarily what Christ prescribed."[55]

A number of trends built bridges across denominations: First, in America's increasingly mobile social environment, people were frequently meeting members of other denominations and thinking, "These people are OK!" Second, the Charismatic movement arose in the late 1950s, the Holy Spirit giving gifts that made it clear, as Willard put it, that "I'm over here where you thought I was not." Third, Billy Graham was unapologetically committed to working with all Christians. "He would be seen," said Willard, "around the world preaching in all kinds of contexts, including Eastern Orthodox, and at first there was great criticism of him for doing this—even from the new evangelicals." His example, however, opened "a kind of practical ecumenism" among evangelicals—the upside of a breakdown of Protestant denominations whose effects we are still seeing today.[56]

Committed evangelicals who recognized that lives were not changing in their churches increasingly began to peer across the Great Divide into Catholic traditions. Willard, who attended a Southern California Evangelical Friends church pastored by the young, fresh-from-Fuller Richard Foster, remembered that in the late 1960s, Foster discovered "a little Catholic nun who played the guitar and sang" and invited her to perform at their church. "A lot of people were worried by this, because they had been raised in opposition to Catholicism. Some people, though, were touched."[57]

A number of events and influences opened the door to Catholic spirituality for American Protestants. The year 1960 saw the election of America's first Roman Catholic president. Vatican II (1962–1965) opened the windows of ecumenical dialogue. Henri Nouwen (1932–1996) came into the consciousness of lay evangelicals, opening up the desert tradition to them. The Charismatic movement crossed confessional boundaries too.

By the 1970s evangelical Protestants began going on retreats at monasteries where they experienced Catholic spirituality on the ground. They came back refreshed, Willard remembered, and others worried about their orthodoxy. The trend of engagement with Catholic spirituality continued, and Foster's 1978 *Celebration* became a great part of that. Nor was the Catholic Church the only magnet for young, dissatisfied evangelicals. Although the defection of Campus Crusade leaders in the 1960s to Orthodoxy was more an isolated event than a bellwether, Willard observed in 2009 that "I constantly find pastors who discover the *Philokalia*—the great treasure on the Christian life of the Greek and Russian church—and people wallow in the riches of it."[58]

Despite the popularity of such historical resources since the 1970s, the evangelical move toward spiritual ressourcement seems to have stalled. Discipline requires, by definition, *submission*. Still marked by the antitraditionalism and pragmatism of their fundamentalist roots, evangelicals seem by and large unwilling to submit their spiritual growth to anything that looks like a mediating practice or tradition. They start from the assumption of unmediated access to the throne of God and rush ahead in fevered activism. Evangelical leadership is not helping. Foster observes that the ABCs of evangelical ministry are still "attendance, buildings, and cash" rather than the basics of discipleship. True, many evangelicals have been opened to the riches of Christian spiritual tradition, but they have barely scratched the surface.[59]

The block against full absorption of Christianity's spiritual heritage has come not just from the pragmatism of church leaders but also from a standoffishness among evangelical academic institutions. According to Willard, a syndrome of disconnection between theology and spirituality marks most seminary programs. He observed, "Most of the programs of spiritual formation in evangelical seminaries remain outside the theology departments, marginalized from the mainstream of seminary life and thought." As a result, although evangelical seminarians have dabbled in the "spiritual classics," their theology has not caught up to their practice. Spiritual formation teachings have not been rooted in theological understandings about who God is and how humans relate to him.[60]

Emblematic of this disconnect is the fact that the most notable champions of evangelical spiritual ressourcement have come from outside the theological guild. Foster and Peterson are pastors, Willard a philosopher, and Regent's James Houston a geologist. Evangelicals owe them much, but without theologians willing to embrace broader definitions of "being saved"—definitions that go beyond "going to heaven" to the "living out" of a graced life on earth—spirituality would seem destined to languish, an orphan among the disciplines of evangelical seminaries.

Yet there is a glimmer of change. We see it in the Sixteenth Annual Theology Conference in 2007 at Wheaton College—evangelicalism's flagship institution of higher learning. Under the guidance of the late Robert Webber, this annual meeting of evangelical theologians took as its theme "The Ancient Faith for the Church's Future." The tone was set by the call for papers, which rejoiced that "one of the most promising developments among evangelical Protestants is the recent 'discovery' of the rich biblical, spiritual, and theological treasures to be found within the early church." Evangelicals, it said, are beginning to "reach back behind the European Enlightenment for patterns and models of how to faithfully read Scripture, worship, and engage a religiously diverse culture."[61]

Conference presenter and Baylor University professor D. H. Williams, author of *Evangelicals and Tradition* (2005), testified to the recent upsurge of evangelical commitment to the theological study of patristics (the study of the "church fathers" in the first seven centuries of the church): "Who would have thought, a decade ago, that one of the most vibrant and serious fields of Christian study at the beginning of the twenty-first century would be the ancient church fathers? There has been an opening of new avenues, especially among free-church Protestants, by the almost overnight popularity of bishops and monks, martyrs and apologists, philosophers and historians who first fashioned a Christian culture 1500 years ago." Two years after this conference, in 2009, Wheaton created a Center for Early Christian Studies in which students can pursue a degree program in patristics. Results? We will see.[62]

To at least some young evangelicals, a reappropriation of the ancient church seems one way around the endless debates about and advertisements for Christianity. Perhaps an "ancient future" journey (Webber's phrase) can help the church stop *talking* about Christianity and just embody it. Perhaps through church fathers, Benedictine monks, and ancient spiritual practices such as the *lectio divina*, evangelicals can find ways to live their faith authentically in community with others—especially others beyond the white suburban world of many megachurch ministries. Perhaps the answer is to embrace ancient symbols and sacraments; to bring candles and incense back into worship; to dialogue with the "other two" historic confessions: Catholicism and Orthodoxy.

Some thoughtful youth have continued, such as Peter Gillquist's (1938–2012) group that defected from evangelicalism to Eastern Orthodoxy in the 1960s, to yearn for a golden time and place (say, before Constantine, or in the medieval monasteries, or the antistate ranks of the sixteenth-century Anabaptists) when the church seemed to have its *own* culture, standing against the stream. And as they come into contact with older, traditional churches, the younger evangelicals believe they have found links to that countercultural church.

Evangelicals read and sometimes write a new subgenre of spiritual books: Kathleen Norris's *Cloister Walk* (Riverhead, 1996), Dennis Okholm's *Monk Habits for Everyday People: Benedictine Spirituality for Protestants* (Brazos, 2007), Karen Sloan's *Flirting with Monasticism: Finding God on Ancient Paths* (IVP, 2006), Leighton Ford's *The Attentive Life: Discerning God's Presence in All Things* (IVP, 2008), Scott Bessenecker's *The New Friars: The Emerging Movement Serving the World's Poor* (IVP, 2006), Tony Jones's *Divine Intervention: Encountering God Through the Ancient Practice of* Lectio Divina (THINK, 2006). There is even a recent spate of Baptist books trying to formulate a "Baptist sacramentology," such as Anthony R. Cross and Philip E. Thompson's *Baptist Sacramentalism* (Paternoster, 2003), Stanley K. Fowler and William H. Brackney's *More than a Symbol: The British Baptist Recovery of Baptismal Sacramentalism* (Paternoster, 2002), Steven Harmon and Paul Avis's *Towards a Baptist Catholicity: Essays on Tradition and the Baptist Vision* (Paternoster, 2006), and Cameron H. Jorgenson's Baylor University Ph.D. dissertation, "Bapto-Catholicism: Recovering Tradition and Reconsidering the Baptist Identity" (2008).[63]

The ancient-future movement has spilled beyond private spirituality to a yearning for, and implementation of, liturgical worship, including use of the rhythms of the traditional "Christian year." Indeed, evangelicals' steady movement into Anglicanism, described years ago in Robert Webber's book *Evangelicals on the Canterbury Trail* (1989), has essentially caused a major split in American Anglicanism, as the old Episcopalian Church has continued along its modernizing path, taking it beyond the theological pale for those liturgy-hungry evangelicals. In his many books on worship, Webber offered evangelicals a way to incorporate the liturgies of the historic Church through a simple order: the Gathering, the Word, the Table, and the Dismissal. He also recommended a restored commitment to the sacraments, especially the Eucharist, as part of the weekly worship event. Such liturgical borrowings open up a greater role in worship for ritual gesture, symbol, and visual art, which point (as they always have) to spiritual realities beyond themselves. They allow evangelicals to "capture the mystery and transcendence of God in a way that modern forms of Protestant worship do not" and, by reentering historic practices, to stress the unity of the church.⁶⁴

CONCLUSION

Whether this ancient-future road proves a thoroughfare or a dead end, if we want to see the "future of evangelicalism," we should cast a careful eye on the forms these younger Christians prefer: every generation's heart is touched differently. Whatever touches the heart of the next generation will shape the style of evangelical worship and spirituality for years to come. Evangelicalism's genius is its plasticity. Look for trends in popular culture and then look for them in similar-yet-different forms in evangelical churches. Free-flowing theology discussions in pubs, social-justice activism, postmodern churches with couches instead of pews and dialogues rather than sermons, "new monastic" communities in the inner cities—each draws from current allergies among evangelical youth to organizational structures and strictures, as well as their desire for an authentic, personal faith that addresses people's real needs where they are.

NOTES

1. "The Alternative Jesus: Psychedelic Christ," *Time*, June 21, 1971, cover story; Robb Redman, *The Great Worship Awakening: Singing a New Song in the Postmodern Church* (San Francisco: Jossey-Bass, 2002), 52.

2. Paul Dienstberger, cited in Elmer L. Towns and Vernon M. Whaley, *Worship Through the Ages: How the Great Awakenings Shape Evangelical Worship* (Nashville: B & H Academic, 2012), 298; Wendy Murray Zoba, *Beliefnet Guide to Evangelical Christianity* (New York: Three Leaves, 2005), 80–81.

3. Towns and Whaley, *Worship Through the Ages*, 303–4; Donald E. Miller, *Reinventing American Protestantism: Christianity in the New Millennium* (Berkeley: University of California Press, 1997), 11–12.

4. Zoba, *Beliefnet Guide*, 82; Torrey Maynard Johnson and Robert Cook, *Reaching Youth for Christ* (Chicago: Moody, 1944).

5. Joel Carpenter, *Revive Us Again: The Reawakening of American Fundamentalism* (New York: Oxford University Press, 1997), 165.

6. According to Carpenter, by the last days of World War II weekly [fundamentalist] youth rallies were thriving in hundreds of cities and towns with hundreds of thousands of people attending. Ibid., 161.

7. Towns and Whaley, *Worship Through the Ages*, 344.

8. Redman, *Great Worship Awakening*, 53–54.

9. Ibid., 41, 51–52.

10. Miller, *Reinventing American Protestantism*, 83.

11. Elmer Towns reported that "as of 2010, more than 85 institutions provide undergraduate degrees in worship studies or worship and music. Nearly 40 graduate degrees in worship are now available at evangelical universities, college, and seminaries. These are primarily vocational degrees that strategically equip students to lead worship in the evangelical community"; Towns and Whaley, *Worship Through the Ages*, 353. See also Miller, *Reinventing American Protestantism*, 83; Redman, *Great Worship Awakening*, 54.

12. Redman, *Great Worship Awakening*, 59, 62, 71; Miller, *Reinventing American Protestantism*, 23.

13. Redman, *Great Worship Awakening*, 29.

14. Miller, *Reinventing American Protestantism*, 13–16.

15. As Miller observed this practice: "After briefly inquiring about the person's needs, a member of the ministry team, or in some cases just a friend, put a hand on the other's shoulder, or sometimes the forehead, and prayed for that person" (ibid., 45–46).

16. Ibid., 88–89.

17. Ibid., 11.

18. Mark Galli, "In the Beginning, Grace," *Christianity Today*, October 2, 2009, http://www.christianitytoday.com/ct/2009/october/13.23.html, accessed August 4, 2015.

19. Lamin Sanneh, *Translating the Message: The Missionary Impact on Culture*, 2nd ed. (Maryknoll, N.Y.: Orbis, 2013).

20. Miller, *Reinventing American Protestantism*, 11.

21. Cecil M. Robeck, *The Azusa Street Mission and Revival: The Birth of the Global Pentecostal Movement* (Nashville: Thomas Nelson, 2006), 111; Gastón Espinosa, *William J. Seymour and the Origins of Global Pentecostalism: A Biography and Documentary History* (Durham, N.C.: Duke University Press, 2014). As for the parallel to the modern Jesus movement churches, Miller says that they "truly did believe in the priesthood of all believers. People were not only having their needs met, but they were finding an avenue for service." Miller, interview with Timothy Sato, "Outrageous Vision: An Interview with Donald Miller About Global Pentecostalism," in *Christian Post*, http://m.christianpost.com/news/outrageous-vision-an-interview-with-donal-miller-about-global-pentecostalism-5972/, accessed August 4, 2015.

22. Mark Noll, *The Old Religion in the New World* (Grand Rapids, Mich.: Eerdmans, 2002), 24; Chris Armstrong, "Tavern Tunes in Church Music and 'Why Should the Devil Have All the Good Music?,'" http://gratefultothedead.wordpress.com/2009/11/02/tavern-tunes-in-church-music-and-why-should-the-devil-have-all-the-good-music/, accessed August 4, 2015; Shay Quillen, "Obituary:

Father of Christian Rock: Musician Larry Norman, 60," *Mercury News*, February 26, 2008, http://www.religionnewsblog.com/20766/larry-norman-2, accessed August 6, 2013.

23. Bruce Hindmarsh, "Is Evangelical Ecclesiology an Oxymoron? A Historical Perspective," in *Evangelical Ecclesiology: Reality or Illusion?*, ed. John G. Stackhouse (Grand Rapids, Mich.: Baker, 2003), 15–38.

24. A thorough and interesting ethnographic survey of the small-group phenomenon as it looked in the 1980s and 1990s—not just in evangelical but also in mainline and non-Christian circles—can be found in a pair of books by Robert Wuthnow, *Sharing the Journey: Support Groups and America's New Quest for Community* (New York: Free Press, 1996) and *I Come Away Stronger: How Small Groups Are Shaping American Religion* (Grand Rapids, Mich.: Eerdmans, 2001). Wuthnow concludes that evangelicals in particular have used small groups to redefine God as "more manageable, more serviceable in meeting individual needs"—perhaps the same sort of domesticated, cash-machine vision of the Almighty that Christian Smith identifies in the thousands of evangelical young people who have pasteurized the older faith into what he calls "Moralistic Therapeutic Deism," and God into an indulgent, supportive, nondemanding grandfather figure. "The deity of small groups is a God of love, comfort, order, and security. Gone is the God of judgment, wrath, justice, mystery, and punishment. Gone are concerns about the forces of evil" (*Sharing the Journey*, 7). Wuthnow's conclusion: small groups are a secularizing force, domesticating the sacred, knocking its rough edges off in service of cultural (therapeutic) agendas.

25. Barry A. Kosmin and Ariela Keysar, *The American Religious Identification Survey (ARIS 2008): Summary Report* (Hartford, Conn.: Trinity College, 2009), http://commons.trincoll.edu/aris/files/2011/08/ARIS_Report_2008.pdf, accessed August 4, 2015.

26. David W. Bebbington, *Evangelicalism in Modern Britain: A History from the 1730s to the 1980s* (London: Unwin Hyman, 1989), 2–17. Related to this observation is the important secondary one that Bebbington's "crucicentrism" (cross-centeredness) is not currently universal among evangelicals—particularly if one includes Pentecostal groups, which still account for a hefty percentage of members in the National Association of Evangelicals. Among many of these, "pneumocentrism" (spirit-centeredness, so to speak) has often replaced crucicentrism to a great degree. And as we have seen, pentecostal styles of worship have deeply influenced much of modern white evangelicalism since the 1970s, so this is not a minor point. On the concept of habitus, see, for instance, Pierre Bourdieu, *The Logic of Practice* (Stanford, Calif.: Stanford University Press, 1990), 66–67.

27. Martin Luther, "The Pagan Servitude of the Church," in *Martin Luther: Selections from His Writings*, trans. and ed. John Dillenberger (New York: Anchor, 1962), 249–362.

28. Miller, *Reinventing American Protestantism*, 15.

29. Tanya Luhrmann, *When God Talks Back: Understanding the American Evangelical Relationship with God* (New York: Vintage, 2012), 74; Grant Wacker, "Hand-clapping

in a Gothic Nave: What Pentecostals and Mainliners Can Learn from One Another," *Christianity Today*, March 11, 2005, http://www.christianitytoday.com/ct/2005/march/31.58.html, accessed August 4, 2015.

30. John Corrigan, ed., *Religion and Emotion: Approaches and Interpretations* (New York: Oxford University Press, 2004).

31. Shara Lee, "Do You Know the Donut Man?" *Converge*, April 11, 2013, http://convergemagazine.com/do-you-know-donut-man-7054/, accessed August 5, 2015. The key line in "The Weight of Glory" is this: "If we consider the unblushing promises of reward and the staggering nature of the rewards promised in the Gospels, it would seem that Our Lord finds our desires, not too strong, but too weak. We are half-hearted creatures, fooling about with drink and sex and ambition when infinite joy is offered us, like an ignorant child who wants to go on making mud pies in a slum because he cannot imagine what is meant by the offer of a holiday at the sea. We are far too easily pleased." C. S. Lewis, "The Weight of Glory," in *The Weight of Glory* (1949; New York, HarperCollins, 2001), 26.

32. Miller, *Reinventing American Protestantism*, 12.

33. See the social analysis, for example, in H. Richard Niebuhr's *Social Sources of Denominationalism* (New York: Meridian, 1957).

34. There are some indications of "revitalization," as demonstrated by Margaret M. Poloma and John C. Green, *The Assemblies of God: Godly Love and the Revitalization of American Pentecostalism* (New York: New York University Press, 2010), 105.

35. Chris R. Armstrong, "Assemblies of God: 1985–Present," in *New International Dictionary of Pentecostal and Charismatic Movements*, ed. Stanley Burgess (Grand Rapids, Mich.: Zondervan, 2002).

36. Candy Gunther Brown, *Testing Prayer: Science and Healing* (Cambridge, Mass.: Harvard University Press, 2012), 21; Poloma and Green, *Assemblies of God*, 1.

37. Thomas Trask, quoted in Corwin E. Smidt et al., "The Spirit-Filled Movements in Contemporary America: A Survey Perspective," in *Pentecostal Currents in American Protestantism*, ed. Edith L. Blumhofer, Russell P. Spittler, and Grant A. Wacker (Urbana: University of Illinois Press, 1999), 129.

38. Ronald J. Sider, *Rich Christians in an Age of Hunger: A Biblical Study* (Downers Grove, Ill.: Intervarsity Press, 1977); Tony Campolo, *Red Letter Christians: A Citizen's Guide to Faith and Politics* (Ventura, Calif.: Regal, 2008); Shane Claiborne, *The Irresistible Revolution: Living as an Ordinary Radical* (Grand Rapids, Mich.: Zondervan, 2006); Jonathan Wilson-Hartgrove, *New Monasticism: What it Has to Say to Today's Church* (Grand Rapids, Mich.: Brazos, 2008); Stanley Hauerwas, *A Community of Character: Toward a Constructive Christian Social Ethic* (Notre Dame, Ind.: University of Notre Dame Press, 1981).

39. Jon Stock, Tim Otto, and Jonathan Wilson-Hartgrove, *Inhabiting the Church: Biblical Wisdom for a New Monasticism* (Eugene, Ore: Cascade, 2007); Avery Dulles, *Models of the Church: Expanded Edition* (New York: Image, 2002), 81–94.

40. Galli, "In the Beginning, Grace."

41. John Perkins, *A Quiet Revolution: The Christian Response to Human Need, A Strategy for Today* (Waco, Tex.: Word Books, 1976); Derek Perkins, Rudy Carrasco, and Phil Ginsburg, *My City, My God: The New Testament* (Colorado Springs, Colo.: International Bible Society, 1999).

42. Christian Smith and Melinda Lundquist Denton, *Soul Searching: The Religious and Spiritual Lives of American Teenagers* (New York: Oxford University Press, 2005).

43. Smith and Benton, *Soul Searching*, 165; Galli, "In the Beginning, Grace"; Collin Hansen, "Death by Deism," *Christianity Today*, April 20, 2009, http://www.christianitytoday.com/ct/2009/aprilweb-only/116-11.0.html, accessed August 4, 2015; Christian Smith, *How to Go from Being a Good Evangelical to a Committed Catholic in Ninety-Five Difficult Steps* (Eugene, Ore: Cascade, 2011).

44. S. Michael Craven, "Willow Creek's Confession," *CP Opinion*, November 27, 2007, http://www.christianpost.com/news/willow-creek-s-confession-30234/, accessed August 4, 2015.

45. Joel Hunter, "Northland: A Church Distributed," http://www.northlandchurch.net/, accessed August, 2015.

46. Shane Hipps, *Flickering Pixels: How Technology Shapes Your Faith* (Grand Rapids, Mich.: Zondervan, 2009), quoted in Sarah Pulliam, "The Art of Cyber Church," *Christianity Today*, September 16, 2009, http://www.christianitytoday.com/ct/2009/september/29.50.html, accessed August 4, 2015.

47. Robert Webber, *The Younger Evangelicals: Facing the Challenges of the New World* (Grand Rapids, Mich.: Baker, 2002); Stanley Hauerwas and William H. Willimon, *Resident Aliens: Life in the Christian Colony* (Nashville: Abingdon, 1989).

48. On the distinction between "emerging" (the more general term) and "Emergent" (referring to an official organization) Christians, see Scot McKnight, "Five Streams of the Emerging Church," *Christianity Today*, January 19, 2007, http://www.christianitytoday.com/ct/2007/february/11.35.html, accessed August 4, 2015.

49. Richard Foster, *Celebration of Discipline: The Path to Spiritual Growth* (San Francisco: Harper & Row, 1978). Lest we think that the Augustinian-Platonic focus on direct inward experience of the divine, so typical of evangelicalism, works only against tradition, however, we need only remember the Reformers' own deep engagement in the thought of the church fathers. The Reformation was precisely the story of a group of people who saw unacceptable (they would have said, "modern") innovations in their church and worked to reform and renew it by reengaging with, yes, the Bible; yes, the New Testament church; but also, and very significantly, the church fathers. When the late evangelical liturgiologist Robert Webber talked about the "ancient-future church," he was saying only what the Reformers themselves were saying.

50. Richard Lovelace, "The Sanctification Gap," *Theology Today* 29, no. 4 (January, 1973): 363–69.

51. D. L. Moody, *The Gospel Awakening* (Chicago: Fairbanks and Palmer, 1885), 667; Nathan Hatch, *Democratization of American Christianity* (New Haven, Conn.: Yale University Press, 1991); Richard Hofstadter, *Anti-Intellectualism in American Life* (New

York: Knopf, 1963); Tim F. LaHaye and Jerry B. Jenkins, *Left Behind* (Wheaton, Ill.: Tyndale House, 1995), and its sequels.

52. Eugene Peterson, interview by author, 2009; Peterson, *The Message: The Bible in Contemporary Language* (Colorado Springs, Colo.: Navpress, 2002).

53. Carl F. H. Henry, *The Uneasy Conscience of Modern Fundamentalism* (Grand Rapids, Mich.: Eerdmans, 1947); Dallas Willard, interview by author, 2009.

54. Peterson, interview.

55. Willard, interview.

56. Ibid.

57. Foster, interview by author, 2009. On the history of evangelicalism's anti-Catholicism and the movement's slow recovery from that prejudice, see Mark Noll and Caroline Nystrom, *Is the Reformation Over?: An Evangelical Assessment of Contemporary Roman Catholicism* (Grand Rapids, Mich.: Baker Academic, 2008).

58. Willard, interview.

59. Foster, interview.

60. Willard, interview.

61. Papers from the conference were published in Mark Husbands and Jeffrey P. Greenman, eds., *Ancient Faith for the Church's Future* (Downers Grove, Ill.: InterVarsity Academic, 2008), which I reviewed at http://www.christianitytoday.com/ch/booksandresources/reviews/alexandriawheaton.html, accessed August 4, 2015.

62. D. H. Williams, "Similis et Dissimilis: Gauging our Expectations of the Early Fathers," paper given at the Sixteenth Annual Wheaton Theology Conference, April 12–14, 2007, and published in Husbands and Greenman, *Ancient Faith*; Williams, *Evangelicals and Tradition: The Formative Influence of the Early Church* (Grand Rapids, Mich.: Baker, 2005).

63. The "Bapto-Catholic" movement seeks to recover the Great Tradition of the church fathers, largely in reaction to growing liberal theology among antifundamentalist exiles from the Southern Baptist Convention, and is promoted by Baptist academics and their students, many now graduated and out in churches or teaching, and associated with specific congregations (such as Dayspring Baptist Church in Waco, Texas, home to D. H. Williams among others); see Jay Smith, "Sojourn: Reflections on a Journey with the Triune God," April 15, 25, 26, 2012, http://theologicalsojourn.blogspot.com/, accessed August 6, 2015.

64. On this, see, for example, *Christianity Today* editor Mark Galli's *Beyond Smells and Bells: The Wonder and Power of Christian Liturgy* (Brewster, Mass.: Paraclete, 2008); Robert Webber, *Evangelicals on the Canterbury Trail: Why Evangelicals Are Attracted to the Liturgical Church* (1985; New York: Morehouse, 2012); Robert Webber, "The Convergence Movement," *The Christian Century* 99 (1982), quoted in Redman, *Great Worship Awakening*, 78–80; Robert Webber, "The Convergence Movement," *The Christian Century* 99 (1982), quoted in Redman, *Great Worship Awakening*, 78–80; Towns and Whaley, *Worship Through the Ages*.

3

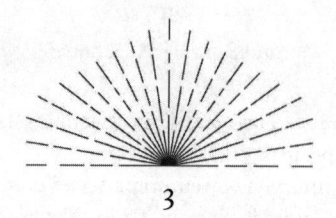

The Emerging Divide in Evangelical Theology

Roger E. Olson

Throughout the 1990s the Evangelical Theology Group of the American Academy of Religion wrestled with the definition of "evangelical." "Who is an evangelical?" and "What does 'evangelical' mean?" were the driving questions of a series of symposiums and panel discussions by scholars of the movement. No consensus appeared. In the last moments of the final session of one such event, as it became clear that the evangelical scholars could not agree, a nonevangelical "mainline" theologian stood in the very back of the room and said, "I propose that an evangelical is someone who loves Billy Graham." The entire room of more than a hundred scholars broke out in applause.

For purposes of this chapter, *evangelical theology* is defined as theology done by evangelicals. *Evangelicals* here denotes those relatively conservative (mostly) Protestant Christians who identify themselves in some way, however indirectly, with the post–World War II, postfundamentalist American evangelical movement. This chapter attends to changes taking place in evangelical theology since 1970, with special interest in the role of tradition in its fragmentation. Because of that fragmentation, for better or worse, there is no viable alternative to defining evangelical theology as theology done by persons associated with the post–World Word II evangelical movement.

Evangelical is an essentially contested concept; outsiders often think they know what it means, but insiders, especially evangelical scholars, debate its nature and especially its theological limits. To outsiders, evangelical often means antimodern, fundamentalist Christianity. Many nonevangelicals, especially journalists, have increasingly used the term to designate politically active conservative Christianity, the so-called religious Right. Insiders know the term designates a much broader range, including many Christians who eschew politics altogether.

One can distinguish six common meanings of evangelical in contemporary American culture. First, it means aggressively evangelistic religion of any tradition. The above-mentioned journalistic equation of it with the religious Right is a subset of this meaning. Second, it means simply Protestant. That is its meaning in German-speaking Europe. Many Lutherans in America continue to use it in that sense, often equating it with their own theological heritage going back to Martin Luther. Third, it means Christian revivalism and renewalism stemming from the continental pietist movements of the late seventeenth and early eighteenth centuries and especially the first and second Great Awakenings in Great Britain and North America. Fourth, it means orthodox, conservative Protestantism, especially Reformed, Calvinistic in flavor. Fifth, it means the antiliberal reaction of conservative and fundamentalist Protestants in Great Britain and North America throughout the late nineteenth century into the twenty-first century. Sixth, and finally, it means the post–World War II, postfundamentalist movement whose figurehead and lodestar has been Billy Graham (b. 1918).

It is important to distinguish between evangelical as an ethos and as a movement. The movement is (or at least was) visible and relatively organized, at least in the sense of networks acknowledging one another as evangelical. The ethos is more difficult to identify. It is a set of convictions, attitudes, beliefs, and practices that extend far beyond the post–World War II movement but also form its center. Much confusion has arisen around evangelicalism and within it by failure to distinguish clearly between the ethos and the movement.

For example, during the 1990s a heated debate arose among Southern Baptist scholars about whether Southern Baptists are evangelicals. The whole debate could have been avoided or at least settled with that distinction (between ethos and movement). For the most part, with notable individual exceptions, Southern Baptists sat outside the formation of the post–World War II, postfundamentalist movement in spite of the fact that the movement's acknowledged leader was Billy Graham, a Southern Baptist. (For many years he held membership in First Baptist Church of Dallas, Texas, even though he lived in North Carolina and attended his wife's family's Presbyterian church.) And yet most scholars of evangelicalism would agree that the majority of Southern Baptists share an evangelical ethos.

THE EVANGELICAL ETHOS

Evangelical historians David Bebbington and Mark Noll have helpfully identified four common features or hallmarks of the evangelical ethos in Great Britain and North America especially, and through them to the rest of the world: conversionism, biblicism, crucicentrism, and activism. *Conversionism* indicates belief that authentic and full Christian life begins with a personal decision to repent, trust in Jesus Christ as Savior and Lord, and turn away from sin. Conversionism among evangelicals emphasizes regeneration, a change of heart, and not just a change of mind. Also, conversionism implies a lifelong process many evangelicals call a "personal relationship with Jesus Christ," or discipleship. *Biblicism* does not denote rigid, literalistic interpretation of the Bible, and certainly not worship of the Bible, but belief in the Bible as the final authority for Christian faith and practice. But the evangelical ethos includes more than just a doctrine about the Bible; it includes love for the Bible, devotional reading of it, preaching from it, and life guidance by means of it.[1]

Crucicentrism is focus and emphasis on the atoning death of Jesus Christ as the only ground for salvation in preaching and piety. Most evangelicals have regarded Christ's death as a "vicarious sacrifice for sins." Some, perhaps the majority, have also believed it to be a "penal substitution for sins," the punishment God requires for reconciliation of sinners with himself. *Activism* refers to any evangelistic activity aimed at bringing about individual conversions and church renewals and, sometimes, social transformation.

Many self-identified evangelicals have rallied around this four-part description of the evangelical ethos as the most helpful one so far for identifying who, meaning individuals and organizations, are truly worthy of the label "evangelical." However, many evangelical movement leaders have expressed dissatisfaction that it does not include a fifth common feature—doctrinal orthodoxy. Traditionally, the evangelical ethos has been doctrinally conservative compared with, say, liberal Protestantism. Belief in Scripture's infallibility, for example, has been common among evangelicals going back to the Reformation itself. All the great founders and leaders of evangelicalism in all its meanings have affirmed Scripture's unique inspiration and authority. Also, evangelicals have always, perhaps without exception, affirmed the deity of Jesus Christ and the Trinity. (One must say "perhaps" to leave the door open to individuals and groups who have denied the Trinity only because they think it implies three gods. So-called Oneness Pentecostals affirm a modalistic view of the Trinity, that Father, Son, and Holy Spirit are manifestations or modes and not distinct persons of the Godhead. Whether they can be evangelicals is much debated.)

Many questions have surrounded the evangelical quadrilateral, even when one adds (as this author has) the fifth common feature of respect for traditional Protestant orthodoxy. Can a person or group be recognized as authentically evangelical in spite of lacking one or more of the features? For example, can an Episcopalian who believes in baptismal regeneration of infants without emphasis on the necessity of personal decision as conversion later be considered authentically evangelical? (Of course, all Episcopalians believe in confirmation for church membership, but evangelical Episcopalians have traditionally emphasized that confirmation must be a profoundly meaningful personal decision and not a formality of confirming one's infant baptism only.) Also, can a hyper-Calvinist who rejects missions and evangelism be an evangelical? Most pressing and controversial since 1970 has been the issue of biblical inerrancy. Can a person or group be authentically evangelical while denying biblical inerrancy, that is, while affirming errors in Scripture?

Recognizing the evangelical ethos does not settle everything; in many cases it has given rise to heated debates about the nature of the common features and about whether all of them are necessary.

THE EVANGELICAL MOVEMENT

Most scholars of evangelicalism agree that no single scholar has done more to identify the evangelical ethos and movement than George Marsden, author of, among other notable books on the subject, *Understanding Fundamentalism and Evangelicalism* (1991). There and in other books on the subject, Marsden recounts and analyzes the rise and development (and perhaps demise) of the post–World War II evangelical movement especially in America. Other scholars who have examined the same phenomenon and contributed to a rough consensus about it include Joel Carpenter, Randall

Balmer, and Gary Dorrien. (Of course, Noll and Bebbington should be included in that list.) Other scholars have muddied the waters of this consensus, demonstrating the radical diversity among self-identified and other-recognized evangelicals in America since World War II. They include notably Donald Dayton and Robert Johnston, editors of *The Variety of American Evangelicalism* (1991), and Kenneth Collins, author of *The Evangelical Moment: The Promise of an American Religion* (2005).[2]

The "Marsden consensus" is that post–World War II, postfundamentalist evangelicalism is predominantly Reformed in terms of its theological orientation. That is, its theological roots lie in Puritan Calvinism, even though that has gone through many permutations. Especially Donald Dayton has argued that Marsden's story of the evangelical movement and its theological roots is only one paradigm of evangelical history and theology—the "Puritan, Presbyterian paradigm." He identifies another paradigm that one might rightly call the "Pietist, Pentecostal paradigm." It emphasizes the revivalistic, experiential roots of evangelicalism and includes as equally formative the Wesleyan heritage. This is one debate among evangelical scholars about the nature of the post–World War II evangelical movement. All agree that the movement bears family resemblances such as those identified by Bebbington and Noll.[3]

Originally the post–World War II, postfundamentalist evangelical movement was called "neo-evangelicalism" by both its leaders and critics, especially separatistic fundamentalists. Most scholars date its birth to the formation of the National Association of Evangelicals in 1942, a broad coalition of individuals, churches, and organizations sharing the rough evangelical ethos and a certain gentle disdain for separatistic fundamentalism that had come to dominate the public's attitude toward evangelicalism throughout the 1930s after the Scopes Trial in Dayton, Tennessee, in 1925. The NAE came to include fifty distinct denominations, ranging from Pentecostal to Reformed to Mennonite. The organization's statement of faith is broad and concise. Almost any denomination or organization that was not affiliated with the Federal Council of Churches (later renamed the National Council of Churches), considered liberal, accommodated to modern culture, could join. Fundamentalists could join but declined. They formed their own umbrella organization and frequently castigated the neo-evangelicals (the fundamentalists considered themselves the "true" evangelicals) as liberals in disguise.

The new evangelicalism was not limited to membership in the NAE, however. The NAE together with the increasingly influential network of organizations affiliated officially or unofficially with the Billy Graham ministry came to represent without encompassing post–World War II evangelicals in America. This new evangelical movement could best be described as an affinity group like the New Thought and New Age movements and the Charismatic movement. It had and has no headquarters or magisterium, even though, over the years since its birth in the 1940s, numerous individuals and organizations have emerged as spokespersons for it. Billy Graham is the only individual who has gained roughly the status of spokesperson for all evangelicals. The only organization that has approximated that status, speaking for the evangelical movement as a whole, is Christianity Today, Inc. (founded 1956).

As an affinity group, American evangelicalism has no boundaries and so its exact membership is uncertain and the subject of much disagreement. All scholars of the movement agree, however, that it has a center even if it has no identifiable circumference. (Whether it has a circumference is a subject of much controversy among evangelicals, but the nature of the movement as an affinity group lacking any magisterium or headquarters requires that it lack one. Those who wish to identify one and patrol it clearly are attempting to take it from being an affinity group or even a movement to being an at least somewhat organized coalition with them as its nominal leaders.)

As an affinity group, American evangelicalism is usually identified by individual leaders and organizations who manage to gain wide influence among self-identified evangelicals who are not separatistic fundamentalists, although separatistic fundamentalists have increasingly entered the evangelical movement beginning especially with Jerry Falwell (1933–2007) in the 1970s. Other influential individuals besides Graham have included the editor-theologian Carl F. H. Henry (1913–2003), the World Vision founder Bob Pierce (1914–1978), the NAE leader Billy Melvin, the Southern Baptist seminary president Albert Mohler, and the Fuller Seminary president Richard Mouw. Influential organizations include publishers such as Eerdmans, Zondervan, Baker, and InterVarsity Press; missionary agencies such as Wycliffe Bible Translators; colleges and universities such as Wheaton, Calvin, and Seattle Pacific; and, of course, the NAE.

Unanswerable questions abound. Are Charismatics evangelicals? The only possible answer is: some are and some are not. Are Oneness Pentecostals evangelicals? Most evangelical leaders would say they are not because of their denial of the orthodox doctrine of the Trinity and their separatism. Can a "welcoming and affirming" church (in favor of membership and ordination) be evangelical? Must a person or organization affirm biblical inerrancy to be authentically evangelical? There is no magisterium or headquarters to settle these questions, so anyone can call himself or herself, or one's organization, "evangelical." The only way to identify the movement is to look to its ethos, its traditional affinities, and its leading spokespersons. Questions will always remain.

EVANGELICAL THEOLOGY

So the only way to identify "evangelical theology" is to say it is theology done by an evangelical, a person affiliated in some way with the evangelical movement. Many evangelical theologians will be upset by such an approach; they want something much more concrete and specific. They will and do propose doctrinal litmus tests. For example, one major turning point in post–World War II evangelicalism and especially evangelical theology was the publication in 1976 of the book *The Battle for the Bible* by evangelical leader Harold Lindsell (1914–1998), former professor of theology at Fuller Seminary and editor of *Christianity Today*. Without doubt, Lindsell was a leading spokesperson for evangelicalism and an influential evangelical theologian. In *Battle*, a book widely read and discussed among evangelicals, he argued that belief in biblical inerrancy is the sine qua non of authentic evangelical theology. The book named individuals and schools that allegedly defected from evangelicalism by default owing to explicit or implicit denial of inerrancy.[4]

The great inerrancy controversy among American evangelicals started a decadelong struggle that began to divide the movement. It became a watershed issue. Conservative evangelicals agreed with Lindsell or at least believed that inerrancy, difficult to define as it may be, is a hallmark of evangelical faith. Progressive evangelicals either denied total, plenary inerrancy or else defined inerrancy so that it did not mean at all what Lindsell intended. Numerous scholarly and not-so-scholarly books were published on each side of the issue.

In spite of suggested and even argued litmus tests for legitimate evangelical theology such as inerrancy (and others have been proposed), it remains the case that the movement lacks any authoritative office or process for deciding who counts as an evangelical theologian. All one can do is argue, and attempt to get others to agree, that a theologian or group of theologians is not "truly evangelical." Others will disagree. The result is simply what was asserted earlier: that an "evangelical theologian" is one who does theology from within the evangelical movement; that is, if one has evangelical credentials, he or she is prima facie an evangelical theologian. "Evangelical theology," then, is simply theology done within the evangelical movement by evangelical theologians.

EVANGELICAL THEOLOGICAL TRIBES AND TYPES

Evangelicalism was from the beginning (1942) a combustible compound. The movement's chief organizer was Boston Congregational pastor Harold John Ockenga (1905–1985), a leader of the New England Fellowship, an organization of concerned conservative pastors and lay leaders. In 1941 he called for a summit of conservative Protestant leaders to create a new umbrella organization for evangelical cooperation. A founding committee met in Chicago that year, but the first meeting of the new organization, the NAE, took place the following year in St. Louis. Ockenga served as the NAE's founding president for several years. He also helped found the flagship evangelical seminary, Fuller Theological Seminary, in Pasadena, California, and the neo-evangelical movement's leading publication, *Christianity Today*.[5]

Ockenga was, by all accounts, the formative organizing influence among neo-evangelicals. His purpose was always to unite moderate conservative Protestants in cooperation and to provide alternative spaces for theological education and reflection to the so-called mainline Protestantism of the Federal Council of Churches (National Council of Churches). Ockenga and his early colleagues believed that separatistic fundamentalism had badly tarnished the public image of evangelical Christianity; it needed a new aspect. Neo-evangelicalism would not be as separatistic or doctrinally narrow as fundamentalism and would engage more publicly and cautiously positively with the wider culture, even entering into dialogue with liberal Protestants and Catholics.

However, Ockenga was himself a study in contrasts and depicts the divisions that were lightly papered over by his organizing efforts. He graduated from Westminster Theological Seminary which was founded by fundamentalist theologians J. Gresham Machen (1881–1993) and Cornelius Van Til (1895–1987), who left Princeton Theological Seminary. Westminster was strongly conservative and theologically Reformed. On the other hand, Ockenga pastored Methodist churches in New Jersey before landing among the Presbyterians and then Congregationalists, two Reformed denominations. Methodists have always been Arminian in theological orientation, believing as their founder John Wesley (1703–1791) did in free will. In other words, Ockenga embodied in himself a division within historic Protestantism. When he founded the NAE, and as he continued organizing neo-evangelicals, he brought into it and them a broad and diverse group of conservative Protestants, including Arminians and Calvinists. In a controversial move, he and other NAE founders invited Pentecostals to join, which was one reason fundamentalist leader Carl McIntire (1906–2002) did not bring his American Council of Christian Churches, founded in 1941, into the NAE.

From its beginning, then, neo-evangelicalism was characterized by theological and doctrinal breadth, excluding the new liberal Protestantism represented in America by pastors such as Harry Emerson Fosdick (1878–1969) and theologians such as Reinhold Niebuhr (1892–1971). (Niebuhr made his reputation opposing an older form of liberal Protestantism and is often associated with neo-orthodoxy, but he was, in fact, quite liberal theologically compared with conservative, revivalist Protestants. He refused even to meet with Billy Graham when the evangelist asked for a meeting.) Neo-evangelicals declined to add premillennialism to the "fundamentals of the faith," something most fundamentalists had done during the 1920s and 1930s. They refused to make opposition to evolution and to communism rallying campaigns as most fundamentalists had done. On the other hand, they also rejected the Social Gospel, which had come to embrace socialism as the Christian economic system, and they held firmly to a supernatural worldview and the basic affirmations of Protestant orthodoxy, including the deity of Christ, the Trinity, Christ's virgin birth, miracles, bodily resurrection and second coming, and salvation by grace through faith alone. Most important, perhaps, they held firmly to the unique inspiration, infallibility, and supreme authority of Scripture, all beliefs they felt mainline Protestantism was neglecting if not rejecting.

What went unrecognized, or at least not dealt with, was the doctrinal, spiritual, and ecclesiastical diversity among neo-evangelicals. Traditionally, Reformed and Arminian conservative Protestants had debated one another, sometimes heatedly, throughout the nineteenth century. Lying in the background of many neo-evangelicals' theological orientation was the monumental influence of the nineteenth-century Old Princeton School of theology represented especially by Charles Hodge (1797–1878) and Benjamin Breckinridge Warfield (1851–1921). Twentieth-century fundamentalist theologian Machen was the last of that dynasty of Reformed theologians. All of them harshly criticized Arminians and Arminianism as a major factor in the rise of liberal Protestantism. Only strongly Reformed theology—Calvinism as it was preached by Jonathan Edwards (1703–1758), for example—could protect conservative Protestantism from doctrinal drift and declension.

On the other hand, many neo-evangelicals came from strongly Arminian traditions that were anathema to the likes of Hodge, Warfield, and Machen. The so-called Holiness churches that arose out of Methodism in the nineteenth and early twentieth centuries formed a strong element within neo-evangelicalism, as did Pentecostals such as the Assemblies of God and the Church of God (Cleveland, Tennessee). This combination was bound to give rise to tensions, which began to appear as Ockenga's and then Billy Graham's unifying powers waned in the 1990s. One leading Reformed evangelical theologian spoke of Arminians as "Christians, barely," while an influential Pentecostal evangelist declared Calvinism the worst heresy in Christian history.

The gulf between these two branches of neo-evangelicalism widened and spawned other controversies increasingly during the late 1950s and 1960s. It was in the background of the great inerrancy debate of the late 1970s and throughout the 1980s. In 1949 Carl F. H. Henry, a protégé of Ockenga and an early theological leader of neo-evangelicalism, founded the Evangelical Theological Society (ETS), whose two requirements for membership were a master's degree in biblical or theological studies (beyond the ordinary seminary degree in pastoral ministry, which was then the bachelor of divinity) and belief in the inerrancy of the Bible. By 2005 the society included over four thousand members, many of them recent graduates of Southern Baptist Seminaries, a relatively new phenomenon as Southern Baptists had not joined the neo-evangelical movement at first. The ETS welcomed both Reformed and Arminian scholars into its ranks, but many Wesleyan and Arminian theological and biblical scholars *perceived* it to be biased toward Calvinism. Thus they founded the Wesleyan Theological Society (WTS) in 1965, not as a rival professional society to the ETS (many belong to both) but as an alternative space for theological reflection for non-Reformed evangelical scholars. The WTS does not require affirmation of biblical inerrancy, a concept largely foreign to the revivalistic Holiness movement rooted in Methodism.

The two main ingredients in the neo-evangelical recipe, so to speak, were Reformed and Arminian, with conservative Presbyterians and some Baptists in the Reformed tribe and Holiness, Pentecostal, and Free Will Baptists in the Arminian tribe. That was one divide papered over by the new evangelical coalition held together largely by Billy Graham and his far-flung influence and by a general antipathy toward liberal Protestantism and separatistic fundamentalism. Another divide, however, was that between what might be called conservative orthodoxy and progressive orthodoxy. Although it is generally true that the former consisted mostly of Reformed theologians and evangelical leaders, some Reformed evangelicals could be found in the latter camp—especially Reformed theologians influenced by Karl Barth (1886–1968) and Dutch Reformed theologian G. C. Berkouwer (1903–1996), who exercised significant influence over some Reformed faculty members of Fuller Seminary in the 1960s especially.

Fuller Seminary was a case study in tensions between conservatives and progressives among neo-evangelical scholars and theologians in the years after the honeymoon period of the 1950s when divisions were largely kept below the surface of the new movement. In 1994 evangelical historian George Marsden published a groundbreaking study of neo-evangelicalism's birth and evolution under the title *Reforming Fundamentalism: Fuller Seminary and the New Evangelicalism*. There the doyen of evangelical historians revealed many interesting details about not only Fuller Seminary but also neo-evangelicalism in general. His research shows that from the very beginning there were tensions, most of them having to do with theological differences. These emerged most notably in the 1960s as Fuller Seminary deleted inerrancy from its statement of faith, a move that shook the evangelical theological world and started a chain reaction that eventually led to the publication of *The Battle for the Bible* and the earthquake that resulted.[6]

The year 1974 saw the publication of a tiny (by standards of theological tomes) volume by Fuller Seminary theologian Jack Rogers, a mainline Presbyterian who had earned his doctorate under progressive Reformed theologian Berkouwer in Amsterdam. The book's intended title was *Confessions of a Post-Conservative Evangelical*, but Presbyterian publisher Westminster Press dropped "Post-" from the title so that the book appeared as *Confessions of a Conservative Evangelical*, a title that did not reflect the author's decidedly progressive message. In it Rogers recounted his theological and spiritual journey from rigid, even mildly fundamentalist, Calvinism to a broader progressive evangelical faith clearly influenced indirectly by Swiss neo-orthodox theologian Barth. Barth was a major influence on Berkouwer, who wrote a groundbreaking study of Barth's theology entitled *The Triumph of Grace in the Theology of Karl Barth* (1955). Many evangelicals, especially younger ones, resonated with Rogers's story and joined him in shedding the last vestiges of fundamentalism and rigid orthodoxy, including biblical inerrancy.[7]

Throughout the 1970s the gap widened between conservative evangelicals and Rogers's tribe of postconservative, progressive evangelicals, for a time known as "the young evangelicals" after the title of a book by Richard Quebedeaux, *The Young Evangelicals: Revolution in Orthodoxy* (1974). The book brought about a harsh backlash from conservatives, including Carl Henry, who published articles attacking this perceived revolt in the ranks of neo-evangelicals. Until the early 1970s most evangelicals had a negative opinion of Barth and his Swiss colleague Emil Brunner's (1889–1966) "dialectical theology." Their type of theology was known in America as neo-orthodoxy because they denied the equation of the word of God with Scripture. Cornelius Van Til of Westminster Seminary labeled it *The New Modernism* (1946) and, in the estimation of many progressive evangelicals, misrepresented Barth's and Brunner's theology as liberal. During the 1970s, however, many younger evangelicals like Rogers studied this "new Reformation theology" (as William Hordern labeled it in a book of that title) and came to different conclusions: they saw it as largely compatible with neo-evangelicalism and as an ally in attempts to shed the last vestiges of fundamentalism.[8]

Henry, founding editor of *Christianity Today* and by all accounts dean of evangelical theologians, reacted negatively to progressive evangelical theology and to Barth and Brunner. Without going so far as Van Til, he treated dialectical, neo-orthodox theology as a Trojan horse among evangelicals and upheld the traditional Reformed equation of revelation with Scripture, including biblical inerrancy, as the only bulwark against encroaching cultural accommodation and liberal theology. He did not side with Lindsell in attacking noninerrantist evangelicals as faux evangelicals, but he did argue vociferously that denial of inerrancy was inconsistent with full faith in Scripture as God's word. On the other hand, progressive evangelicals such as Donald Bloesch (1928–2010) and Bernard Ramm (1916–1992), prolific and influential evangelical theologians, gave cautious endorsement to the growing attraction of younger evangelicals to Barth's and Brunner's neo-orthodoxy.[9]

THE PERCEIVED FRAGMENTATION OF EVANGELICAL THEOLOGY

Marsden declared in *Understanding Fundamentalism and Evangelicalism* that by 1967 neo-evangelicalism was no longer "a single coalition with a more or less unified and recognized leadership." Internal factures were splitting the movement apart. According to Marsden, "The transdenominational movement to reform fundamentalism was thus irreparably split over a combination of political and doctrinal issues. [Here the emphasis has been and will remain primarily on the doctrinal ones, but see chapter 4 in this volume.] 'Neo-evangelicals' were so divided among themselves that the term lost its meaning. By the late 1970s, no one, not even Billy Graham, could claim to stand at the center of so divided a coalition."

Many observers would regard Marsden's pronouncement as too pessimistic. Without doubt the movement was fractured, but there was still a relatively identifiable movement of evangelicals in America. If nothing else, the media said so. And *Christianity Today* remained its primary unifying force. The NAE continued to exist and provide a certain unifying voice. The ETS grew. Evangelical publishers, mission agencies, and "ministries" flourished. Theologically, however, evangelicalism continued to fracture and fragment. By the turn of the century there was no even relatively identifiable evangelical theology. Still, ironically and paradoxically, mainline publishers then began to discover evangelical theology and pump out books by evangelical theologians and about the subject.¹⁰

A whole new crop of evangelical theologians grew, but what made them all "evangelical" became increasingly difficult to say. All claimed to do their theologizing from within an evangelical heritage, rooted in the post–World War II postfundamentalist, neo-evangelical movement. All also claimed to adhere to the evangelical ethos identified by Bebbington and Noll. It is relatively safe to say that all, from neofundamentalists to postconservatives, look like one tribe from the view of mainline Protestantism dominated increasingly by special interest theologies only distantly related to orthodoxy and eschewing revivalism, such as feminist theology and process theology. From inside the fragmenting evangelical movement, however, it became increasingly difficult to see how they could all be equally evangelical when they had difficulty even talking to one another.

A series of events illustrates this internal struggle and even (nonviolent) civil war among evangelical theologians. The year 1990 saw the publication of a bombshell article in *Christianity Today* entitled "Evangelical Megashift: Why You May Not Have Heard About Wrath, Sin, and Hell Recently" by Canadian evangelical theologian Robert Brow (1924–2008). The subtitle, if not the article's content, made an evangelical brouhaha inevitable. The article was followed by brief responses by "five noted evangelical scholars" offering "a spectrum of opinion on the perils and promise of this 'new-time religion.'" The responding theologians represented the new warring tribes of evangelical theologians: D. A. Carson (b. 1946) of Trinity Evangelical Divinity School, Clark Pinnock (1937–2010) of McMaster Divinity College, David Wells (b. 1939) of Gordon-Conwell Theological Seminary, Robert Webber (1933–2007) of Wheaton College, and Donald Bloesch (1928–2010) of Dubuque Theological Seminary.¹¹

In his article, Brow summarized the thrust of a book he coauthored with fellow Canadian evangelical Pinnock: *Unbounded Love* (1994). Both the article and the book announced a new paradigm of evangelical theology that veered far from traditional Reformed theology, stressed what Pinnock called "the Arminian option" with pronounced emphasis on God's universal love, and demoted the doctrines of God's judgment and hell to secondary status. The clear implication was a move toward universalism, although neither Brow nor Pinnock actually affirmed it.¹²

Brow's article developed further a methodological piece written by Pinnock and published earlier in *Christianity Today* (1979) as "An Evangelical Theology: Conservative and Contemporary," the thesis of which was "Scripture is normative, but it always needs to be read afresh and applied in new ways." That article made conservatives nervous, but Brow's 1990 article made them furious. It led to convulsions at *Christianity Today* and in the evangelical academy generally. (This can be compared to a similar book and response in 2011: *Love Wins* by emerging church pastor Rob Bell [b. 1970], which resulted in several reactionary books by conservative evangelical theologians.) Brow's article might be interpreted as an experiment in "progressive orthodoxy," a label scholars attached to the theology of nineteenth-century pastor Horace Bushnell (1802–1876), the most influential American Protestant theologian of his time. Nothing in the article openly contradicted basic Protestant orthodoxy *unless* one considers the penal substitution theory or Calvinism in general endemic to such orthodoxy. Brow (and Pinnock) clearly did not. Evangelical Calvinists especially reacted swiftly with condemnation, labeling the new paradigm announced by Brow and embodied in Pinnock as accommodated to modernity.[13]

After the Brow debacle (which some considered the *Christianity Today* debacle even though the magazine did not endorse Brow's new paradigm and published critical responses), a slew of articles and books fell from publishers' presses critically examining the state of evangelicalism and evangelical theology. Historian and theologian D. G. Hart analyzed the evangelical malaise in "The Mid-life Crisis of American Evangelicalism" in *Christian Century* (1992). Roger Olson announced and examined a new evangelical engagement with postmodernity in "Postconservative Evangelicals Greet the Postmodern Age," also in *Christian Century* (1995). Peter Leithart asked, "What's Wrong with Evangelical Theology?" in *First Things* (1996). Conservative evangelical theologian D. A. Carson decried the perceived evangelical theological defections from orthodoxy in *The Gagging of God* (1996), while fellow conservative Wells complained that there was *No Place for Truth* (1993) in the postconservative evangelical movements.[14]

On the other hand, progressive, postconservative evangelical theologian Stanley J. Grenz (1950–2005) called for *Revisioning Evangelical Theology* (1993), and Methodist postconservative evangelical theologian Henry H. Knight announced *A Future for Truth: Evangelical Theology in a Postmodern World* (1997). Notably, the above-mentioned conservative evangelicals were all

Calvinists, whereas the postconservatives were all non-Calvinists. It is a rule of thumb, but not an absolute rule, that conservative evangelicals with heightened concern about evangelical theological doctrinal drift are Calvinists, whereas progressive, postconservative evangelicals are not.[15]

Nothing better illustrates the great divide opening up among evangelical theologians in the early twenty-first century than the great controversy over open theism beginning in the 1990s and coming to a head in the first decade of the new century. It provides a case study in what ails evangelical theology in America. "Open theism" and "openness of God" are terms for a belief that, although God is omnipotent, God does not infallibly know all that will happen in the future. Evangelical philosopher Nicholas Wolterstorff set the stage for open theism to emerge among evangelicals with his essay "God Everlasting," published in *God and the Good* (1975). (Interestingly, the lead essay was by Berkouwer.) There Wolterstorff, a highly regarded philosopher of religion, argued that it is illogical to conceive of God interacting with creatures while being outside of time. Also, according to him, the biblical narrative portrays God as temporal rather than "eternal" in the traditional Augustinian and Boethian sense in which all times are simultaneous to God. Wolterstorff's essay barely caused a ripple among theologians, but it helped open the door to the appearance of open theism among evangelicals.[16]

Although there had been deniers of God's omniscience as comprehensive, exhaustive, and infallible foreknowledge before the evangelical open theists published their manifesto *The Openness of God* (1994), it brought open theism to public attention. The book's five authors, all well-known evangelical scholars such as Clark Pinnock, argued philosophically, biblically, and theologically that traditional belief in God's omniscience is untenable. They affirmed God's knowledge of all possibilities and God's ability to control all events, but they appealed to God's self-limitation as the explanation for why God does not control events or know the future exhaustively.[17]

Most scholarly readers of *The Openness of God* and other books advocating open theism knew that process theology, a form of liberal theology, denied God's exhaustive and infallible foreknowledge, and many of them immediately, and wrongly, associated open theism with process theology. In fact, however, process theology was not the catalyst for open theism among evangelicals, and the two views of God had little in common, which was eventually demonstrated in a dialogue between process theologians and open theists published as *Searching for an Adequate God* (2000). A major difference is that process theology denies creation *ex nihilo* and God's omnipotence; open theism affirms both. In subsequent books responding to their critics, open theists flew their flag of orthodoxy high, including belief in the supernatural, the deity of Christ, the Trinity, biblical infallibility, Christ's virgin birth, miracles, bodily resurrection, second coming, etc. Still, evangelical critics were not satisfied.[18]

A flurry of books and articles followed the publication of *The Openness of God*. Many of them misrepresented open theism as barely disguised process theology and dismissed open theists as nonevangelicals. Almost all the critics of open theism were Calvinists; a few conservative Arminians, such as Methodist Thomas Oden, joined the attack. Among the leading evangelical open theists were Gregory Boyd, John Sanders, Clark Pinnock, David Basinger, and William Hasker. The open theists insisted they were not attempting to alter the doctrine of God but only to redefine "omniscience." Their view, they argued, was not about God but about the nature of the future—open or closed, settled or not yet settled. They all affirmed that the end of history is settled but not all that happens between the present and that end is settled, so even God cannot know all that will happen.[19]

Many evangelical Arminians read the critics of open theism and recognized two main lines of argument. For some evangelical critics, open theism cannot be true because it is nontraditional. For them it is acceptable to tinker with tradition's details, but such a major overhaul of classical theism is not permitted. Oden seemed to be of that mindset, which surprised no one as his reputation was built (at least among evangelicals) on what he called "paleo-orthodoxy"—the call for all Christians to heed the ancient Christian consensual tradition of the church fathers and early Christian councils. Other critics simply dismissed open theism as violating the "received evangelical tradition." A second line of argument was that open theism denies the sovereignty of God. The problem is that most of these critics presented arguments against open theism that, if true, would equally undermine traditional Arminian belief in free will. For example, some Calvinist critics charged that open theism makes it impossible for God to control events such as the cross of Christ and the inspiration of the Bible.

The Emerging Divide in Evangelical Theology

Between 1995 and 2005 numerous books appeared from evangelical publishers either defending or attacking open theism. The controversy polarized evangelical scholars when it became clear that some critics were working to get open theists fired from their teaching positions in evangelical colleges. Eventually two of the leading evangelical open theists were terminated by their evangelical college's administration even though nothing in those colleges' statements of faith explicitly required belief in the traditional idea of God's omniscience (or of the nature of the future). Also, the ETS started an investigation of open theists' memberships even though the only two doctrinal requirements by that time were belief in biblical inerrancy and the Trinity. The two objects of the investigation, Pinnock and Sanders, affirmed both. Eventually both evangelical theologians were allowed to keep their membership in the ETS but only because a two-thirds majority is required to expel a member. Many observers felt that the attack on open theism was riddled with mean-spiritedness and misrepresentations of what open theists actually believe. Other observers and participants in the controversy felt open theists were being disingenuous about the influence of process theology on their own thinking about God.

Nothing demonstrated the divide among evangelical theologians as clearly as the open theism controversy. By the time it died down, many were no longer even speaking to each other. By that time many were blogging about their theologies and using their blogs to argue that many evangelical theologians were retreating to a new form of fundamentalism; others argued that many were flirting with liberal Protestantism. The lines had been fairly clearly drawn, and few stood in the middle.

Other controversies added to the fragmentation of evangelical theology throughout the 1990s and first decade of the twenty-first century. Growing interest in postmodern thought brought some progressive, postconservative evangelical theologians to critically embrace some aspects of it. Most notable was Stanley Grenz, who emerged as an evangelical star, a prolific author and speaker to whom many, especially younger, evangelicals looked for leadership toward a new evangelical openness to culture and theological reconstruction. Many younger evangelicals in the so-called emerging church movement regarded him as their theological prophet, the one who would lead them out of the Egypt of fundamentalism (which is what they considered conservative evangelicalism to be) into the promised land of a new, neither conservative nor liberal, postmodern form of Christianity. Conservative evangelicals treated him as dangerous to orthodoxy, even going so far as to accuse him of "cultural relativism," something he adamantly denied. Unfortunately, Grenz died at the peak of his influence at age fifty-five.[20]

EVANGELICALS DIVIDE OVER TRADITION

Many conservative evangelicals, such as David Wells and D. A. Carson, tried to argue that the problem with progressive, postconservative evangelicals was biblical infidelity. They portrayed them as defectors from biblical authority, implicitly, if not explicitly, operating out of cultural accommodation rather than faithfulness to Scripture. The problem with that interpretation of the fragmentation of evangelicalism is twofold. First, most of the progressives, including the open theists such as Pinnock and critical postmoderns such as Grenz, affirmed biblical inspiration, authority, and even inerrancy. (Some did not affirm inerrancy or argued that it is a meaningless concept given all the qualifications that surround it, even among conservatives.) The leading progressive evangelicals used Scripture to defend their views but argued that hermeneutics is the issue. One can affirm even inerrancy and come up with different interpretations. Some conservatives attempted to argue that there is only one reasonable interpretation of Scripture—their own—and that those who disagreed with them were playing fast and loose with Scripture under the influence of an impulse toward cultural accommodation.

One noted evangelical sociologist who engages with theology shed a great deal of light on the underlying problems of evangelical theology in his book *The Bible Made Impossible* (2011). Christian Smith argued that traditional evangelical biblicism is literally impossible. His main point was that the Bible is a not-yet-systematized doctrinal system and speaks with diverse, multiple voices even on important doctrinal matters. This is one of the reasons for what he called "pervasive interpretive pluralism" among evangelicals. So long as equally sincere, intelligent, and educated evangelical scholars continue to arrive at significantly varying interpretations on issues such as God's sovereignty in history and salvation (viz., Calvinism versus Arminianism), appeals to biblical authority alone, *sola scriptura*, will fail. It is simply not the case, as many conservatives believe and argue, that

III
The Emerging Divide in Evangelical Theology

there is only one reasonable interpretation of Scripture such that anyone who does not adhere to it is being unfaithful to Scripture itself.[21]

Here the details of Smith's analysis and solutions need not detain us. The upshot of his argument, however, was that without something like the U.S. Supreme Court's role vis-à-vis the Constitution, as an authoritative organ of interpretation, even the most devout believers in holy Scripture will fail to come to agreement on important doctrinal issues. The open theism controversy illustrates this. Open theists made their case not primarily from logic, although they thought logic was on their side, but from Scripture. So did their critics. Many of the latter as much as said that Scripture is so clearly on the side of the traditional interpretation of God's omniscience and sovereignty that open theists (and, at least in some cases, Arminians in general) are simply denying the truth of the Bible. This accusation against the open theists almost got them expelled from the ETS. Even many critics of open theism and Arminianism, however, recognized that open theists could support their view of God's knowledge and control of events from Scripture and were not merely denying the truth of the Bible. Such critics rejected open theists' claim to be evangelical on the basis of tradition, an argument Christian Smith's critique of biblicism could not touch. This appeal to tradition to settle theological controversies flew in the face of traditional evangelical biblicism (Scripture *over* tradition).

What was gradually becoming apparent, even to many conservative evangelical theologians, was that tradition is a necessary arbiter of truth in theological debates. But how can those be settled if evangelicalism has no magisterium? For decades evangelicalism did have an informal, though unrecognized, magisterium: living founders of the post–World War II, postfundamentalist, neo-evangelical movement. One of their voices was *Christianity Today*, especially its editorials. Trouble really began when Harold Lindsell replaced founding editor Carl Henry because some board members perceived the latter as too lenient toward deniers of inerrancy. That was the beginning of a neofundamentalist movement among evangelicals. It was not enough to believe in inerrancy; one had to express doubts about noninerrantists' evangelical credentials. Another early evangelical magisterial voice was Billy Graham; nearly all evangelicals looked to him and his surrogates to settle theological disputes. He and they did not always choose to do that, however, so evangelicals had to try to discern what Graham thought, and which side he would be on if he spoke up. Another unofficial magisterium was, at least for a while, Henry himself, widely perceived to be the dean of evangelical theologians and even anointed as that by *Time* magazine in an article badly titled "Theology for the Tent Meeting" (1977).[22]

Beginning with his tenure as the founding editor of *Christianity Today* and continuing well past his ouster from that position by neofundamentalists, Henry remained the one most evangelicals perceived as the closest to an evangelical theological pope. Feeling that burden and, no doubt, wishing to carry it responsibly, Henry wrote a series of volumes on evangelical theological method under the overarching title *God, Revelation, and Authority*, the first volume of which was *God Who Speaks and Shows: Preliminary Considerations* (1976). The set was not a systematic theology but Henry's attempt to lay out a universal evangelical theological method. Along the way, among the numerous essays on a wide range of theological and ethical subjects, he provided guidance to evangelicals who wanted to know what their own tradition ruled in and ruled out in terms of innovations. Many conservative and moderate evangelicals perceived Henry's work as the "received evangelical tradition." In a situation of pervasive interpretive pluralism, it could serve as a kind of high court. For the most part his vision of evangelical orthodoxy was generous. On certain issues, however, he took positions unsettling to both conservatives and progressives. He affirmed inerrancy but refused to make it a litmus test for evangelical authenticity. That dismayed many conservatives such as Lindsell but pleased many, for example, Wesleyans whose own evangelical tradition did not include inerrancy. On the other hand, he affirmed classical theism, leaning heavily toward the conservative Reformed view of God's sovereignty, which dismayed many evangelical Arminians, including Wesleyans, and especially open theists.[23]

Henry's, Graham's, and even *Christianity Today*'s abilities to function as evangelical magisteriums to settle theological disputes ultimately failed as they either moved off the scene with death or retirement or, as in the case of the magazine, declined to take a position on the most heated controversies dividing evangelical theologians, such as open theism and postmodernity. As of 2016 American evangelicalism has no pope; it has several. Gradually, throughout the 1990s and the early twenty-first century, several prominent conservative evangelical theologians stepped forward, offering, for all practical purposes, to function as the magisterial voice of authentic evangelicalism. Evangelical theologians either lined up behind them or went their own, independent ways. This is one way contemporary evangelical theology handles pervasive interpretive pluralism. In some cases these pontifical voices continue to argue that they are unaffected by any particular tradition and simply "know" the mind of God through a correct interpretation of Scripture. To believe that, however, one has to dismiss many apparently profoundly devout and scholarly evangelicals as pretenders or dumb.

This situation has led some evangelicals to defect from Protestantism to either Eastern Orthodoxy or Roman Catholicism. A long series of evangelical leaders, mostly theologians, joined one of those two ancient traditions out of frustration with evangelical pervasive interpretive pluralism. In 2007 Francis Beckwith, then president of the ETS, joined the Catholic Church, which led to his resignation as president even though he continued to affirm biblical inerrancy and the Trinity. A similar but different response is Thomas Oden's paleo-orthodoxy. Without joining the Catholic Church or Eastern Orthodoxy, many evangelical theologians have attempted to overcome pervasive interpretive pluralism by retrieving ancient Catholic and Orthodox doctrine as the authoritative lens for interpreting Scripture. Many of them admit that Scripture can be interpreted many ways, especially when it is cut loose from the ancient Christian doctrinal consensus, which they regard as having begun with the "rules of faith" found in the antiheretical writings of Irenaeus (c. 130–202), Origen (c. 184–253), and Tertullian (c. 160–225) and coming to conclusion in the doctrinal declarations of the ecumenical councils.

Paleo-orthodoxy is not a completely unified group of scholars; it is more of a research project with practical implications. The acknowledged leader of this approach among evangelicals is Oden, whose three-volume *Systematic Theology* (1987) attempted to perform a magisterial function among Christians by retrieving the ancient consensus of the undivided church. Oden later edited and contributed heavily to the *Ancient Christian Commentary* series (1998), whose purpose was the same—to attempt to bring an end to pervasive interpretive pluralism by appeal to the consensus of the church fathers.[24]

One problem of Oden's project is the possible conclusion that Baptists are heretics because they "rebaptize" persons already baptized as infants. Oden's manifesto of paleo-orthodoxy was *The Rebirth of Orthodoxy* (2003). There he sided with Pope Stephen of Rome against the Donatists for baptizing persons already baptized. His assertion was that "when an unprecedented claim [viz., the Donatists' rebaptism practice] on such an important subject as baptism stands in direct contrast to the previous consensual memory, it has to be rejected promptly and firmly." At least half of all American evangelicals belong to churches that baptize only believers old enough to confess faith for themselves; that includes rebaptizing converts with only infant baptisms. Oden's paleo-orthodoxy raised the specter of excluding them as not truly orthodox and therefore, in his and fellow paleo-orthodox theologians' eyes, not truly evangelical.[25]

Three other leading evangelical theologians joined Oden in treating the ancient Christian consensus as a kind of magisterium for uniting evangelicals in orthodoxy. Wheaton College theologian and liturgist Robert Webber spent his career introducing evangelical students to ancient Christian faith and worship and ushering them out of independent, Bible churches and into the Episcopal Church. His book *Ancient-Future Faith* (1999) called for "rethinking evangelicalism for a postmodern world" by retrieving the original Christianity of the church fathers. Baylor University theologian Daniel H. Williams published two volumes recommending that evangelicals return to the Great Tradition and especially the church fathers for unification and avoid cultural accommodation and liberal theology. His main work in this regard was *Retrieving the Tradition and Renewing Evangelicalism* (1999). With Oden, Williams argued that evangelicals have no right to interpret Scripture independently of the church fathers, but that the consensual tradition of the first few Christian centuries must be the lens through which Scripture is read and interpreted. Finally, in series of books with similar titles, including *Learning Theology with the Church Fathers* (2002), Eastern University theologian Christopher Hall urged evangelicals to read Scripture with the church fathers, worship with them, and do theology with them.[26]

Paleo-orthodoxy is one influential evangelical proposal for overcoming pervasive interpretive pluralism. These theologians admit that Scripture alone can be made to mean many different things; only the magisterial voice of the ancient Christian consensus, which they argue was heeded by the magisterial reformers, can guide evangelicals back from the brink of pluralism to doctrinal correctness and unity. Critics of paleo-orthodoxy wonder, however, what happened to *sola scriptura*, a basic tenet of Protestantism. All the evangelical traditionalists, however, argue that the ancient

Christian church fathers developed their consensual teachings out of Scripture, so adhering to them did not threaten *sola scriptura*.

Another traditionalist approach to solving the problem of pervasive interpretive pluralism among evangelicals is more Reformation-centered. Throughout the 1990s and the first decade of the twenty-first century, many conservative evangelicals troubled by innovations such as open theism and postmodern nonfoundationalism (Grenz's contribution) called for evangelicals to recognize the consensus of the Protestant magisterial reformers as the evangelical magisterium. April 1996 witnessed the first meeting of the Alliance of Confessing Evangelicals, which produced the Cambridge Declaration calling for a renewal of evangelicalism through retrieval of Protestant orthodoxy and especially monergism, belief that God is the sole decider of who will be saved. Most of the signers of the declaration were conservative Reformed theologians, and both the organization and the declaration clearly emphasized a high view of God's sovereignty. There can be little doubt that this was at least in part a response to open theism, but it also excluded classical Arminians. Associates of the Alliance of Confessing Evangelicals have, since 1992, published the journal *Modern Reformation*, which tends to lay the problem of evangelical defection from strong Reformation doctrines at the feet of Arminianism. Two evangelical theologians emerged as spokespersons for this traditionalist approach: Michael Horton of Westminster Theological Seminary in California and David F. Wells of Gordon Conwell Theological Seminary. In 1974 Wells published an article in *Christianity Today* holding up "The Stout and Persistent Theology of Charles Hodge" as the paradigm for evangelical theology.[27]

Paleo-orthodoxy and Alliance theology are two traditionalist approaches to renewing evangelical unity by magisteriums. Innovations such as open theism are, according to both approaches, unacceptable because they fly in the face of some authoritative tradition *even if* they can be supported by Scripture. Critics of both, however, argue that they concede too much to tradition, thus weakening *sola scriptura*—a major hallmark of classical Protestantism and especially evangelical Christianity. The majority of evangelicals were "simple biblicists," people who love the Bible and seek to believe whatever it says even against any "man-made tradition." Most evangelical scholars give greater weight to tradition than that, but these evangelical traditionalisms may not wash with the majority of evangelicals in the pews or the pulpits. They want to know "What say the Scriptures?"

Many conservative evangelical theologians sympathize with the paleo-orthodox and Reformation traditionalists but feel that Scripture itself must remain the sole magisterium for evangelicals. Tradition can be a tool of interpretation and have a voice in doctrinal disputes, but the final word must be spoken by Scripture itself.

During the first decade of the twenty-first century a group of mostly Reformed conservative evangelical theologians and pastors under the name the Gospel Coalition launched a major effort to avoid or correct pervasive interpretive pluralism among evangelicals. Some of them were also members of the Alliance of Confessing Evangelicals, but the thrust of the new coalition was to restore the supremacy of Scripture in evangelical theology and rule out innovations by sound biblical exegesis. In 2012 evangelical publisher Crossway issued a major volume of essays by coalition authors under the title *The Gospel as Center*. The volume, edited by coalition leaders D. A. Carson and Timothy Keller, contained sermonic essays on all major doctrinal loci. Each one attempted to demonstrate that Scripture does speak with one voice on the subject at hand. The clear implication of *The Gospel as Center* was that pervasive interpretive pluralism is absolutely unnecessary and not even inevitable insofar as evangelicals are guided by reasonable biblical exegesis. Those who introduce innovations such as open theism, then, are simply departing from the plain meaning of Scripture. Although this approach could hardly be called "simple biblicism," as it involves high-level exegesis of the Hebrew and Greek texts of Scripture, it resonates with many grassroots evangelical pastors and laypeople because it does not depend on some tradition. As early as 1991 George Marsden, in *Understanding Fundamentalism and Evangelicalism*, argued of evangelicalism that "little seems to hold it together other than common traditions, a central one of which is the denial of the authority of traditions."[28]

All three of these traditionalist approaches to avoiding or correcting pervasive interpretive pluralism and unifying evangelicals doctrinally can fairly be labeled "conservative." All, including the third one, the Gospel Coalition, wish to conserve some tradition. In spite of their vaunted talk of returning to Scripture as the sole supreme source and norm for theology, the coalition members all enshrine a particular evangelical hermeneutical heritage: Calvinism. For many of them, the specific Calvinism enshrined is that of Jonathan Edwards; for others, it is that of the great Princeton theologians Charles Hodge and Benjamin Warfield. This is largely unacknowledged but discernable by anyone familiar with those people and their theologies. In spite of claims to the contrary, it seems that something considered "the received evangelical tradition" really drives the coalition and its proposal. Tellingly, Arminians and Wesleyans are absent from the coalition.

Not all evangelicals are as concerned about pervasive interpretive pluralism as others. Throughout the 1990s and the first decade of the twenty-first century, progressive, postconservative evangelical theologians worked to put tradition in its rightful place and leave open the possibility of "new light" breaking forth from Scripture.

PROGRESSIVE, POSTCONSERVATIVE EVANGELICAL THEOLOGIES

Much could be said about progressive, postconservative evangelical theologians, but here the analysis will be of their approach to Scripture and tradition and their rejection of any human magisterium for settling evangelical theological controversies.

Throughout the 1970s and into the 1980s, "progressive evangelicals" were those who, like Donald Bloesch, found allies in Karl Barth and Emil Brunner and made critical use of their dialectical, neo-orthodox theologies. "Progressive" indicated cautious, critical openness to higher critical scholarship of the Bible, which usually presupposed a degree of discomfort with biblical inerrancy. As noted earlier, many self-proclaimed progressive evangelicals taught at Fuller Seminary and were disciples of Dutch theologian G. C. Berkouwer, who openly denied inerrancy. Many affirmed "infallibility" of Scripture, distinguishing it from inerrancy in that the former simply meant that Scripture, as a form of God's word (Barth), does not fail to communicate truth needed for salvation. These progressive evangelical theologians were cautiously comfortable with limited interpretive pluralism and doctrinal innovation while holding firmly to the major tenets of orthodoxy, such as the deity of Christ and the Trinity.

Perhaps the most influential of such progressive evangelical theologians was Bloesch, who published two not very systematic theological systems. His seven-volume *Christian Foundations* (1992–2004) series constituted a comprehensive critical survey of Christian doctrines with a strong evangelical flavor. Bloesch's appeal was to Scripture first, but his interpretations of Scripture and doctrine were clearly guided by his own "great cloud of witnesses," including the church fathers, the reformers (including some radical reformers), the pietists Edwards and Wesley, Søren Kierkegaard (1813–1855), the British theologian P. T. Forsyth (1848–1921), Barth, Brunner, and the Scottish theologian T. F. Torrance (1913–2007). Although he worked out of a broadly Reformed theological orientation, Bloesch was not bound to Calvinism. Some of his doctrinal constructions broke with classical Calvinism. Most revealing was his treatment of biblical inerrancy, a concept he rejected as rationalistic. While Bloesch held very strong opinions, especially about liberal theology, including feminist theology, he refused to be drawn into polemics and retained an irenic spirit with regard to those with whom he disagreed. His sympathy for the theology of Barth became increasingly clear as he compared the relationship between Scripture and the word of God to that between a lightbulb and the light. This caused some conservative evangelicals to regard him as a "mediating theologian" rather than a traditional evangelical. (Carl Henry communicated this estimation of Bloesch to this author in personal correspondence.)[29]

Bloesch was extremely wary of doctrinal magisteriums; he was a classical Protestant who upheld what he understood to be the classical Reformation pattern of authority of God's word and Holy Spirit. He did not deny, however, having favorite theologians and gave special credibility, if not authority, to those mentioned above. The point is, however, that he did not think there was any possibility of resolving pervasive interpretive pluralism besides persuasion, and he did not absolutely eschew doctrinal innovation insofar as it was grounded in Scripture.

Postconservative evangelical theology was best represented by Stanley Grenz and Clark Pinnock, who both rejected closed systems of theology and viewed theology as a pilgrimage of following the light of Scripture wherever it may lead. Both admitted theology's inevitable influence from culture and urged cautious appropriation of culture, not uncritical accommodation to it, in theological construction. Perhaps the best way to describe postconservatism is that Grenz and Pinnock and others like them believed that the constructive task of theology is always open, whereas conservative traditionalists believe that the only task of theology is criticism and translation. Grenz, for example, rejected classical Chalcedonian, hypostatic union Christology in favor of a Christology inspired by his mentor Wolfhart Pannenberg's (1928–2014) eschatological ontology. Pinnock, of course, promoted open theism and also inclusivism as the possibility of salvation of the unevangelized. These postconservative theologians believed tradition always gets a vote in doctrinal controversies but never a veto. Scripture alone holds veto power, but Scripture is not as clear as conservatives tend to think it is. And traditions are all open to varying interpretations and are fallible.

Although many postfundamentalist evangelical theologians studied in countries outside the United States and received some influences from non–North American theologies, progressive, postconservative theologians have been especially eager to learn from and interact with global theological communities. Pinnock, for example, earned his doctorate under New Testament scholar F. F. Bruce (1910–1990) in England. Barth, Brunner, Pannenberg, and Jürgen Moltmann have been major influences on postconservatives' theologies. Some, including this writer, have listened to and been informed by Latin American liberation theologies.[30] An early postconservative theologian, Jack Rogers of Fuller Seminary, wrote about how studying theology abroad (in his case the Netherlands) changed him from "conservative" to postconservative as an evangelical.[31] Almost without doubt, their interests in and influences from abroad helped progressive, postconservative evangelicals break further from fundamentalism than many of their evangelical counterparts.

CONCLUSION

If present trends continue, evangelical theology will further fragment so that, if it is not already the case, there will soon be no such thing. There will only be evangelical theologians, and an honest, objective person will simply have to admit that "evangelical theology" is nothing other than theology done by persons who have some right to own the label "evangelical." No magisterium will prevail; pervasive pluralism will continue.

The upshot of this rather dreary forecast is that evangelical theology must be understood *descriptively* in relation to the evangelical movement and ethos and *not prescriptively* in terms of doctrinal boundaries. To be sure, "evangelical" has evolved as a Christian tradition and form of life in Great Britain and North America (and from there throughout the world), but it is a boundary-less tradition, like "New Age" or "esoteric Christianity" and

"Charismatic." These are defined by common interests and family resemblances rather than by boundaries.

This situation will pose a problem for administrators of evangelical colleges, universities, seminaries, and other organizations. They will have to rely on their own confessional standards rather than on the amorphous concept "evangelical" in hiring. Or, alternatively, they will have to use the minimalist NAE Statement of Faith if their institution or organization has no formal confessional statement. Publications such as *Christianity Today* will increasingly take on the role of gatekeeper of evangelical thought, which will inevitably create controversy. No doubt alternative publications will appear among evangelicals attempting to define the movement and its theology differently, probably more narrowly. Already *Modern Reformation* (founded 1992) and *World* (founded 1986) are publications associated with conservative wings of evangelicalism, both seeking to steer evangelical theology toward a conservative consensus. The result will be further fragmentation by perceived exclusion.

Two possible shifts may appear in the meaning of evangelical theology in the twenty-first century. The common journalistic tendency to use "evangelical" as a synonym for politically conservative and activist Protestantism may gradually prevail so that progressives will find it increasingly difficult to hold on to that label. That was already happening as of 2016 as many progressive evangelicals, especially younger ones, readily dropped the label without having anything with which to replace it. "Emerging Christian" and "missional Christian" are two alternative labels gaining popularity among young postevangelicals. If that trend catches on and becomes a sea change, it would leave evangelical theology to the traditionalists, something they see as positive.

A second possible shift is that evangelical theology may become as amorphous, and therefore nearly meaningless, as "liberal theology." That label is used to cover so much that Union Theological Seminary historical theologian Gary Dorrien has written three massive volumes on its history and vast range—from the "progressive orthodoxy" of Horace Bushnell to the radical feminist theology of Elisabeth Schüssler Fiorenza. Virtually no evangelical theologian wants their label to become that vacuous.

In the meantime, the only way to invest evangelical theology with meaning that makes sense is to keep it tied to the post–World War II, neo-

The Emerging Divide in Evangelical Theology

evangelical movement. That will satisfy neither the most conservative of the conservatives, who insist on a prescriptive definition, nor progressives who seek to open evangelical theology to include any and every scholar who, as one blogger put it, "has the aroma of Jesus."

NOTES

1. David W. Bebbington, *Evangelicalism in Modern Britain: A History from the 1730s to the 1980s* (London: Unwin Hyman, 1989), 2–17; Mark A. Noll, D. W. Bebbington, and George A. Rawlyk, eds., *Evangelicalism: Comparative Studies of Popular Protestantism in North America, the British Isles, and Beyond, 1700–1990* (New York: Oxford University Press, 1994).

2. George Marsden, *Understanding Fundamentalism and Evangelicalism* (Grand Rapids, Mich.: Eerdmans, 1991); Donald W. Dayton and Robert K. Johnston, eds., *The Variety of American Evangelicalism* (Knoxville: University of Tennessee Press, 1991); Joel A. Carpenter, *A New Evangelical Coalition: Early Documents of the National Association of Evangelicals* (New York: Garland, 1988); Randall Balmer, *Blessed Assurance: A History of Evangelicalism in America* (Boston: Beacon, 1999); Gary J. Dorrien, *The Remaking of Evangelical Theology* (Louisville: John Knox, 1998); Kenneth J. Collins, *The Evangelical Moment: The Promise of an American Religion* (Grand Rapids, Mich.: Baker Academic, 2005).

3. Donald W. Dayton, "The Search for the Historical Evangelicalism: George Marsden's History of Fuller Seminary as a Case Study," *Christian Scholar's Review* 23, no. 1 (September, 1993): 12–34.

4. Harold Lindsell, *The Battle for the Bible* (Grand Rapids, Mich.: Zondervan, 1976).

5. Joel A. Carpenter, ed., *Two Reformers of Fundamentalism: Harold John Ockenga and Carl F. H. Henry* (New York: Garland, 1988).

6. George M. Marsden, *Reforming Fundamentalism: Fuller Seminary and the New Evangelicalism* (Grand Rapids, Mich.: Eerdmans, 1987).

7. Jack Bartlett Rogers, *Confessions of a Conservative Evangelical* (Philadelphia: Westminster, 1974); G. C. Berkouwer, *The Triumph of Grace in the Theology of Karl Barth* (Grand Rapids: Eerdmans, 1955).

8. Richard Quebedeaux, *The Young Evangelicals: Revolution in Orthodoxy* (New York: Harper & Row, 1974); Cornelius Van Til, *The New Modernism: An Appraisal of the Theology of Barth and Brunner* (Philadelphia: Presbyterian & Reformed, 1946); William Hordern, *The Case for a New Reformation Theology* (Philadelphia: Westminster, 1959).

9. Donald G. Bloesch, *The Future of Evangelical Christianity: A Call for Unity Amid Diversity* (Garden City, N.Y.: Doubleday, 1983); Bernard L. Ramm, *After Fundamentalism: The Future of Evangelical Theology* (San Francisco: Harper & Row, 1983).

10. Marsden, *Understanding Fundamentalism and Evangelicalism*, 74, 76; Molly Worthen, *Apostles of Reason: The Crisis of Authority in American Evangelicalism* (New York: Oxford University Press, 2014), 15–26, 36.

11. Robert Brow, "Evangelical Megashift: Why You May Not Have Heard About Wrath, Sin, and Hell Recently," *Christianity Today*, February 19, 1990, 12–14.

12. Clark H. Pinnock and Robert Brow, *Unbounded Love: A Good News Theology for the 21st Century* (Downers Grove, Ill.: InterVarsity, 1994).

13. Clark H. Pinnock, "An Evangelical Theology: Conservative and Contemporary," *Christianity Today*, January 5, 1979, 23–29; Rob Bell, *Love Wins: A Book About Heaven, Hell, and the Fate of Every Person Who Ever Lived* (New York: HarperOne, 2011).

14. D. G. Hart, "The Mid-life Crisis of American Evangelicalism: Identity Problems," *Christian Century*, November 11, 1992, 1028–31; Roger E. Olson, "Postconservative Evangelicals Greet the Postmodern Age," *Christian Century*, May 3, 1995, 480–83; Peter Leithart, "What's Wrong with Evangelical Theology?," *First Things* (August/September 1996): 19–20; D. A. Carson, *The Gagging of God: Christianity Confronts Pluralism* (Grand Rapids, Mich.: Zondervan, 1996); David F. Wells, *No Place for Truth; Or, Whatever Happened to Evangelical Theology?* (Grand Rapids, Mich.: Eerdmans, 1993).

15. Stanley J. Grenz, *Revisioning Evangelical Theology* (Downers Grove, Ill.: InterVarsity, 1993); Henry H. Knight, *A Future for Truth: Evangelical Theology in a Postmodern World* (Nashville: Abingdon, 1997).

16. Nicholas Wolterstorff, "God Everlasting," and G. C. Berkouwer, "Essays in Christian Ethics," in *God and the Good: Essays in Honor of Henry Stob*, ed. Clifton Orlebeke and Lewis Smedes (Grand Rapids, Mich.: Eerdmans, 1975).

17. Clark H. Pinnock et al., *The Openness of God: A Biblical Challenge to the Traditional Understanding of God* (Downers Grove, Ill.: InterVarsity, 1994).

18. John B. Cobb and Clark H. Pinnock, eds., *Searching for an Adequate God: A Dialogue Between Process and Free Will Theists* (Grand Rapids, Mich.: Eerdmans, 2000).

19. Thomas Oden, "The Real Reformers and the Traditionalists," *Christianity Today*, February 9, 1998, 46.

20. Stanley J. Grenz and Roger E. Olson, *20th Century Theology: God & the World in a Transitional Age* (Downers Grove, Ill.: InterVarsity, 192).

21. Christian Smith, *The Bible Made Impossible: Why Biblicism Is Not a Truly Evangelical Reading of Scripture* (Grand Rapids, Mich.: Brazos, 2011).

22. "Theology for the Tent Meeting," *Time*, February 14, 1977, 82.

23. Carl F. H. Henry, *God, Revelation, and Authority*, 6 vols. (Waco, Tex.: Word, 1976–1983); Henry, *God Who Speaks and Shows: Preliminary Considerations* (Waco, Tex.: Word, 1976).

24. Thomas C. Oden, *Systematic Theology* (1987–1992; Peabody, Mass.: Hendrickson, 2006); Oden, *Ancient Christian Commentary on Scripture: New Testament*, rev. ed. (1998; Downers Grove, Ill.: InterVarsity, 2005).

25. Thomas C. Oden, *The Rebirth of Orthodoxy* (San Francisco: HarperSanFrancisco, 2003), 77.

26. Robert Webber, *Ancient-Future Faith: Rethinking Evangelicalism for a Postmodern World* (Grand Rapids, Mich.: Baker, 1999); Daniel H. Williams, *Retrieving the Tradition and Renewing Evangelicalism* (Grand Rapids, Mich.: Eerdmans, 1999); Christopher A. Hall, *Learning Theology with the Church Fathers* (Downers Grove, Ill.: InterVarsity, 2002).

27. David F. Wells, "The Stout and Persistent Theology of Charles Hodge," *Christianity Today*, August 30, 1974, 10–15.

28. D. A. Carson and Timothy J. Keller, *The Gospel as Center: Renewing Our Faith and Reforming Our Ministry Practices* (Wheaton, Ill.: Crossway, 2012); Marsden, *Understanding Fundamentalism and Evangelicalism*, 81.

29. Donald G. Bloesch, *Christian Foundations* (Downers Grove, Ill.: InterVarsity, 1992–2004).

30. See Joao B. Chaves, *Evangelicals and Liberation Revisited: An Inquiry Into the Possibility of an Evangelical-Liberationist Theology* (Eugene, Ore.: Wipf & Stock, 2013).

31. Rogers, *Confessions of a Conservative Evangelical*.

4

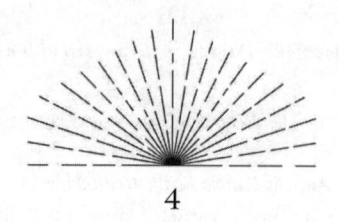

Evangelicals, Politics, and Public Policy

LESSONS FROM THE PAST, PROSPECTS FOR THE FUTURE

Amy E. Black

From the Native American civilizations that preceded the arrival of European settlers centuries ago to present-day skirmishes on Capitol Hill, religious adherents from many different perspectives have made their mark on American politics. Activists motivated by religion have been part of all major social movements in the United States, and, more often than not, organizers on opposing sides of contentious issues have used religious arguments to build support for their perspectives on politics and public policy.

Although religion itself has been a consistent feature in public debate, the cast of religious groups and actors participating in politics has varied. The Christian believers broadly classified as contemporary evangelicals, those under discussion in this volume, were largely absent from public politics for much of the twentieth century. Only in recent decades have evangelicals rejoined the national political debate with full force. This chapter examines the recent history of evangelical political activity to assess their participation in public life and to chronicle their greatest political successes and failures.

After a brief discussion of religious groups and their political behavior, the chapter provides an overview of the history of the Christian Right that coalesced in the late 1970s, describing the central political issues, organizations, and personalities that originally shaped the movement. Next, it charts the development of new organizations and political coalitions that entered the public square as the traditional leaders and movements began to lose influence. The subsequent section explores the role of evangelicals in contemporary politics. The final section analyzes the most recent transformations of evangelical political engagement, considering what these trends suggest for the future of evangelicalism in American politics and public policy.

EVANGELICALS AND OTHER RELIGIOUS GROUPS IN POLITICAL CONTEXT

Discussions of the role of evangelicals in politics inevitably encounter two problems: defining the term *evangelical* and identifying which people or organizations fit this label. As the chapters in this volume demonstrate, neither of these tasks is simple or uncontested.

The Changing Definition of Evangelical

The definition of the term *evangelical* has shifted over the course of American history. In the nineteenth century the term applied to groups that emphasized spiritual conversion, while largely presuming conservative theology; as such, most Protestant denominations were part of the evangelical movement. As described in more detail in the introductory chapter, theological differences between Protestants in the early twentieth century led to their division into two major camps: fundamentalists and modernists. Political controversies over how best to confront the social and economic problems of the growing nation emerged from this theological debate. Proponents of liberal theology, or modernists, held a more optimistic view of human nature, believed that the kingdom of God would be revealed through the improvement of society, and embraced modern scientific thinking. Fundamentalism arose as a reaction against liberal theology and the growing secularism of the culture. Believing that the sinful nature of humankind makes it difficult or impossible to achieve the kingdom of God in history, fundamentalists focused on individual salvation and called for a return to the "fundamentals" of the faith.

Even as many fundamentalist leaders were still separating from the dominant culture, the movement originally called neo-evangelicalism emerged. In 1942 a national conference of 147 leaders gathered in St. Louis and founded the National Association of Evangelicals, an organization created to combine traditional theological principles and a renewed concern for "social engagement." Over time, Christian believers who shared these convictions became known simply as evangelicals.

Much like its predecessors, the contemporary evangelical movement is a loose and diverse coalition that developed over time and continues to change in composition and character. Some people and organizations self-identify as evangelical; others are given the label even if they do not use it for themselves. The fluidity of the movement makes precise definition difficult. For the purposes of this chapter, I will describe evangelicals in one of two ways. When reporting survey data, I will group together the views of those respondents who answer a question probing if they are "born again" or "evangelical," regardless of church affiliation. In the larger discussion of the role of evangelicals in American political life, the definition becomes even less precise. I will focus on those leaders, movements, and political actors who identify with theologically conservative Protestant Christians and are generally recognized as part of the evangelical movement. Such a broad definition will include self-identified evangelicals as well as some fundamentalists and pentecostals.

Religion by the Numbers

The process of categorizing people by religion is more an art than a science; every attempt to do so will necessarily be incomplete in some way. Even so, sample surveys are the best tools available for studying relationships between religion and political behavior. In the early years of survey research, typical polls included one religion question at most, asking respondents if they were Protestant, Catholic, or Jewish. In recent decades, however, scholars of religion and politics have convinced survey organizations to include more religion-related questions, thus increasing the amount and improving the quality of data available for exploring the relationship between religion and politics. Despite the limitations of such data collection, however, a long line of research on religion and politics indicates that grouping survey respondents by religious identity and affiliation consistently generates robust and statistically significant findings. Such measurement is clearly imperfect, but it still manages to capture politically relevant patterns.

Most contemporary survey research compares religious adherents by grouping them into one of seven categories: Catholic, mainline Protestant, evangelical, black Protestant, Jewish, other religious, and secular. Although the number of Americans describing themselves as belonging to a religion other than Christianity or Judaism is increasing, surveys rarely include large enough samples of these groups to allow for reliable analysis. Thus most political profiles of American voters compare the five Judeo-Christian groups and seculars.

Although the exact percentages vary slightly from survey to survey, data sources, including Pew Research Center surveys and polling conducted in the course of national campaigns, report similar distributions of religious voters. About one-fourth of American adults identify themselves as Roman Catholics. One in five adults are best categorized as mainline Protestant, those who worship in the historic Protestant churches in the United States. Another quarter of American voters are best classified as evangelical Protestants.[1] Because of the unique history and traditions of African American churches, most researchers categorize black Protestants separately. This group includes about 7 percent of the adult population; another 2 percent are Jewish. The group researchers call seculars or Nones—those who do not identify with a particular religion—is the fastest growing religious segment of the American electorate. Depending on how researchers measure this group, religious Nones constitute about 15 to 20 percent of the voting population.

A Profile of American Evangelicals

Data from the American Religious Identification Survey provide a useful profile of American evangelicals, identified as those adult respondents in a national survey who answered yes to the question, "Are you an evangelical or born again Christian?" and who were not African American, Catholic, or members of a mainline Protestant denomination.

Although in many respects evangelicals look much like other Americans, the ARIS data reveal some differences. Compared with the national sample, evangelicals are less educated (22 percent of evangelicals and 17 percent of national adults have not earned a high school diploma) and have slightly lower annual household incomes (51 percent of evangelicals compared with 45 percent nationally report earning incomes less than $50,000). Evangelicals are less likely to live in the Northeast (10 percent, compared with 18 percent nationally) and West (16 percent, compared with 23 percent nationally). A majority of evangelicals (55 percent) live in the South, compared with 37 percent of the adult population.

More than 80 percent evangelicals say they are registered to vote compared with three of four national adults in the survey (76 percent). Evangelicals are much more likely to identify as Republicans (42 percent, compared with 24 percent nationally) than as Democratics (24 percent, compared with 33 percent nationally).

Another significant source, the U.S Religious Landscape Studies conducted by the Pew Forum on Religion and Public Life in 2007 and 2014, provides additional data to compare the political views of various religious groups. Of the major religious groups surveyed, evangelical Protestants were the most Republican, most conservative, most likely to favor restrictions on abortion, and least accepting of homosexuality. In 2014, 68 percent of evangelicals surveyed described themselves as Republican or leaning Republican, compared with 48 percent of mainline Protestants, 40 percent of Catholics, 31 percent of Jewish and 25 percent of unaffiliated respondents, and 10 percent of respondents from historically black churches.[2]

Religion, Voting, and Presidential Elections

Analysis of exit polls from recent presidential elections offers insights into how evangelicals fit into the larger landscape of religion and American politics. The data reveal interesting trends that persist across elections: religious affiliation is a significant factor that shapes voting decisions, and the differences between theological conservatives and their more theologically liberal counterparts have enduring political consequences.

Religious affiliation correlates highly with partisan voting patterns. In recent presidential elections, three religious groups have voted overwhelmingly Democratic, two have been more evenly divided, and only one, evangelicals, has voted overwhelmingly Republican.

Mainline Protestants and Catholics are most likely to divide their vote evenly between the two parties and are thus targeted as potential swing voters. The mainline Protestant vote has recently leaned slightly Republican. In 2004 George W. Bush won 59 percent of their vote. John McCain won 54 percent in 2008, and Mitt Romney won 57 percent in 2012. Although Catholic voters have historically tended to be Democratic, this vote has shifted in recent decades to a more even split between the two parties. In 2004 Bush won a slim majority (52 percent) of the Catholic vote; Barack Obama won a slight majority (54 percent) in 2008 and just half (50 percent) in 2012.[3]

Three religious groups are core Democratic voters. Black Protestants, known for theological conservatism and political liberalism, represent a solid Democratic voting bloc. John Kerry received 86 percent of the black Protestant vote in 2004; Obama won 94 percent of this group in 2008 and 95 percent in 2012. Jews are also strong supporters of Democratic candidates. Almost three of four Jewish voters (74 percent) voted for Kerry in 2004, and Obama received 78 percent of their votes in 2008. Jewish support for Obama slipped to 69 percent in 2012. In recent elections Democrats have made significant gains with religious Nones, a third group important for Democratic success. In 2004 about two-thirds of religiously unaffiliated voters chose Kerry; Obama received 75 percent of their vote in 2008 and 70 percent in 2012.

Only one religious group, evangelicals, has been a consistently strong voting bloc for the Republican Party in recent decades. In the 2004 election 79 percent of self-identified white evangelical voters chose Bush; McCain won 73 percent of their support in 2008; and Romney won 79 percent in 2012. Continuing this trend, 78 percent of evangelical or born-again Christians voted Republican in the 2014 midterm elections.[4]

Research on religion and partisanship reveals a strong connection between white evangelicals and Republicans. Party elites strategically court the evangelical vote by emphasizing issues of concern to them, and voters appear to respond. For example, evidence from experiments suggests that white evangelicals (but not mainline Protestants or Catholics) pick up subtle cultural and religious cues designed to engender the support of religious conservatives without ostracizing others.[5] One of the few studies that analyzes race, religion, and partisanship found significant differences in the ways that blacks, Latinos, and whites translated their faith into politics. Political scientist Eric McDaniel and sociologist Christopher Ellison compared survey responses of individuals who said they interpret the Bible literally, dividing the sample by race and ethnicity. Their findings suggest that cultural background affects the ways Christians apply their faith to politics. Among those who say they interpret the Bible literally, white evangelicals and, to a lesser extent, Latinos have developed stronger identification with the Republican Party in recent years; by contrast, black biblical literalists have not changed in their Democratic identification.[6]

Analysis of election data consistently reveals distinctive voting patterns among religious groups, but another measure, religious observance, has become an increasingly important factor dividing American voters. The question survey researchers call "church attendance," one that probes how often a respondent attends religious services, has been one of the strongest predictors of the presidential vote since the 2000 election. Christians, Jews, and Muslims who frequently attend religious services are more likely to vote for Republicans; by contrast, Christians, Jews, and Muslims who rarely or never attend are more likely to vote for Democrats. Journalists coined the catchy phrase the "God gap" to describe this division between voters.

In the 2004 presidential election about three of five voters (61 percent) who reported attending religious services more than once a week voted for George W. Bush, while 62 percent of those who reported never attending religious services voted for John Kerry. In the 2008 election the numbers took a slight turn. John McCain's support from weekly attenders (55 percent) was down 6 percentage points from 2004, yet Barack Obama's share of the vote from those who never attend religious services increased 5 points to 67 percent. After factoring in the 4-point overall gain in votes for the Democratic candidate in 2008, the God gap decreased slightly. The 2012 election followed a similar pattern. Almost three of five (59 percent) weekly attenders voted Republican, and 62 percent of voters who never attend religious services voted Democratic.[7]

THE ROOTS OF EVANGELICAL POLITICS

Observers of contemporary American politics can easily forget that the current pattern of active evangelical political engagement and alignment with the Republican Party is actually quite recent. The history of evangelicals and politics in the twentieth century is a story of fluctuation, changing patterns of partisan allegiance, and movement in and out of the public square.

Methods of Public Engagement

Political scientist John Green identifies three approaches to public engagement found within the evangelical tradition: movement politics, quiescent politics, and regularized politics. *Movement politics* arise when a particular issue or problem engages a new group of people and mobilizes them to challenge the status quo. When public concern about the issue eventually wanes, some movement activists may stay involved in politics. In contrast, those who affirm *quiescent politics* decide not to engage in political activity for theological or pragmatic reasons. Some theological traditions emphasize detachment from politics, calling the church to focus on spiritual issues more than temporal concerns or privileging individual transformation over collective action. Others may disengage for pragmatic reasons, determining that they cannot achieve their goals through the normal political process. The third model of engagement, *regularized politics*, calls for participation in regular political processes that are not distinctively religious, such as voting, joining or working in interest groups, campaigning, or even running for elected office.[8]

Evangelicals and their immediate predecessors have alternated among these three modes of public engagement. At the turn of the twentieth century, the precursors of contemporary evangelicals were involved in movement politics including Progressive Era reforms and the prohibition movement. A series of defeats, however, led many former activists toward quiescent politics. In particular, the caricatures of fundamentalists following the Scopes Trial convinced many to redirect their energies. Those who became identified with the fundamentalist movement pulled away from the wider culture and focused their efforts on serving the faithful, establishing their own institutions, and seeking conversions.[9] Only later did these same emphases point them to political reengagement. As the story of the emergence of the Christian Right will demonstrate, many contemporary evangelicals and fundamentalists returned to the public square and engagement via movement politics; by the end of the twentieth century, some of these organizations and actors had chosen the path of regularized politics.

God in the Grass Roots: The Emergence of the Christian Right

Although not a strong presence in national politics for much of the twentieth century, theologically conservative Christians regained an interest in political activity in the post–World War II era and began returning to movement politics. The work of historians such as Daniel Williams (2010) and Darren Dochuk (2010) reveals ways that evangelical interests and concerns affected political processes far before the emergence of the Christian Right.[10] Churches, educational institutions, and other religious organizations helped like-minded believers gain skills and experiences that paved the way for future political activism.

A range of issues captured the attention of evangelicals. Some grew disillusioned with New Deal policies. Others were concerned by the cultural and political changes associated with the tumultuous 1960s. The sexual revolution and the erosion of traditional gender roles, for example, threatened core teachings of many conservative churches, while the Cold War fight against "godless" communism highlighted a religious dimension to foreign policy, reinvigorating debate over the scope and purpose of national defense.

The resulting movement, originally called the "New Christian Right" and later shortened to Christian Right or religious Right, grew out of grassroots political advocacy on a variety of issues. Fundamentalists and evangelicals first mobilized nationally in opposition to sex education in public schools in the late 1960s and in the legal battles to protect the tax-exempt status of Christian schools. The movement expanded in 1974 when Christians organized in Kanawha County, West Virginia, to confront the perceived anti-Christian bias in public school textbooks. The newly formed conservative think tank, the Heritage Foundation, supported the local protestors and helped them to garner the attention of the national media.[11] In 1977 the Miss America finalist and pop singer Anita Bryant gained notice for organizing Christian activists in Dade County, Florida, to repeal a gay rights ordinance. After her success in Florida, Bryant began a national campaign to assist other groups fighting against employment protections for gays and lesbians.[12] In both instances, a national organization or prominent spokesperson transformed a local grassroots campaign into a high-profile national movement. This pattern repeated itself so that, by the early 1980s, religious activists were achieving success in movement politics across the country as they raised concerns about what they saw as threats to traditional values.

As theologically conservative Christians began to organize single-issue-based political movements across the country, a few high-profile religious leaders founded multi-issue organizations designed to connect and energize like-minded activists. The most famous of these groups, the Moral Majority, was established in 1979 by Reverend Jerry Falwell (1933–2007), pastor of what was then the largest independent Baptist church in the United States. Contending that supporters of profamily issues comprised a silent majority of the American public, Falwell encouraged political participation and voter registration to build support for socially conservative policies. He also attracted significant media attention. Other Christian Right organizations founded around this time included Ed McAteer's (1926–2004) Religious Roundtable, later shortened to the Roundtable, designed to organize like-minded pastors, and Christian Voice, a national lobbying organization that became known for its "Congressional Report Cards."

Forging an Alliance with the Republican Party

Through much of the 1970s evangelicals were more likely to identify as Democrats than Republicans, reflecting their general support for New Deal programs and the high percentages of evangelicals in the heavily Democratic South. Evangelicals were beginning to reenter grassroots politics as particular issues captured their attention, but, owing to their quiescent tendencies, they were not especially active in party politics. The presidential election of 1976, however, was an important catalyst for change. In the wake of the Watergate scandal and President Nixon's resignation, Jimmy Carter's biographical campaign attracted evangelical support. Carter spoke openly of Christian faith, describing himself as "born again." At a time when both parties had legitimate opportunity to compete for the conservative Christian vote, Carter energized religious voters, encouraged them to focus on electoral politics, and captured much of their support.[13] The perceived influence of evangelicals in Carter's election raised their national profile, leading *Newsweek* magazine to devote a cover article to the "Year of the Evangelicals." Theologically conservative Protestants were moving back onto the national political scene.

Evangelical support for Carter and the Democratic Party, however, was short-lived. Many evangelicals who regained interest in politics with Carter's 1976 campaign became more politicized in their opposition to abortion during his presidency. Although evangelicals had been reluctant to join the right-to-life movement in the immediate aftermath of *Roe v. Wade* (1973), in part because of the association of the movement with Catholicism, the efforts of several high-profile leaders brought the issue to the fore.[14] The publication of Hal Lindsey's best seller *The Late Great Planet Earth* (1970) reflected and stimulated theologically conservative Protestants' increasing concerns about the erosion of traditional values. Lindsey popularized premillennial dispensationalism, a reading of biblical prophecy that predicted a period of moral decline leading to the end times and Christ's return. Popular theologian Francis Schaeffer (1912–1984) wrote extensively about society's moral decline and the movement away from God toward what he deemed "secular humanism." In *Whatever Happened to the Human Race* (1979), a book, film series, and national speaking tour with the pediatrician C. Everett Koop, Schaeffer brought attention to the religious importance of the political controversies surrounding *Roe v. Wade*, proclaiming that "of all the subjects relating to the erosion of the sanctity of human life, abortion is the keystone."[15] Gradually, these and other influences led evangelicals to connect concern for the unborn with the central tenets of their faith.

By the end of the 1970s the abortion issue was at the center of Christian Right politics, and evangelical activists had begun pressuring elected officials to change abortion policy. Although he openly expressed his personal opposition to abortion, Carter held to the traditional Baptist belief in the separation of church and state, and he viewed the president's role as substantially limited by separation of powers and federalism. As a consequence, he viewed abortion as primarily a personal issue most appropriately addressed by state governments, if at all. He thus did little as president to deal with pro-life concerns directly. Carter opposed public funding of abortion, but he alienated conservative Christians who expected him to be more proactive in working against *Roe v. Wade*. By late 1979 the growing cadre of evangelical political leaders voiced increasing dissatisfaction with Carter.

In a deliberate effort to expand their political base, Republican Party elites seized the opportunity and built alliances with disaffected Christian conservatives, encouraging them to support Ronald Reagan. Beginning with the 1980 election, the Republican Party platform included planks appealing to the Christian Right, such as support for constitutional amendments permitting organized prayer in public schools and defining human life as beginning at conception. Although not as open and clear about his evangelical faith as the other two candidates in that year's presidential race, Jimmy Carter and John Anderson, Reagan supported the newly broadened conservative agenda, which included a set of policy positions that were being relabeled as "profamily" issues.[16] In a now-famous speech to a group of ten thousand evangelical pastors, candidate Reagan won the crowd with the line: "I know you can't endorse me, but I want you to know that I endorse you and all that you are doing."[17]

The outreach efforts were successful. Evangelicals constituted an important Republican voting bloc in the federal elections of 1980 and 1984. Although it would take a few election cycles for the transformation to be complete, Christian Right leaders and activists were forging a close connection with the Republican Party, thus making the transition from movement politics to regularized politics.

The Triumph (and Peril) of Morality Politics

Initially, Christian Right activists found great success by adopting the language of morality and sinfulness to discuss political issues. In a certain sense, all legislation reflects an underlying morality, charting a path seen as the best or right way over less-favored alternatives. But certain issues earn the moniker "moral issues" because they are framed in terms of values. As political scientist Kenneth Meier starkly but aptly characterized the resulting politics: "Rather than redistributing income, however, morality politics seeks to redistribute values, to put the government's stamp of approval on one set of values and to abase another."[18]

By framing their priority issues in moral terms, Christian Right leaders primed their followers to think of politics as an all-or-nothing process. Following the theoretical work of Edward Carmines and James Stimson (1980) political scientists call such issues "easy issues" because they focus on the policy ends, not means, and are usually framed in dichotomous terms: one is either for the issue or against it.[19] These issues appear simple to voters who think that they understand the two competing sides and know their position instinctively. An alternative category of issues, that which Carmines and Stimson labeled "hard issues," includes those that concern the means of achieving a shared goal, not the end itself. On such issues, legislators and activists debate which of a range of options is best to pursue, so it is more difficult for voters (or elected officials, for that matter) to determine their position easily. Examples of such issues include reducing poverty and combating terrorism. Almost everyone shares the policy goal; the conflict arises when seeking how to achieve it.

Activists have many incentives to frame issues in simple, dichotomous terms. It is far easier to rally the troops, mobilize voters, and raise money when the policy debate seems clear and the lines are sharply drawn. In practice, however, the public policy issues addressed in a representative democracy are almost always multifaceted and require willingness to compromise in order to reach agreement. The two sides on the end goal of an "easy issue" are often quite clear, but public debate over the various ways elected officials might address the issue is much murkier. By choosing to build support using the rhetoric of morality politics, Christian Right leaders followed a path that would likely lead to short-term rewards but long-term frustrations.

Out with the Old, In with the New

On the heels of Reagan's election, the Christian Right entered a period of dramatic change. In the early 1980s Christian Broadcasting Network founder Pat Robertson (b. 1930) organized the Freedom Council, a national network of local groups designed to train political activists and educate voters. When Robertson began exploring a possible bid for the presidency in 1988, he drew key support from the grassroots networks built by the Freedom Council and its successor groups. Although he did not win the Republican nomination, Robertson's strong showings in several early states, including a surprise second-place finish in the Iowa caucus, demonstrated the growing political strength of religious conservatives. His campaign had other significant ripple effects; many of his supporters stayed involved in politics, forming a resilient network of activists that would become the backbone of future outreach efforts.

By the 1990s evangelical politics was beginning to divide into two camps. Most of the older-style organizations were hierarchical in structure and typically centered on a charismatic (sometimes controversial) leader. In practice, many were little more than large mailing lists. Conversely, the newer organizations were often decentralized, with a strong emphasis on grassroots networking and mobilization. Many of these second-generation Christian Right groups found great success developing state and local chapters.

What would become the most significant evangelical political organization of the 1990s, the Christian Coalition, grew out of the Robertson network. Founded by Robertson in 1989 and directed by a young and ambitious political operative, Ralph Reed (b. 1961), the Christian Coalition created a new model for evangelical political activity. The national office quietly built a network of state and local affiliates to train and prepare individuals for political advocacy and pursuit of political office, especially positions in state and local government. Reed moved the emphasis away from direct religious appeals and instead advocated a more pragmatic approach, broadening the organization's policy agenda and building coalitions with nonreligious groups. The organization became famous for utilizing a network of churches each election year to distribute tens of millions of voter guides that compared candidates on a range of issues they defined as profamily. Although technically nonpartisan, the guides typically prompted voters to select Republican candidates. At its peak in 1995, the Christian Coalition boasted 1.6 million members and 1,600 local chapters.[20] Reed left after the election of 1996, and the organization never recovered. After losing an expensive legal battle for tax-exempt status and facing sharp membership decline, it lost its place as an influential player in domestic politics.[21]

In addition to grassroots organizations such as the Christian Coalition, evangelical leaders created another vehicle for political influence, the advocacy think tank. Such organizations focus their attention on public policy, researching policy issues, educating elected officials, and helping to write legislation. In 1983 Focus on the Family's James Dobson (b. 1936) founded the Family Research Council (FRC), a Washington-based policy organization for promoting and researching profamily issues. By 1999 the FRC had a $14 million budget and a mailing list of 500,000. National advocacy groups such as the Traditional Values Coalition and the American Family Association also grew in size and influence during the 1990s. Even more significantly, activists across the country founded state-level research foundations modeled after their national counterparts that devoted resources and called attention to the work of state governments.

As newer, more robust advocacy groups emerged, some of the earliest Christian Right organizations declined or even folded. Many lacked the deep grassroots networks and outreach strategies necessary for longer-term survival. Organizations claimed large membership bases, but most operated as centralized groups with small staffs and large mailing lists of people who sent donations and received newsletters but rarely or never gathered to work collectively. Additionally, high-profile scandals involving televangelists Jim Bakker (b. 1940) and Jimmy Swaggart (b. 1935) created image and fundraising problems for other well-known media evangelists and their affiliated groups. The most prominent of the early Christian Right organizations, Jerry Falwell's Moral Majority, closed in 1989.

Rallying Around the Opposition: The Clinton Years

As is often the case for lobbying groups, nothing seems to energize grass-roots members quite like the perception of a threat. The election of Bill Clinton in 1992 provided the burst of energy needed by languishing national Christian Right organizations. Democrats gained unified control of the presidency and both houses of Congress for the first time since the Christian Right aligned with the Republican Party, paving the way for an aggressive Democratic legislative agenda. Clinton's reversal of Reagan's abortion-related executive orders, advocacy for gays in the military, and push for health-care reform were among many political moves that prompted a conservative backlash.

Evangelical organizations that found renewed unity in the opposition to Clinton and Democratic policy proposals successfully rallied the grass roots for the 1994 midterm congressional election. The Christian Coalition, at the height of its power, distributed an estimated 33 million voter guides that tacitly supported Republican candidates.[22] Republican leaders in the House of Representatives crafted the "Contract with America," a set of proposed internal congressional reforms and list of ten pieces of legislation to be passed in the first hundred days that promised an agenda for change. Although it avoided controversial issues such as abortion, the contract included language designed to appeal to conservatives throughout the party, including profamily groups. The election was a major Republican victory. The party added eight seats and secured majority control of the Senate. In a dramatic win that astonished most pundits, Republicans gained fifty-four seats in the House, a move that transferred party control of the chamber for the first time in forty years. Several factors contributed to the strong Republican gains, but researchers agree that the mobilizing efforts of Christian Right organizations and increased evangelical turnout played a pivotal role in the victory.[23]

The revelation in January 1998 that Bill Clinton had a sexual relationship with intern Monica Lewinsky added ammunition for groups that already opposed many of the Clinton administration's policies. Rumors of Clinton's marital infidelity were nothing new, but the confirmation of the Lewinsky affair and the release of the sexually explicit Starr Report gave profamily groups even more reasons to oppose the president and prompted many evangelical leaders to call for his resignation. Clinton's sworn testimony concerning his relationship with Lewinsky eventually led to his impeachment in the House of Representatives on charges of perjury and obstruction of justice, but he was found not guilty in the Senate trial. In the end, the impeachment harmed Republican morale. In an ironic twist, Clinton's approval ratings reached an all-time high after the House impeachment vote, and support for the Republican Party plummeted. Many of the organizations that publicly scorned President Clinton during the Lewinsky scandal faced criticism for what some viewed as overzealous attacks.

EVANGELICALS IN CONTEMPORARY POLITICS

Yet all was not lost. Even as national organizations faced setbacks at the end of the Clinton years, statewide groups were making steady progress bringing attention to cultural issues and winning significant victories with state constitutional amendments and ballot initiatives defending traditional marriage and restricting abortion. In many states, the work grew out of the decentralization of Christian Right organizations and the founding of "profamily" research organizations.

The Sweet Smell of Victory: George W. Bush and Evangelicals

On the national level, the evangelical political tide turned once again in 2000. Although evangelical turnout dipped slightly in the 2000 election, George W. Bush's eventual victory energized evangelical leaders and organizations. For the first time since the rise of the Christian Right, the movement could claim a president who shared its members' central policy goals and was openly faithful. Although he never described himself as an evangelical, Bush's frequent references to his life-changing religious conversion and open discussion of his faith aligned him firmly with this tradition. Bush was a strong advocate for many issues of principal concern to evangelical groups, especially upholding the right to life and appointing conservative judges.

After a generation of Democratic dominance, the Republican Party controlled the presidency and both houses of Congress. The prospects seemed bright for promoting the Christian Right agenda in Washington. In the campaign, Bush named three top priorities: tax cuts, public education reform, and the faith-based initiative. Many Christian Right groups promote fiscal conservatism, so they welcomed the tax-reform package. Bush's success in winning tax cuts came at a very high cost, however; Senator Jim Jeffords left the Republican Party after the congressional battle to pass the legislation, a move that switched party control of the Senate to the Democrats. Bush also succeeded in passing a bipartisan education bill, No Child Left Behind, but many evangelical groups disliked the emphasis on national educational standards and thus strongly opposed the measure. His third policy priority, a proposal to encourage more government partnerships with faith-based organizations, failed in Congress but found some success with policy changes that Bush could make within the executive branch. Despite the religious nature of the initiative, evangelical support of the faith-based legislation was lukewarm at best. Religious responses varied widely, from a few groups who actively promoted the effort to those who expressed vehement opposition to the plan, which they said might result in tax dollars supporting the wrong kind of religion.[24]

No single event affected the Bush presidency more than the terrorist attacks on September 11, 2001. As one Bush adviser explained, in the aftermath of the attacks, "we went from domestic policy to domestic consequences. It totally changed our lives."[25] National security took center stage; soon the United States was involved in wars in Afghanistan and Iraq. Christian Right groups rallied around the president and his foreign policy as what was necessary to protect the homeland and fight against "radical Islam."

In 2004 Bush's supporters did not want to repeat the narrow election result and thirty-six-day recount battle from 2000. Evangelical organizations aggressively rallied their supporters to assist with Bush's reelection effort and encourage voter turnout, a move that helped him to secure his narrow victory. For the first time, Focus on the Family's influential leader James Dobson officially endorsed a presidential candidate, publicly announcing his support for Bush. In return, Bush campaigned on many issues of importance to the Christian Right, including giving his vocal support for a constitutional amendment defining marriage as between one man and one woman.

The Growing Divide Between Purists and Pragmatists

Although Bush's domestic policy agenda in his first term had not given high priority to many Christian Right issues, evangelical leaders hoped for and expected more aggressive action on their agenda after the victory in 2004. Increasing hostilities in Iraq, the return of Democratic control of the House of Representatives, and Bush's plummeting approval ratings were among several factors that limited Bush's productivity.

As his second term in office progressed, Bush faced increasing criticism from many Christian Right leaders. From their vantage point, Bush was not giving enough attention to the most important issues, particularly the battles against abortion and gay marriage. Amid growing concern that the Republican Party was taking the evangelical voting bloc for granted and thus ignoring their issues, James Dobson and other leaders publicly warned the White House to take heed or face the consequences for Republicans in the next election.

To some extent, the criticism was valid. The Bush administration was not particularly proactive in the battles against abortion or gay marriage. But the proponents of morality politics failed to acknowledge the limits of the presidential office to force change on these issues. Under Supreme Court precedents at the time, most of the limited abortion regulations that were allowed, along with all marriage laws, were left to state governments—and presidential power in such matters only lessened after a landmark Supreme Court ruling in 2015 declared gay marriage a constitutional right that even state legislatures must not abridge. Bush had, and future presidents may be expected to have, little power to implement the policy agenda Christian Right activists most desired.

Even as criticism mounted from old guard leaders with their purist approach to politics, a newer wave of activists, one that came of age politically while working on campaigns for candidates and ballot initiatives, was gaining power. They were directly involved in regularized politics, so they understood the written and unwritten rules of the process. Given their experience on the ground, most of these activists approached politics more pragmatically than did their purist counterparts.

This new style of leadership moved away from bold demands for change in favor of advocating more incremental (and politically feasible) legislation. Often willing to compromise some of their end goals in order to win part of what they wanted, the pragmatists found more political success than their purist counterparts.[26] For example, instead of demanding an immediate constitutional amendment to ban abortion, many pro-life groups actively supported legislation that made incremental steps toward their final goal. This pragmatic approach during the years of unified Republican control of Congress and the White House led to a series of victories for abortion opponents, including the passage of three largely symbolic pro-life bills.

Traditional Christian Right organizations also adopted new strategies as they adjusted to the changing political environment. Most significantly, their leaders developed new coalitions of like-minded organizations to coordinate efforts. In May 1998 a group of Republicans in Congress sponsored a "Values Summit" that brought pastors and leaders of well-known evangelical organizations to Washington to offer their input on public policy. Momentum from the summit led to the formation of the Values Action Team (VAT) spearheaded by Representative Joe Pitts. The VAT gathered representatives from Christian Right organizations to meet weekly on Capitol Hill to coordinate political strategy and exchange information about profamily legislation. The Arlington Group, described by investigative journalist Dan Gilgoff as "a secret society of the Religious Right's top power brokers," began meeting in June 2003 with the purpose of discussing their political agenda and resolving disagreements away from public scrutiny. Composed of leaders from approximately seventy organizations, the group convenes every six weeks to plan political strategy and encourage a united front.[27]

The Rise of the Evangelical Left?

Although Christian Right organizations capture most of the public attention (both positive and negative) focused on evangelicals in politics, a smaller yet relevant evangelical Left has also gained influence in the public square. Several organizations that offer a counterpoint to religious conservatives have worked for decades at promoting a different set of policy priorities. Some of these organizations, such as Sojourners, grew out of Vietnam-era antiwar efforts, but many of the evangelical Left organizations active today emerged in response to the growing power of the Christian Right.

Groups that align on the evangelical Left are similar to Christian Right organizations in their emphasis on the authority of the Bible, but they differ significantly from them in what biblical passages and concepts they emphasize. Whereas groups on the right tend to focus on issues of personal morality such as abortion and homosexuality, those on the left prioritize social justice issues such as poverty, war, and racism. Much like the Christian Right organizations that claim they are nonpartisan yet typically support policies aligned with the Republican Party, many of those on the evangelical Left describe themselves as nonpartisan but advocate for positions commonly associated with the Democratic Party.

Although evangelicals would generally agree that the Bible speaks about both individual and collective sin, the political Right and Left typically emphasize different sources of sin and its social effects and thus have divergent views about the role of government in addressing political and social problems. Activists on the evangelical Right are most likely to focus on individual behavior and thus see government as most helpful guiding individual decisions. The religious Left places more emphasis on collective sin and the structural problems that can result, so they are most likely to advocate for a stronger role for government and programs that try to redistribute resources.

In a pattern similar to that found in the Christian Right, many organizations and movements on the evangelical Left center around a magnetic and captivating personality. Prophetic figures such as Tony Campolo (b. 1935), the now-retired Eastern University sociologist, gained popularity on the evangelical lecture circuit. Campolo founded the Evangelical Association for the Promotion of Education (EAPE), a social justice organization focused on caring for the poor. The EAPE began its work in inner-city Philadelphia and the Dominican Republic and has since expanded to include a range of programs such as Cornerstone Christian Academy and Mission Year, a program to encourage young people to serve as urban missionaries. More recently Campolo founded Red Letter Christians, a blog that emphasizes living out the teachings of Jesus.

Likely the most recognized activist from the evangelical left is Jim Wallis (b. 1948), author of several best sellers, including *God's Politics* (2005). Written in part as a response to evangelical leaders who claimed victory in securing George W. Bush's reelection in 2004, this book argued against the tactics of the political and religious Right and challenged the secular Left to pay more attention to religious voters who share progressive values. Although Wallis had spent several decades as the head of Sojourners, a Washington-based antipoverty and social justice organization, the timing of the book and its success garnered significant media attention and gave him new visibility. Capitalizing on increased disaffection with the Iraq War and Republican leadership in Washington, Wallis offered a public counterpoint to the Christian Right, emphasizing social justice issues instead of the cultural issues associated with religious conservatives. Although evangelicals are still a minority presence in Wallis's organization, the number of self-identified evangelicals who subscribe to the flagship publication *Sojourners* has grown significantly in recent years, increasing from 5 percent of its readership in 2002 to 18 percent in 2011. Another 15 percent of the readership identify themselves as part of the emerging church movement, a group that includes some evangelicals.[28]

Another advocacy group that has been offering a counterpoint to the Christian Right is Evangelicals for Social Action (ESA), a network of moderate and progressive evangelicals founded in 1978 by Ronald Sider (b. 1939). The ESA network grew out of the work of evangelical leaders concerned about social justice issues who gathered in Chicago in November 1973 and together penned the Chicago Declaration of Evangelical Social Concern. This statement spoke out against racism and materialism and called evangelicals to care for the poor and the oppressed. ESA has been a lower-profile but significant voice for the evangelical Center and Left for more than three decades.

A popular figure who has influenced the evangelical Left is Shane Claiborne (b. 1975), an activist, author, and founding member of The Simple

Way community in Philadelphia. Claiborne has gained notice for his call to simple living, concern for and unity with the poor, and commitment to nonviolence. The most recognized figure of the New Monasticism movement, Claiborne is a sought-after speaker who travels the world sharing his message of social justice and peacemaking. In 2008 he coauthored with Chris Haw his most directly political book, *Jesus for President: Politics for Ordinary Radicals*.[29] Their postmodern approach does not follow standard party lines as it calls for the church to "embody a social alternative," but it offers a radical departure from the themes and motifs of the Christian Right.

Several other smaller organizations have an active presence in Washington to lobby in favor of issues more traditionally aligned with the Democratic Party. Bread for the World is an advocacy group dedicated to ending domestic and global hunger. The Evangelical Environmental Network raises awareness of climate change and other environmental issues. The New Evangelical Partnership for the Common Good was founded by Richard Cizik after he was ousted from his role as vice president for governmental affairs at the NAE for discussing his evolving views on gay rights in a national interview.

Several prominent organizations and activists thus provide a voice for politically moderate and liberal evangelicals. But the size, scope, and influence of these groups is quite small when compared with the Christian Right. The largest and best-financed Christian advocacy groups at work today are on the opposite side of the policy spectrum, advocating for socially and economically conservative policies.

The Response of Political Parties

Party leaders are well aware of the importance of activating religious voters, so they pay attention to influential religious organizations and also track voting trends. Recent patterns of religion and political behavior have created political dilemmas for both major political parties. Leaders and activists want to reach across the God gap while still satisfying religious voting blocs in their own parties. Republicans do not want to appear to be too tied to religious voters, yet at the same time they need to maintain and build support from the evangelicals who constitute an essential part of their electoral base. Conversely, Democrats need to engage more openly in religious discussions without alienating their important voting bloc of religious Nones.

As the 2008 election approached, Democratic-leaning evangelicals were seeking new ways to present a visible and viable alternative to the Christian Right, and Democratic Party leaders wanted to reach out more effectively to religious voters. Candidates and consultants responded, making significant public efforts to connect with religious voters and build new links between more progressive Christians and the Democratic Party. Every major Democratic presidential candidate in 2008 hired at least one full-time staff member for religious outreach, and the candidates spoke openly, often at some length, about their personal faith. Common Good Strategies, the first major political consulting firm to specialize in connecting Democratic candidates with religious voters, found ample work assisting clients with races across the country. The 2012 Obama campaign continued the pattern established in 2008 and hired a faith vote director, Michael Wear, to spearhead religious outreach.

As the Democrats wrestle with new ways of connecting with religious voters, Republicans face different dilemmas. In the wake of significant political losses in the elections of 2006 and 2008, various factions within the party vied for control as they sought to rebuild party strength. The rise of the Tea Party movement in the 2010 election cycle added a new and vocal bloc of voters that framed the political agenda in terms of economic policy and reducing the size of government. The extended economic crisis and ongoing military action in the Middle East kept most attention focused on "peace and prosperity" issues, leaving little room for discussion of issues of greatest concern to social conservatives.

Republican Party leaders recognize the importance of evangelical voters, but they also want to be responsive to other voting blocs that can mobilize votes and raise money. As different blocs within (and outside of) the Republican Party vie for influence, party leaders face significant questions about what path is best to rebuild the party and secure its base. The direction party leaders eventually choose to take will have strong implications for the relative influence of Christian conservatives in the party.

THE FUTURE OF EVANGELICAL POLITICAL ENGAGEMENT

The preceding analysis of the recent history of evangelicals and political activism reveals patterns and trends that point toward a possible future for evangelicals in politics and public policy. One thing is for certain: this is a time of significant transition. Several of the leaders who were essential in shaping the Christian Right have died in recent years, and still others are retiring from public life. New pastors and activists appear well positioned to lead a fresh wave of activism, but, as of this writing, none have clearly emerged to take such definitive leadership roles. The future of evangelicals in public life thus depends in large part on the actions and decisions of those currently in their twenties and thirties. What policy issues engage these younger evangelicals, which style of political activism they adopt, and which public figures they choose to follow will shape the contours of evangelical politics for much of the twenty-first century.

New Generation, New Perspectives?

Although high percentages of evangelicals continue to vote Republican, survey research suggests that some generational change may be on the horizon. Polls conducted in the months preceding the 2008 election revealed that younger evangelicals, although overwhelmingly Republican, had weaker connections to the Republican Party than did their older counterparts. Even so, a full 40 percent of young evangelicals in a survey in 2007 identified as Republicans, more than twice the percentage who said they were Democrats (19 percent) and double the number of Republican-identifiers in their age-group as a whole.[30]

Although the generational differences in partisan affiliation are striking, many measures of younger evangelicals' views on policy issues suggest that, as a group, they remain politically conservative. In the Millennial Values Survey of 2012, for example, college-aged white evangelicals were the most conservative religious group on almost all political questions asked. Only one in ten (11 percent) younger white evangelicals said they wanted President Obama to win reelection. A majority (53 percent) said the government should do more to narrow the gap between rich and poor, yet 86 percent agreed that "poor people have become too dependent on government assistance programs." Almost nine of ten (88 percent) said abortion should be illegal in almost all cases, and slightly more than one in four (27 percent) favored same-sex marriage.[31]

The views of older and younger evangelicals diverge in interesting ways on the two issues that have long been central to the Christian Right: abortion and gay rights. On the abortion issue, younger evangelicals are significantly more *conservative* than their elders. The pattern reverses, however, on the gay marriage issue. Younger evangelicals are much more likely to report having a gay or lesbian friend or family member, and they are also more supportive of gay marriage or civil unions.

Not as tied to the traditional Christian Right organizations or their leaders, younger evangelicals are more engaged in grassroots politics on a wider range of issues than are those from older cohorts. Data also suggest that younger cohorts may have a different sense of which issues should have the highest priority. The increasingly globalized economy coupled with the rapid spread of new technology helps bridge gaps of distance, language, and culture. Perhaps as a result, the younger generation expresses increased interest in international affairs and the global reach of domestic politics.[32]

In sum, younger evangelicals are not as closely tied to the Republican Party as are older generations, yet many (but not all) of their underlying beliefs best fit the Republican agenda. Analysis of polling trends suggests that much of the younger generation's disaffection is a reflection of their dissatisfaction with George W. Bush. As memories of the Bush presidency fade, new figures will emerge to fill the party leadership role. If a new leader can recapture the hearts of younger evangelicals, the party will likely regain some strength. In the meantime, Democratic elites will need to redouble their efforts to attract younger evangelicals while the present opportunity remains.

The Old Guard and the Politics of Disengagement

In recent years the old purist/pragmatist split has reemerged as well. As we have seen, younger evangelicals include a wider range of issues among their priorities and are more liberal on gay rights than their older counterparts. The leaders of the traditional Christian Right organizations, however, are still waging culture wars, issuing warnings of gloom and doom on the horizon. Speaking to the National Religious Broadcasters in 2008, for example, James Dobson raised questions about generational change: "It causes me to wonder who will be left to carry the banner when this generation of leaders is gone.... Who in the next generation will be willing to take the heat, when it's so much safer and more comfortable to avoid controversial subjects? What will be the impact on the conservative Christian church when the patriarchs have passed?"[33] Old guard leaders such as Dobson are concerned about future leadership for the Christian Right.

Looking back on three decades of advocacy for issues typically associated with the Republican Party, some old guard leaders are now expressing frustration that their entry into regularized politics did not yield enough policy success. From their vantage point, the party and its candidates promised them a lot, relied on their help in mobilizing voters during each election cycle, but in the end did very little to promote Christian Right priorities once they were in office.

The strong Democratic gains in the 2008 election weakened the Republican Party and created internal dissention about how to rebuild electoral strength. Although the Republican resurgence in the 2010 elections gave party leaders hope for future electoral successes, the emergence of the Tea Party movement and its focused agenda diverted attention from social issues many evangelicals want to emphasize. The current political climate is less favorable to social conservatives, so the policy purists whose tendencies are more uncompromising may choose to disengage from the public square, moving again toward quiescence.

Regularized Politics Reborn: Mainstream Evangelical Activism Moving Forward

Even as many old guard leaders and organizations fade in importance or exit politics completely, a new guard of evangelical leadership is emerging that seems likely to chart a new path of regularized politics. Familiar with and comfortable working through regular political processes that are not distinctively religious, evangelical activists in the coming decades will be active, if slightly wary, participants in American politics. In particular, mainstream evangelical politics will likely include three defining features: (1) activists will advocate for a wider range of issues, resulting in weaker ties to either political party; (2) movement leaders will adopt a new, more conciliatory leadership style, with an expanded role for megachurch pastors; and (3) activists will approach politics more pragmatically. Let us consider each of these features in turn.

The Expanding Evangelical Policy Agenda

The new millennium has been marked by various efforts to expand the evangelical political agenda. In 2004 the NAE, an umbrella group representing over sixty evangelical denominations and related organizations, issued *For the Health of the Nations*, a document calling evangelicals to civic engagement on a broad range of policy issues. Designed to extend and redefine the agenda for evangelical politics, the statement was well received by many in the larger movement who advocated such change. At the same time, the statement angered some older guard Christian Right leaders who believe that evangelicals should focus their advocacy work on cultural issues such as abortion and gay marriage.

Many evangelicals, especially the younger cohorts, appear to support the broadening agenda. Issues such as the AIDS pandemic, religious freedom, sex trafficking, and global poverty are among the key priorities for many evangelical organizations that are currently gaining strength and visibility. As the issue agenda broadens, many new guard leaders are distancing themselves from ties to a particular political party and advocating a multifaceted response to public policy issues.

A key step in this movement toward a less partisan and less strident approach occurred in May 2008 when a group of evangelical pastors, academics, and leaders gathered in Washington, D.C., to release "An Evangelical Manifesto: A Declaration of Evangelical Identity and Public Commitment." Addressing audiences inside and outside of evangelicalism, the signatories sought to counter negative stereotypes by reclaiming and redefining the term *evangelical* while encouraging more civil and humble political participation. In effect, the document issued a warning against the potential dangers of regularized politics: "Called to an allegiance higher than party, ideology, economic system, and nationality, we Evangelicals see it our duty to engage with politics, but our equal duty never to be completely equated with any party, partisan ideology, or nationality."[34] Evangelicals can and should participate in the public square, the signers argued, but they should never put party or ideology before their faith commitments.

Inspired in part by increased interactions with immigrant churches and the growing ethnic diversity of evangelical congregations, evangelical leaders have become increasingly active on the politically contentious immigration issue. In 2009 the NAE issued a statement in favor of immigration reform, and in 2010 the organization spearheaded a publicity campaign highlighting the issue. A theologically and ideologically diverse group of evangelical Christian leaders issued a bipartisan call for immigration reform that included a plank advocating "a path toward legal status and/or citizenship for those who qualify and who wish to become permanent residents."[35]

These shifts in focus will weaken evangelical connections with the Republican Party. To be sure, the Republican Party is still the most natural political home for most white evangelicals, but the wide array of issues moving onto the agenda cross party lines. Some issues, such as international religious freedom, can attract bipartisan support, but most of the issue positions are a mix between core Republican and core Democratic stances. In coming elections, neither party can take the evangelical vote for granted, and both parties will have significant reasons for courting this sizable voting bloc.

And Who Will Speak for Them? New Styles of Public Advocacy

A second important transformation of evangelical politics is the emergence of leaders who are gaining resonance and a large popular following by offering a more tempered approach to political advocacy. Many megachurch pastors and other new guard leaders are moving away from black-and-white moral language and following a more moderate path. In a reversal from old-style morality politics, they are much more willing to acknowledge and even embrace the complexity of issues that do not offer simple, binary solutions. Instead of looking to the political system for the solution, this new style of leader is more likely to raise awareness of a policy issue, address the issue in sermons or other writings that connect it to biblical themes, and call the church to direct action that addresses some aspect of the problem.

More than any other group, megachurch pastors are emerging as the new spokespeople for the evangelical movement. Pastors of large, nationally recognized congregations command notice, so many are beginning to use their name recognition and prominence to raise awareness of a new array of policy issues and call the church to action. Although prominent pastors will not be the only significant spokespeople for politically engaged evangelicals, they will likely lead the way in setting trends and attracting the lion's share of media attention.

No megachurch leader has been more influential than California pastor Rick Warren (b. 1954), founder of Saddleback Church and author of *The Purpose Driven Life* (2002), which has sold more than 30 million copies, topping *Publisher's Weekly*'s all-time best-seller list. Warren self-consciously maintains a politically neutral stance even as he calls attention to a range of politically significant issues. In 2005 he unveiled the "PEACE Plan," a blueprint for addressing global poverty with an emphasis on planting churches, equipping leaders, assisting the poor, caring for the sick, and educating the next generation. He revised the plan three years later, replacing the focus on church planting with a new plank, promoting reconciliation, and invited other churches to join the global effort.[36]

In August 2008 Warren convened the Civil Forum on the Presidency, a nationally televised event (discussed in more detail by Michael Hamilton in chapter 1 of this volume) that featured the pastor asking a series of political and religious questions to the two major party presidential candidates. The event was televised by several cable networks and marked the first time candidates Obama and McCain shared a national stage. Warren planned a similar forum for the 2012 presidential election but canceled it in protest against the rancor in the presidential campaign.

Joel Hunter (b. 1948) is another example of a megachurch leader who has sought many different platforms for advocating broader and more moderate political views. In books such as *Right Wing, Wrong Bird* (2006) and *A New Kind of Conservative* (2008), Hunter argued for broadening and expanding the evangelical political agenda. In 2006 he made national news headlines after he agreed to take the helm of the Christian Coalition and then abruptly resigned before beginning his work. Hunter explained that he accepted the job with the intention of expanding the coalition's issue agenda but then discovered resistance from the organization's board. As he summarized in a media interview afterward, "When we really got down to it, they said: 'This just isn't for us. It won't speak to our base, so we just can't go there.'"[37] Hunter found more positive reception connecting with both parties during the 2008 election. He was an early supporter of

Mike Huckabee's campaign for the Republican presidential nomination; later he delivered a prayer at the Democratic convention and served on President Obama's initial faith-based council.

The Triumph of Pragmatism

Pragmatism is a third defining feature of the new wave of evangelical public engagement. Many evangelical political activists who are gaining influence in contemporary debates engage in a different style of politics than their predecessors did. Pragmatists begin with the intention of working with the system, not against it, and they seek results, even when doing so requires acceptance of compromise and gradual progress. Whereas some policy purists resist all forms of compromise as immoral, pragmatists argue that incremental change need not compromise fundamental values. By moving slowly toward a goal, they hope to build support for further changes as the political opportunities arise.

Aware that working with other groups increases the likelihood of achieving political success, many organizations and their representatives build coalitions with groups outside of traditional evangelical circles, seeking political partners on an issue-by-issue basis. Political scientist Allen Hertzke uses the phrase "strange bedfellows" to describe the most jarring of these resulting partnerships. In his work chronicling religious activism on human rights issues, he offers examples such as the coalition created to build support for antitrafficking legislation, in which Charles Colson's Prison Fellowship, the NAE, and the Salvation Army partnered with Gloria Steinem, Eleanor Smeal, and other key figures from the feminist movement.[38]

Although this more nuanced policy approach has gained popularity with many evangelical leaders, some of those who are seeking to expand the evangelical policy agenda are still relying on morality politics in their quest to shift focus from one group of issues to another. Even as they decry the practices of their conservative counterparts, they apply religious principles and moral rhetoric in an attempt to reframe classic "hard issues" into dichotomous "easy issues." The federal budget, for example, becomes a "moral document" that reflects whether national priorities are biblical. The complex process of determining the annual allocations for budget line items is thus described simplistically as either right or wrong.

In a movement as fluid and multifaceted as American evangelicalism, there will always be outliers, particularly in the form of larger-than-life figures who compete for public attention to their efforts. But recent trends suggest that evangelical political leaders in coming decades will approach politics pragmatically, wary of dangers from the past but intent on building a multifaceted issue agenda for the future.

CONCLUSION

The emergence of the Christian Right in the late 1970s ended decades of ambivalence toward politics and reestablished organized efforts to encourage evangelical political participation. The election of 1980 began an uneasy but significant alliance between this burgeoning social movement and the Republican Party. Given the importance of evangelical voters helping to secure Republican victories early into the twenty-first century, it is easy to forget that they could have found a political home in the Democratic Party.

This recent alignment between evangelicals and Republicans, although still quite strong, is showing some signs of weakening. Many of the key figures who attracted significant media attention and large followings have died, and older Christian Right organizations are fading in influence. At the same time, new organizations and spokespeople are expanding the range of issues of concern to evangelicals, and younger voters seem less tied to the Republican Party. The mode and tone of evangelical engagement in politics and public policy are undergoing small but significant shifts that will have lasting influence on the Republican and Democratic Parties. In the meantime, the influence of the Christian Right will endure for decades in the work of an entire generation of activists who now serve in staff positions and in elected office at all levels of government.

NOTES

1. Because most researchers classify black Protestants as a politically relevant group, almost all discussions of "evangelical" voters in social science research are actually describing the political behavior of white evangelicals. The reasons for doing so in large part reflect the statistical problems of analyzing data with small sample sizes, not a conscious decision to exclude racial and ethnic minorities for substantive reasons.

2. Dan Cox, "Young White Evangelicals: Less Republican, Still Conservative," Pew Forum on Religion and Public Life, September 28, 2007, http://pewforum.org/docs/?DocID=250, accessed August 4, 2015; Pew Research Center, "A Deep Dive Into Party Affiliation," April 7, 2015, http://www.people-press.org/2015/04/07/a-deep-dive-into-party-affiliation/2, accessed November 25, 2015.

3. Pew Research Center, "How the Faithful Voted: 2012 Preliminary Analysis," November 7, 2012, http://www.pewforum.org/Politics-and-Elections/How-the-Faithful-Voted-2012-Preliminary-Exit-Poll-Analysis.aspx#rr, accessed August 4, 2015.

4. Pew Research Center, "How the Faithful Voted: 2014 Preliminary Analysis," November 5, 2014, http://www.pewforum.org/2014/11/05/how-the-faithful-voted-2014-preliminary-analysis/, accessed August 7, 2015.

5. Brian R. Calfano and Paul A. Djupe, "God Talk: Religious Cues and Electoral Support," *Political Research Quarterly* 62, no. 2 (2009): 329–39.

6. Eric L. McDaniel and Christopher G. Ellison, "God's Party? Race, Religion and Partisanship Over Time," *Political Research Quarterly* 61, no. 2 (2008): 180–91.

7. Pew Research Center, "How the Faithful Voted: 2012."

8. John Green, "Seeking a Place," in *Toward an Evangelical Public Policy*, ed. Ronald J. Sider and Diane Knippers (Grand Rapids, Mich.: Baker, 2005), 15–34.

9. See Joel Carpenter, *Revive Us Again: The Re-Awakening of American Fundamentalism* (New York: Oxford University Press, 1999), for a rich description of how the apparent isolationism of American fundamentalists gave them an opportunity to build organizations and develop skills that would prepare them for later political participation.

10. Daniel K. Williams, *God's Own Party: The Making of the Christian Right* (New York: Oxford University Press, 2010); Darren Dochuk, *From Bible Belt to Sunbelt: Plain-Folk Religion, Grassroots Politics, and the Rise of Evangelical Conservatism* (New York: Norton, 2010).

11. George Hillcocks, Jr., "Books and Bombs: Ideological Conflict and the Schools: A Case Study of the Kanawha County Book Protest," *School Review* 86, no. 4 (August 1978): 632–54.

12. Tina Fetner, "Working Anita Bryant: The Impact of Christian Anti-Gay Activism on Lesbian and Gay Movement Claims," *Social Problems* 48, no. 3 (2001): 411.

13. Andrew R. Flint and Joy Porter, "Jimmy Carter: The Re-Emergence of Faith-Based Politics and Abortion Rights Issues," *Presidential Studies Quarterly* 35, no. 1 (2005): 28–51.

14. George M. Marsden, *Fundamentalism and American Culture* (New York: Oxford University Press, 2006), 243; Ed Dobson, quoted in Michael Cromartie, *No Longer Exiles: The Religious New Right in American Politics* (Washington, D.C.: Ethics and Public Policy Center, 1993), 52.

15. Francis Schaeffer and C. Everett Koop, *Whatever Happened to the Human Race* (Wheaton, Ill.: Good News, [1979] 1983), 13.

16. See, e.g., Richard A. Holmes, *The Faiths of the Postwar Presidents* (Athens, Ga: University of Georgia Press, 2012).

17. Richard V. Pierard, "Religion and the 1984 Election Campaign," *Review of Religious Research* 27, no. 2 (1985): 100.

18. Kenneth J. Meier, "Drugs, Sex, Rock and Roll: A Theory of Morality Politics," *Policy Studies Journal* 27, no. 4 (1999): 681.

19. Edward G. Carmines and James A. Stimson, *Issue Evolution: Race and the Transformation of American Politics* (Princeton, N.J.: Princeton University Press, 1990).

20. Andrea E. Moore, "Christian Coalition," in *Encyclopedia of American Religion and Politics*, ed. Paul A. Djupe and Laura Olson (New York: Checkmark Books, 2008). The Christian Coalition membership numbers are small when compared with the tens of millions of evangelical Americans, but these same numbers are quite large when compared with the membership of most interest groups active in American politics.

21. Organizations that receive tax-exempt status must comply with Internal Revenue Service regulations that significantly limit their political activities and directly forbid formal endorsement of candidates for elected office. The Christian Coalition sought tax-exempt status for almost a decade. In June 1999 the IRS made its final decision, ruling that the organization did not qualify as a tax-exempt organization. Following this ruling, many churches were less willing to partner actively with the Christian Coalition for fear of jeopardizing their own tax-exempt status.

22. Richard L. Berke, "The 1994 Campaign: Religion; at Church, the Sermon Is Often How You Vote," *New York Times*, November 7, 1994.

23. Mark J. Rozell and Clyde Wilcox, "The Past as Prologue: The Christian Right in the 1996 Elections," in *God at the Grassroots: The Christian Right in the 1994 Elections*, ed. Clyde Wilcox and Mark J. Rozell (Lanham, Md.: Rowman and Littlefield, 1995).

24. Amy E. Black, Douglas L. Koopman, and David K. Ryden, *Of Little Faith: The Politics of George W. Bush's Faith-Based Initiatives* (Washington, D.C.: Georgetown University Press, 2004).

25. Ibid., 215.

26. I use the term "pragmatists" stylistically to refer to those leaders and activists who have adopted a more practical approach to politics and to distinguish them from their more "purist" counterparts. My discussion here is distinct from that of the historic pragmatists such as Charles Sanders Peirce and John Dewey and the philosophical movement of which they were a part.

27. Dan Gilgoff, *The Jesus Machine: How James Dobson, Focus on the Family, and Evangelical America Are Winning the Culture War* (New York: St. Martin's, 2007), 157.

28. These data were provided by Cynthia Martens, Sojourners' director of circulation and production, in email communication.

29. Shane Claiborne and Chris Haw, *Jesus for President: Politics for Ordinary Radicals* (Grand Rapids, Mich.: Zondervan, 2008).

30. Cox, "Young White Evangelicals."

31. Robert Jones, Daniel Cox, and Thomas Banchoff, "Millennial Values Survey Report," Berkley Center for Religion, Peace and World Affairs, April 19, 2012, http://berkleycenter.georgetown.edu/millennialvaluessurvey, accessed August 4, 2015.

32. Faith in Public Life, "The Faith and American Politics Survey: The Young and the Faithful, Appendix A: Selected Profile of Young White Evangelicals," October 8, 2008, http://media.npr.org/documents/2008/oct/young_religiousvoters.pdf, accessed August 4, 2015.

33. Rose French, "Dobson: Christian Right Needs Leadership," *USA Today*, March 12, 2008.

34. Evangelical Manifesto Steering Committee, "An Evangelical Manifesto: A Declaration of Evangelical Identity and Public Commitment," May 7, 2008, http://www.anevangelicalmanifesto.com/docs/Evangelical_Manifesto.pdf, accessed August 4, 2015.

35. The NAE unveiled the statement in a full-page ad in *Roll Call*, "An Evangelical Call for Bipartisan Immigration Reform," http://nae.net/wp-content/uploads/2015/05/Immigration_NAE-Ad-Urges-Bipartisan-Immigration-Reform.pdf, accessed August 4, 2015.

36. Timothy C. Morgan, "Rebooting PEACE," *Christianity Today*, May 28, 2008, http://www.christianitytoday.com/ct/2008/july/1.1.html, accessed August 4, 2015.

37. Neela Banerjee, "Pastor Chosen to Lead Christian Coalition Steps Down in Dispute Over Agenda," *New York Times*, November 28, 2006.

38. Allen D. Hertzke, *Freeing God's Children: The Unlikely Alliance for Global Human Rights* (Lanham, Md.: Rowman and Littlefield, 2004), 328–30.

5

The Changing Face of Evangelicalism

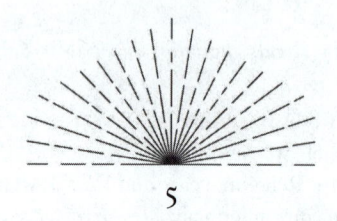

Timothy Tseng

Since the mid-1960s immigration has fundamentally altered the composition of American evangelicalism. Historians usually trace the roots of American evangelicalism to Protestant denominations shaped by the Reformation in Europe and the trans–North Atlantic revivals of the eighteenth century. African American Christianity has been recognized recently to be a distinct and central part of the larger story. Historians are just beginning to explore the growing number of American evangelicals with ethnic traditions and histories that originate in Latin America or Asia. The latter's styles of worship, political priorities, cultural taboos, and perceptions of outsiders often differ from those of the Anglo evangelicals who shaped the tradition in the United States. Their social concerns are molded by the distinct experiences they bring. Many migrate from places where religious freedom and human rights are severely curtailed and where Christianity is not the dominant religion. Others come from predominantly Catholic or secular societies. Indeed, the growing numbers of Latinos are swelling evangelical ranks such that their political concerns and spirituality are already influencing the movement. In addition, a significant number of Asian immigrants and their children are pursuing higher education in America's leading universities and seminaries and making their presence felt in multiethnic congregations and mainstream evangelical organizations. They are bringing their own convictions and particular theological interests into American religious discourse.[1]

Evangelical Latino and Asian (as well as more recent African) immigrants demonstrate both ethnic and religious allegiances. Many immigrant evangelicals retain firm ties to their homelands and devote their resources to evangelizing their countries of origin through informal relational networks and denominational programs. They have succeeded at evangelizing their American ethnic compatriots. As a result, the percentage of evangelical identification is higher for many ethnic groups in the United States than in their home countries. First-generation ethnic evangelicals negotiate identity in ways that may not satisfy their offspring who become more Americanized. The separate worlds of ethnic and English-speaking evangelicals converge on American campuses where ministries such as InterVarsity Christian Fellowship and Cru (formerly Campus Crusade for Christ) attract an ethnic mix that reveals the evangelical movement's growing diversity.

American evangelicalism remains largely Anglo in its formal institutional presence. But on the ground it is increasingly diverse. Generational change and growing global awareness are changing the face of American evangelicalism. In fact, the face has already changed. Nevertheless, mainstream evangelicals have been slow to engage the presence of racial-ethnic people within their organizations or consider the implications for theology and ministerial practice that this new face has for the future. Not until recently (and especially with the stunning results of the 2012 presidential election) have many evangelical political, organizational, and church leaders seriously entertained the priorities and aspirations of black, Hispanic, or Asian American evangelicals.

This chapter explains why the American evangelical movement has been slow and ill-equipped to engage its own racial-ethnic diversity no less than the diversity that has transformed the face of America today. This failure is largely a consequence of pre–World War II fundamentalist separation from their denominations and retreat from mainstream American culture. In the middle decades of the twentieth century, as mainline Protestant leaders grappled with the assimilation of Latinos and Asians into churches and society, and as they wrestled with racial integration and civil rights, neo-evangelicals observed from a distance and rarely engaged racial-ethnic people. In Bible institutes and evangelical seminaries where Latinos and Asian Americans interacted with Anglo evangelicals, most of the focus centered on sending missionaries to Latin America or Asia rather than supporting ethnic diversity within the evangelical churches in America. Unconsciously, perhaps, evangelicals considered themselves the custodians of Anglo Christian America and could not imagine a truly multiethnic United States. Thus the explosive growth of Latino and Asian Americans in the later twentieth century has at times been associated with the demise of an evangelical vision for a Christian America.

Nevertheless, if recent demographic shifts and efforts of many evangelicals to rethink their theology of culture and to intentionally build multiethnic organizations are any indication, it appears that evangelical institutions are moving to embrace a multiracial vision. In any case, if existing institutions fail to reckon with that change, they will become obsolete, and new networks and voluntary associations that reflect current realities will emerge.

THE NEW EVANGELICAL DEMOGRAPHIC?

The changing racial-ethnic composition of American evangelicalism, to some extent, mirrors the demographic changes of the United States. Since 1970 Asians and Latinos have significantly augmented the African American population to such an extent that the American racial landscape has been altered dramatically. By 2040 it is projected that the white population will no longer be in the majority (see table 5.1).

These changes are not reflected in most Anglo-dominated evangelical and mainline Protestant institutions. Black Christians tend to avoid the "evangelical" label despite embodying an evangelical ethos in their churches. More Latinos and Asian Americans identify as evangelicals than as mainline Protestants. But they, like African American Christians, often organize congregations and institutions independent of white evangelicals. Many of their leaders received training from Anglo teachers in American evangelical Bible institutes or seminaries, but their communities have grown and, in many cases, flourished with little interaction with white evangelicalism. In part, this racial-ethnic segregation is a result of regional barriers. Most well-known evangelical organizations and congregations are located where there are generally fewer nonwhite people. Conversely, evangelical organizations with much greater racial-ethnic visibility are usually found in large metropolitan regions (or on campuses where the Asian American student population tends to be overrepresented). Furthermore, linguistic barriers prevent greater interaction between mainstream and immigrant evangelicals since many of the latter do not communicate well enough in English.

TABLE 5.1
Population Growth of Racial Minorities in the United States Since 1970

YEAR	U.S. TOTAL	HISPANIC	ASIAN	BLACK
1970	203,211,926	9,072,602 (3.94%)	1,538,721 (0.76%)	22.6 million (11.12%)
1980	226,545,805	14,609,000 (6.45%)	3,500,439 (1.55%)	26.5 million (11.69%)
1990	248,709,873	22,354,000 (8.98%)	6,908,638 (2.77%)	30.0 million (12.06%)
2000	281,421,906	35,305,818 (12.54%)	11,896,828 (4.22%)	34.6 million (12.29%)
2010	308,745,538	50,477,594 (16.35%)	17,320,856 (5.61%)	38.9 million (12.59%)

Source: U.S. Census (2010), http://www.census.gov/2010census/, accessed August 6, 2015.

Although regional and linguistic barriers are major factors for the insignificant presence of nonwhite immigrants in mainstream evangelical organizations, race also plays a role. As recent immigrants, Latinos and Asians share a narrative similar to that of Americans of European ancestry. Their experiences are usually interpreted through the lens of migration. Race is often neglected despite being a central part of their stories and those of their offspring. The race factor explains, in large part, why black Christians historically have charted a course quite separate from that of their white counterparts. Race also has explanatory power for the persistence of Anglo dominance and racial segregation within American evangelicalism today.

Before I describe and explore the race factor, I will briefly discuss the results of two important surveys of Latinos, Asian Americans, and African Americans. The American Religious Identification Survey conducted in 1990, 2001, and 2008 by researchers at Trinity College is considered one of the largest and most comprehensive sources on religious identity in America. The 2008 survey contains data from a large, nationally representative sample of 54,461 U.S. adults in the forty-eight contiguous states. In 2007 and 2014 the Pew Research Center conducted Religious Landscape

Studies that surveyed over 35,000 respondents across the United States. These findings largely confirmed the ARIS results.

Because ARIS was conducted three times in the last twenty years, it tracks changes in American religious practices and affiliation. Among its overall findings is that Christianity is becoming less dominant in the United States. In 1990, 86 percent of American adults identified as Christians. But in 2008, that figure dropped to 76 percent. The greatest challenge to Christianity has been the rise of "Nones," a largely younger adult population that has rejected all forms of organized religion. Roman Catholicism and mainline Protestant denominations have experienced the most significant losses. At the same time, respondents who identify as evangelicals now make up 45 percent of all Christians (or 34 percent of the total national adult population). There is evidence of declining black and Asian mainline Protestant and Catholic affiliation. Latino mainline Protestant identification has also diminished. It is important to note, however, that evangelical belief and practice have become more prevalent among those who also identify as mainline Protestant (38.6 percent) or Catholic (18.4 percent). In sum, evangelicals and Nones appear to be gaining the most overall. Nevertheless, the changes in the first decades of the twenty-first century have been moderate compared to the 1990s.[2]

In discussing the demographics of black, Latino, and Asian American evangelicalism, I draw largely from the Pew Research Center's Religious Landscape Studies from 2007 and 2014 and refer to the ARIS report for additional findings. The proportion of Pew-defined evangelicals from racial and ethnic minorities rose from 19 percent in 2007 to 24 percent in 2014. Despite declines among white Christians, the numbers claimed by historically black Protestant churches remained stable, accounting for nearly 16 million adults. In the 2014 Pew study just 4 percent of African Americans identified as mainline Protestants and 5 percent as Catholic. Fully 53 percent indicated that they belonged to a historically black church, and 14 percent could be identified as evangelical. According to the ARIS report, however, when asked if they considered themselves "born again" or "evangelical," 58 percent of African American religious believers said "yes." Furthermore, the main trend in the 1990s among African Americans was similar to that of whites—a move into the Nones (in this case mostly by former Baptists), with 18 percent so identifying in 2014. Since 2001 black self-identification has shifted toward a generic Christian identity and slightly toward conservative Protestantism. The movement out of the mainline has mainly been in the African Methodist churches.[3]

There is a distinct black evangelical movement that developed separately from other African American traditions. Its roots are in the black Plymouth Brethren churches (and their distinctive dispensational theology) that emerged in the early nineteenth century, the Christian and Missionary Alliance and other Holiness churches of the later nineteenth century, and a host of twentieth-century black Pentecostal movements (including the Church of God in Christ). Theologically conservative leaders organized the National Black Evangelical Association (NBEA) in 1963. But, as a whole, the black church is so broadly evangelical that those who represent the NBEA do not exhaust African American evangelical identity.[4]

Complicating the matter of African American religious identity, immigration from sub-Saharan Africa and the Caribbean has accelerated since the 1990s. Post-1990 black African immigration total now exceeds the U.S. total for the two previous centuries—1.1 million people, or 3 percent of the total foreign-born population. Nigeria, Egypt, Ethiopia, Ghana, and Kenya rank among the largest source countries. Another 1.7 million blacks have recently arrived from the Caribbean. Many new immigrants are theologically conservative Protestants who embrace pentecostal spirituality. Some of them form African migrant churches, while others join predominantly white evangelical congregations. Recent African migrants, though still a small percentage of the total U.S. black population, may be less reluctant than descendants of African American slaves to identify with the label "evangelical" or to affiliate with explicitly evangelical institutions.[5]

The Pew Research Center's two recent surveys of Latino and Asian American religion gives us a glimpse into two populations that are most dramatically changing the face of American evangelicalism today. In *Changing Faiths: Latinos and the Transformation of American Religion* (2007), 16 percent of the Hispanic population polled identified as evangelical, 5 percent as mainline Protestant, and while 58 percent said they are Catholic, another 14 percent reported no religious identification. This translates to about 7.5 million Latino Protestants and evangelicals, 1.5 million of whom belong to mainline Protestant churches. Hispanics comprise one-third of all American Catholics and are projected to become an ever-increasing segment of the church. When compared to Hispanic evangelicals, they are a more heavily immigrant population. Furthermore, 54 percent of Hispanic Catholics consider themselves Charismatic, and 28 percent say that they are born again. According to the ARIS 2008 survey, 60 percent of Hispanics self-identified as Catholic, while 12 percent claimed to have no religion. Pew 2014 reveals growth among evangelicals and decline in Catholic affiliation (19 percent evangelical, 5 percent mainline Protestant, 48 percent Catholic, and 20 percent religiously unaffiliated).[6]

Among the Protestants and evangelicals, there were a number of demographic distinctions. More mainline Protestant Hispanics were born in the United States and were more likely to have been here for a few generations. The opposite was true of evangelicals and pentecostals. Dominant language use also correlates with this pattern (see table 5.2).

When one looks at country of origin, with the exception of Mexicans and Central Americans, the breakdowns for mainline Protestants and pentecostal/evangelicals do not differ much (see table 5.3).

A closer look at the national background of Hispanic Christians reveals additional patterns of religious affiliation. According to the most recent

TABLE 5.2
Religious Affiliation of Hispanics by Level of Acculturation

	PENTECOSTAL/ EVANGELICAL (%)	MAINLINE PROTESTANT (%)
Born in U.S./other countries	45/55	65/35
First generation	55	35
Second generation	23	37
Third generation	21	28
English dominant	31	45
Bilingual	32	28
Spanish dominant	38	26

Source: Juan Francisco Martínez, Los Protestantes: An Introduction to Latino Protestantism in the United States (Santa Barbara, Calif.: Praeger, 2011), 8–10, based on Pew survey.

TABLE 5.3
Origin of Protestant Hispanic Americans

ORIGIN	PENTECOSTAL/ EVANGELICAL (%)	MAINLINE PROTESTANT (%)
Central America	14	6
Cuba	4	6
Dominican Republic	1	3
Mexico	50	56
Puerto Rico	15	16
South America	6	4
Other	8	8

Source: Martínez, Los Protestantes, 8–10.

census, 66 percent of the Hispanic population is of Mexican background and 9 percent is of Puerto Rican descent. But the percentage of Protestant and evangelical affiliation among Puerto Ricans is higher than it is among Mexican Americans. This reflects the larger percentage of Protestant affiliation in Puerto Rico (40 percent) than in Mexico (6 percent). Thus Mexican immigrants are more likely to be and remain Roman Catholic once they come to the United States even though the percentage of Protestants is growing in Mexico. Because Mexico sends the most migrants from Latin America who have strong transnational ties, the religious tendencies there have a strong influence on religious practices of U.S. Hispanics. The Puerto Rican population, however, is overrepresented among Hispanic Protestants. Furthermore, the two countries in Central America that have sent the most migrants to the United States also have high percentages of Protestants (40 percent from Guatemala and 21 percent from El Salvador).[7]

Another transnational factor to consider is the presence of a higher percentage of agnostics and atheists from Cuba and the southern cone of South America. Whereas the Pew and Trinity studies correlated secularization to the influence of living in the United States, it is likely that these migrants may not have practiced any religion in their countries of origin. Furthermore, those who engage in syncretic practices that blend Catholicism with indigenous or African spirituality may not be easily classified in the two studies. Scholar Juan Martínez concludes that because religious practices in Latin America are diverse and changing dramatically, one should expect to see changes in the Hispanic American religious experience as well. Much study is needed in this area.[8]

Hispanic American diversity is also a function of differing U.S. policy in various countries of Latin America. These differences affect Hispanic American interactions with the majority population. For example, not only have people of Mexican background had the longest relationship with the United States, but that relationship has also been linked to the conquest of the Southwest and the bracero (or manual laborer) program. Many in the Chicano movement consider these historical interactions to be the cause of the social inequality that many Mexican Americans still face. Indeed, Mexicans are the single largest group of noncitizen workers and the largest group of people deported from the United States because of a lack of legal documentation. Cuban Americans, on the other hand, are more likely to express a favorable view of the United States. In the aftermath of the Cuban Revolution, waves of immigrants were welcomed to the United States as political exiles and given support to establish themselves. As late as 2015, any Cuban who arrived in the United States received refugee status. Undocumented Dominicans, who came to the United States in the 1960s as political refugees, are not treated with the same openness as Cuban immigrants are. Although Puerto Ricans are U.S. citizens and have complete freedom to travel between the mainland and the island, they are often viewed and treated like immigrants. The Central American civil wars, in which the United States played a fairly direct role, are a major cause of immigration from El Salvador and Guatemala. The United States has granted temporary protected status (TPS) for many who come from El Salvador, Nicaragua, and Honduras, and Guatemala has requested that its nationals also be considered for TPS. A person granted TPS can live and work legally in the United States but is not eligible for permanent residency. So if TPS were to be removed, those nationals would lose their legal status and could be subject to deportation. Because U.S. policy approaches Latin American countries differently, Hispanic migrants embrace a variety of attitudes towards assimilating into mainstream America.[9]

As we consider the development of evangelicalism among Hispanics in the early twenty-first century, conversion from Catholicism is a key factor. It is noteworthy that 51 percent of Hispanic evangelicals are converts, and more than four-fifths of them (43 percent of Hispanic evangelicals overall) are former Catholics. Ninety percent of the evangelicals affirm that a spiritual search for a more direct, personal experience with God drove their conversion. Although 61 percent of evangelical converts said that the typical Catholic mass is "not lively or exciting," only 36 percent cited that as a reason for their conversion.[10]

Two significant attributes of Hispanic Christianity in the United States merit special attention. The first is the prevalence of spirit-filled (or pentecostal) religious expressions of worship in all the major religious traditions. Although this is especially true of evangelical Hispanics, more than 50 percent of Catholics are Charismatic (compared to one-eighth of non-Hispanic Catholics). The growth of the Hispanic population is leading to the emergence of Latino-oriented pentecostal churches across the country and is gradually reshaping American evangelicalism.[11]

Second, Hispanic American evangelicalism is "ethnic oriented," though to a lesser degree than Catholicism. Two-thirds of Latino Christians select Spanish-language services led by and predominantly attended by Latinos. Foreign-born Hispanics are more likely than native-born and English-speaking Latinos to attend Hispanic-oriented worship services, yet the tendency is strong for both groups, 77 percent and 48 percent, respectively. The Pew report concludes that this pattern "strongly suggests that the phenomenon is not simply a product of immigration or language but that it involves a broader and more lasting form of ethnic identification."[12]

Although Hispanic Catholics and evangelicals share similar religious expressions, their political affiliations differ significantly. Among those eligible to vote, 48 percent of Hispanic Catholics identify with the Democratic Party, while only 17 percent are Republican. Nevertheless, although Hispanic evangelicals are twice as likely as Catholics to identify with the Republican Party (37 percent), almost as many say they are Democrats (32 percent). Overall 70 percent of all Hispanic eligible voters who identify as Democrats are Catholics. Hispanic evangelicals are also significantly more conservative than Catholics on social issues, foreign policy issues, and attitudes toward the poor. Catholics, in turn, are somewhat more conservative than seculars when it comes to gay marriage, government-guaranteed health care, and increases in government services.[13]

In a 2012 survey of Asian Americans, the Pew Research Center reported that Christians are the largest religious group, at 42 percent, among U.S. Asian adults. At 26 percent, the unaffiliated represented the next highest group of respondents (highest among all races). Buddhists accounted for about one in seven Asian Americans (14 percent), though white Buddhists outnumbered Asian Americans by almost two to one. This was followed by Hindus (10 percent), Muslims (4 percent), other religions (2 percent), and Sikhs (1 percent). Buddhists and Hindus accounted for about the same share of the U.S. public as Jews (roughly 2 percent).[14]

Asian Americans are much more religiously diverse than the rest of the predominantly Christian U.S. population. Despite sizable contingents of Christians and the unaffiliated, the Pew report asserts that Asians are "largely responsible for the growth of non-Abrahamic faiths in the United States, particularly Buddhism and Hinduism," and are increasing the diversity of the U.S. religious landscape. Pew 2014 reports that 11 percent of Asians are evangelical, 17 percent Catholic, 5 percent mainline Protestant, 16 percent Hindu, 6 percent Buddhist, 3 percent other world religions, and 31 percent unaffiliated.[15]

A closer look at each of the six largest Asian subgroups reveals differing religious complexions. A majority (65 percent) of Filipinos in the United States are Catholic, while most (61 percent) Korean Americans are Protestants. About half (51 percent) of Indian Americans are Hindu, while approximately half (52 percent) of Chinese Americans are unaffiliated. A plurality (43 percent) of Vietnamese Americans are Buddhist, while Japanese Americans are a mix of Christians (38 percent, including 33 percent who are Protestant), Buddhists (25 percent), and the unaffiliated (32 percent; see fig. 5.1).

The 2012 Pew report also provides data on the growth of Asian American Protestantism through the switching of religious affiliation. Conversion rates are higher among Japanese, Chinese, and Korean Americans than among other U.S. Asian groups, which may factor into Protestant growth. Approximately 22 percent of Asian Americans identified as Protestant in 2012, compared with 17 percent who say they were raised Protestant. However, Asian American Catholics (with a net loss of only 3 percentage points) and Hindus (with a net loss of only 2 percentage

Chinese Americans
- 31% All Christian
- 22% Protestant
- 8% Catholic
- 15% Buddhist
- 52% Unaffiliated

Filipino Americans
- 89% All Christian
- 8% Unaffiliated
- 1% Buddhist
- 21% Protestant
- 65% Catholic

Indian Americans
- 18% All Christian
- 11% Protestant
- 5% Catholic
- 10% Unaffiliated
- 2% Jain
- 5% Sikh
- 10% Muslim
- 51% Hindu

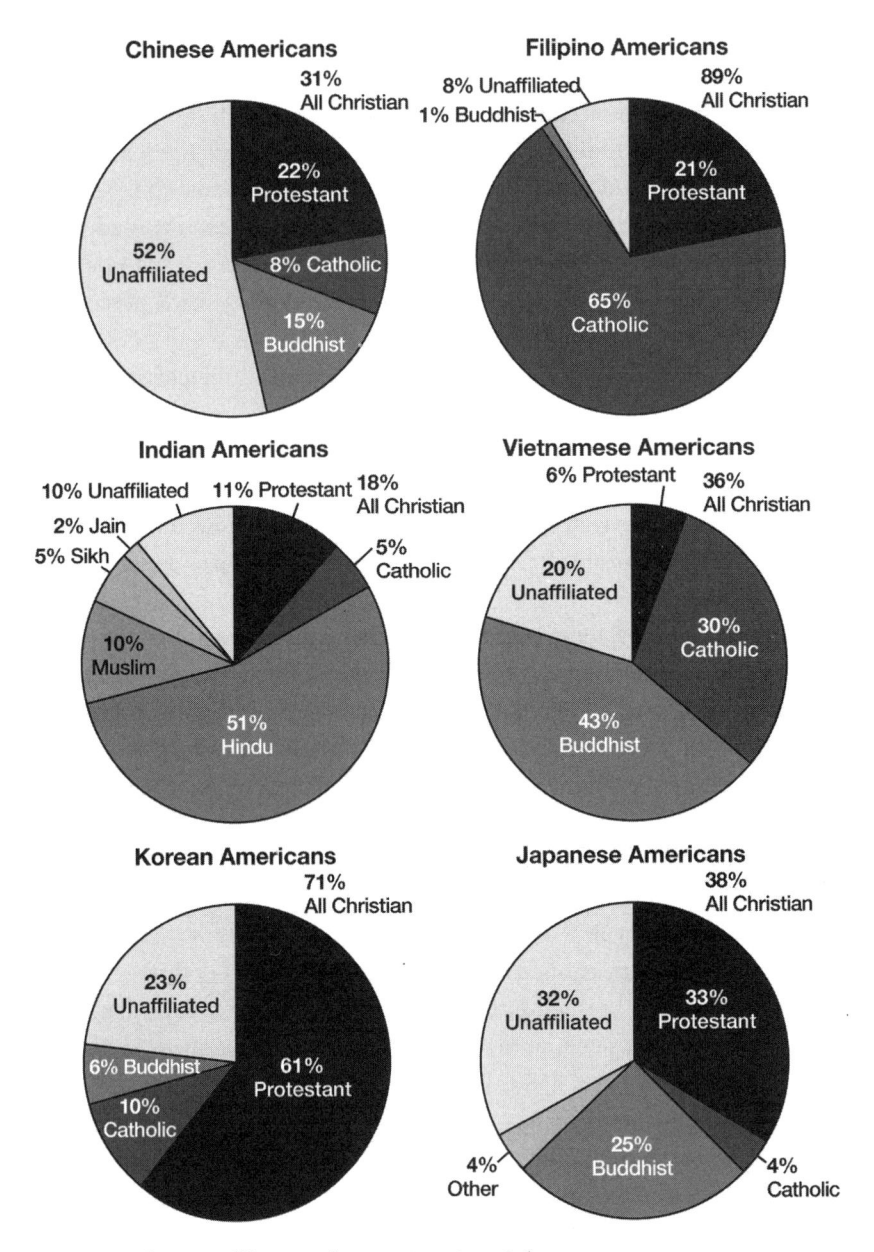

Vietnamese Americans
- 36% All Christian
- 6% Protestant
- 30% Catholic
- 20% Unaffiliated
- 43% Buddhist

Korean Americans
- 71% All Christian
- 23% Unaffiliated
- 6% Buddhist
- 10% Catholic
- 61% Protestant

Japanese Americans
- 38% All Christian
- 33% Protestant
- 4% Catholic
- 25% Buddhist
- 4% Other
- 32% Unaffiliated

Figure 5.1 Religious Affiliation of Asian American Subgroups

Note: The "All Christian" category includes Protestants, Catholics, and other Christians. Subgroups are listed in order of the size of the country-of-origin group in the total Asian American population. Those who did not give an answer are not shown. Other religions, Hindu, and Buddhist are not shown for some subgroups.

Source: Pew Research Center.

points) have experienced little net impact from switching. By contrast, Asian American Buddhists have experienced the biggest net losses from religious switching. Roughly one in five Asian Americans (22 percent) say they were raised Buddhist, and 2 percent have switched to Buddhism from other faiths (or from having no particular religion). But 10 percent of Asian Americans have left Buddhism, for a net loss of 8 percentage points.[16]

Asian Americans have low rates of religious intermarriage. It is striking that 94 percent of married Hindus have a spouse who is also Hindu. Still noticeable is that 81 percent of Asian American Catholics and Protestants are married to fellow Catholics or Protestants, respectively, and 70 percent of Buddhists are married to fellow Buddhists. Of those with no religious affiliation, 61 percent have a spouse who is also unaffiliated.[17]

Although a very large percentage of Asian Americans today were born overseas, fewer Christians (73 percent) and unaffiliated (70 percent) are foreign born (see table 5.4). Mainline Protestant Asian Americans provide a substantially lower percentage of foreign-born than other Christians (60 percent). A larger percentage of mainline Protestants are over fifty-five years old. Furthermore, when asked whether they think of themselves as "typical Americans" or "very different from a typical American," only mainline Protestants had a larger percentage respond that they thought of themselves as "typical Americans" than "very different." Evangelicals scored almost as high as Buddhists and Hindus in the "very different from a typical American" response. One can infer from these data that older mainline Protestants are more acculturated than the younger and more foreign-born evangelical and Catholic populations.

Asian Americans also range more widely than the total population between highly religious and highly secular. For example, unaffiliated Asian Americans tend to express lower levels of religious commitment than unaffiliated Americans in the general public (according to Pew 2014, 70 percent say religion is not too important or not at all important in their lives, compared with 56 percent among unaffiliated U.S. adults as a whole). Some critics have noted, however, that these surveys did not adequately take into account the practice of family-centered cultural rituals among unaffiliated Asian Americans. Since many understand "religious" to mean

TABLE 5.4
Acculturation of Asian Americans by Religious Affiliation

PERCENTAGE ASIAN AMERICAN	NATIVE BORN (%)	FOREIGN BORN (%)	ARRIVED 2000– 2012 (%)	ARRIVED BEFORE 2000 (%)	AGE 18– 24 (%)	AGE 33– 54 (%)	AGE 55+ (%)	TYPICAL/VERY DIFFERENT FROM TYPICAL AMERICAN (%)
Christian (overall)	27	73	16	55	24	38	36	44/49
Protestant	32	68	17	50	25	38	36	41/50
Evangelical	26	73	20	53	34	42	33	36/57
Mainline	40	60	13	46	24	34	40	48/41
Catholic	21	79	16	62	24	37	37	46/49
Buddhist	21	79	20	58	26	35	36	32/59
Hindu	4	96	42	52	42	39	17	27/59
Unaffiliated	29	70	25	45	41	36	19	41/52

Source: Kohut, Rise of Asian Americans, 190, 195.

a commitment to a church community, the religiosity of unaffiliated Asian Americans may not be measured accurately.[18]

Asian American evangelicals, by contrast, rank among the most religious groups in the United States (76 percent attend church weekly compared with 64 percent of white evangelicals). In fact, all three Asian American Christian groups attend services more frequently than do their counterparts in the general public. Of Asian American Catholics, 60 percent attend at least once a week, as do 42 percent of mainline Protestants.[19]

Asian American Christians, particularly evangelicals, are also strongly inclined (72 percent) to believe that their religion is the one, true faith leading to eternal life. Among white evangelicals, 49 percent say the same, whereas 47 percent say many religions can lead to eternal life. The Asian American evangelical pattern also contrasts sharply with Buddhists, Hindus, and unaffiliated Asian Americans, who are relatively unlikely to make exclusive truth claims.[20]

Asian American evangelicals are also more inclined than white evangelicals to believe that there is only one true way to interpret the teachings of their faith (53 percent versus 43 percent). Although just as likely as white evangelicals to say that the Bible is the word of God, Asian American evangelicals are somewhat less inclined to claim that everything in Scripture should be taken literally, word for word. Korean American evangelicals are in this respect exceptional, since 68 percent say the Bible should be interpreted literally, compared with 44 percent of non-Korean Asian American evangelicals who hold to this view. This is an important exception since 34 percent of Asian American evangelicals are of Korean descent (25 percent are Chinese, 14 percent Filipino, 11 percent Indian, 10 percent Japanese, 2 percent Vietnamese, and 5 percent others; see fig. 5.2). Koreans are nevertheless similar to other Asian American evangelicals on most measures of religious commitment.[21]

In politics and on social issues, Asian American evangelicals express views that are closer to those of white evangelicals than do Hispanic and African Americans. Approximately 56 percent identify as Republicans versus 28 percent as Democrats. Catholics are almost evenly split (42 percent Republican, 41 percent Democrat), while mainline Protestants lean Democrat at 44 percent (versus 37 percent Republican). Asian Americans on the whole, however, identify with Democrats (52 percent to 32 percent) and are more liberal on social issues.[22]

The Changing Face of Evangelicalism

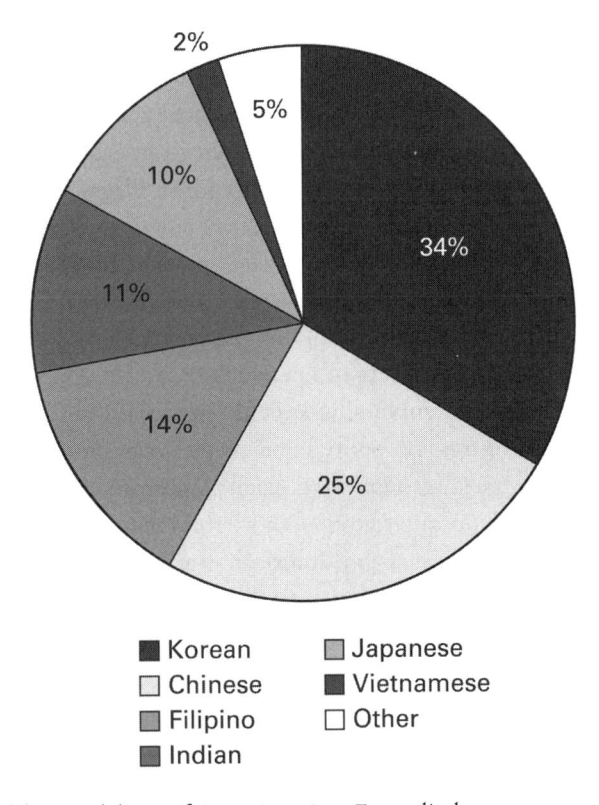

Pie chart showing: Korean 34%, Chinese 25%, Filipino 14%, Indian 11%, Japanese 10%, Vietnamese 5%, Other 2%.

Figure 5.2 Ethnic Breakdown of Asian American Evangelicals

Source: Jerry Z. Park, "Asian American Christians in the Twenty-First Century," presentation for the Seventh National Lighting the Community Summit of the AAPI Faith Alliance, Washington, D.C., May 20, 2014. Data: Pew Research Center 2012 Asian-American Survey.

Taking views on homosexuality as an example, 53 percent of all Asian Americans believe that society should accept homosexuality, while 35 percent say it should be discouraged (by comparison, 58 percent among the general public say homosexuality should be accepted, while 33 percent say it should be discouraged). The preponderance of Asian American evangelical opinion, however, is reversed: 65 percent say society should discourage homosexuality, and 24 percent say it should be accepted. Unaffiliated U.S. Asians lean most strongly toward acceptance of homosexuality (69 percent). Smaller majorities or pluralities of Asian American Catholics (58 percent), Buddhists (54 percent), Hindus (54 percent), and mainline Protestants (49 percent) accept homosexuality.[23]

Similarly, Asian Americans as a whole tend to support abortion rights. More than half (54 percent) say it should be legal in all or most cases; 37 percent say it should be illegal in all or most cases. Among the general public, by comparison, 51 percent say abortion should be legal in all or most cases, while 43 percent say it should be illegal. But the majority of Asian American Catholics (56 percent) and evangelical Protestants (64 percent) say abortion should be illegal in most or all cases. Support for legal abortion is highest among Asian Americans who are religiously unaffiliated (74 percent), followed by Hindus (64 percent), Buddhists (59 percent), and mainline Protestants (50 percent).[24]

Based on the recent surveys, it appears that black and Latino evangelicals stand in contrast on politics and social issues compared with the majority of their racial groups. But Asian American evangelicals stand even further apart from their group as a whole. One might also infer that younger black, Latino, and Asian American evangelicals may differ on issues such as abortion or homosexuality compared with earlier generations, but more data needs to be studied; if younger nonwhite evangelicals follow the pattern of younger white evangelicals (see chapter 4), it may be in the direction of increasingly conservative views on abortion, coupled with more liberal views on homosexuality. Race, economic issues, and immigration reform appear to be issues that these evangelicals share with their own ethnic populations, whereas such issues have been of less interest to white evangelicals.[25]

BEFORE EVANGELICALISM: AMERICAN PROTESTANTISM AND RACE

Many religion scholars have noted that the media focus on "white evangelicals" in electoral politics reinforces a perception that evangelicalism is exclusively identified with conservative politics and older white men. In fact, we have seen, evangelicalism is varied by ethnicity, race, and politics. Unfortunately, media attention to "nonwhite" evangelicals has been rather spotty. But it seems reasonable to believe that nonwhite evangelical leaders and organizations may begin to receive greater coverage. Indeed, American evangelicalism, when viewed as a religious ethos rather than an organized movement, has always been multiracial and multiethnic, and it will become increasingly so in the future.

To fully appreciate the multiracial, multiethnic characteristic of American evangelicalism, one must momentarily pivot away from the narrative lens that a generation of groundbreaking scholars have shaped. Historians such as George Marsden, Mark Noll, Joel Carpenter, and Margaret Bendroth have broadened the definition of evangelicalism beyond that of an antimodern religiously fundamentalist fringe. They have also repositioned it into the heart of American religious history as a popular and pervasive cultural ethos. Nevertheless, historians have yet to incorporate adequately the histories of African, Hispanic, Native, and Asian American Christianity into their narratives. Consequently, it often comes as a surprise to many when the point is made about the multiracial, multiethnic character of American evangelicalism. Many readers may also be surprised to discover that Hispanic and Asian American Christianity have had long histories. One needs to explore mainline Protestantism's encounter with racial diversity in previous centuries to see more clearly that Hispanic and Asian American Christians were also part of the larger story of American Protestantism, despite their marginalization.[26]

I will therefore take a brief look at American Protestantism and race before the twentieth century. Prior to the fundamentalist-modernist controversy, all of "white" Protestantism appeared very "evangelical." As modernist-dominated mainline Protestant denominations became identified with the "establishment," they increasingly mirrored American culture at large and its changes. Thus mainline Protestants turned their backs on a legacy of missionary and political engagement on behalf of racial minorities (for example, the abolitionist movement) and embraced the practice of racial segregation. It would take two generations before mainline Protestants recommenced the fight against racism by opposing segregation.

Nevertheless, mainline Protestants could make the case that their legacy includes a tradition of engaging and uplifting the racial "other." For instance, African American Christianity took shape in the fires of eighteenth-century transatlantic revivals and became the first successful nonwhite evangelical movement. In the nineteenth century the American foreign missionary enterprise planted evangelical Christianity in many regions of Latin America, Africa, the Pacific basin, and Asia (though many Christian communities in the global South have much longer histories that are largely independent of Western missionary influences).

The years between the Mexican-American War (1846–1848) and the American Civil War (1860–1864) ushered in new opportunities to build a multiracial Protestantism in the United States. The Treaty of Guadalupe Hidalgo (1848) ended the Mexican-American War and ceded the southwestern territories, Texas, and California to the United States. This proved to be a pivotal point for Protestant home missions. Ninety percent of the Mexicans who resided in the ceded territories chose to become American citizens. White Protestants articulated a sense of spiritual and material obligation toward the peoples of the region and sent missionaries. White Protestants also hoped that conversion to Protestant Christianity would Americanize the Mexican American citizens. Most nineteenth-century Latino churches were Methodist or Presbyterian, along with a few Baptists and Congregationalists. By the twentieth century there were about 150 Latino Protestant congregations throughout the Southwest, along with a handful of Spanish-language congregations on the Eastern Seaboard that ministered to immigrants from Puerto Rico, Cuba, and Spain.[27]

At the same time, prospectors and merchants from China were drawn to the newly acquired territory of California because of the Gold Rush. Missionaries, with an eye to China, saw in the emerging Chinese diaspora in California (and the Kingdom of Hawaii) a golden opportunity for Christianization and Americanization. In subsequent decades they saw similar opportunities among Japanese, Korean, and Filipino laborers and immigrants. As with Hispanic missions, Presbyterian, Methodist, Baptist, and Congregationalist missionaries (along with Asian pastors) were central figures in the establishment of over one hundred Asian American congregations in the United States by the turn of the twentieth century.[28]

Furthermore, Protestant reformers saw an opportunity to Christianize and Americanize Native Americans. Given the failure of the U.S. government's Indian Removal policy and the ineffectiveness of the Office of Indian Affairs, the government enacted a new policy of assimilation, the high point of which was President Ulysses S. Grant's short-lived "Peace Policy." Protestant missionaries, often under government contract, were sent to the Indian Territory to operate schools for teaching citizenship, English, and agricultural and mechanical arts.[29]

Finally, the missions to the freedmen during and after Reconstruction were expressions of Protestant hopes of African American assimilation and evangelization in the aftermath of the Civil War. Although all these efforts were relatively short-lived, they left a legacy of Protestant participation in an early version of multiculturalism and racial integration in the South and Southwest and on the West Coast (and in the Kingdom of Hawaii, which was annexed in 1900). Many mainline Protestant educational institutions and congregations that served these populations survived into the twentieth century, leaving a somewhat paradoxical legacy of segregationism and racial-ethnic empowerment.

Through these encounters, it can be argued that the "color line," a term coined by Frederick Douglass (1818–1895) and reiterated by W. E. B. DuBois (1868–1963), was born. Although this term is normally identified with relations between blacks and whites, it was not just about blacks and whites. For many Protestants (particularly northerners) in the late nineteenth century, the struggle over the abolition of slavery, racial equality, the uplift and civilization of non-Anglos, and the evangelization of souls converged around the question of embracing Asian and Hispanic "strangers" as well as "freedmen."[30]

Yet by the end of the century, in a quest for national union and international prominence, northern white Protestant leaders embraced a compromise with southern whites regarding racial uplift. Henry Ward Beecher (1813–1887), Dwight L. Moody (1837–1899), and Frances Willard (1839–1898) accepted racial segregation. According to the historian Edward Blum, "From the end of the Civil War to the War of 1898, northern religion—its spokesmen and spokeswomen, practitioners, ideologies, and movements—played a critical role in reuniting northern and southern whites, in justifying and nourishing the social and spiritual separation of whites and blacks, and in propelling the United States into global imperialism."[31] The abandonment of abolitionism, along with the "scientific" legitimization of white supremacy, emboldened the practices of Jim and Jane Crow segregationism, lynching, and nativism throughout the nation. By the time fundamentalists battled modernists, racial segregation and white superiority were embedded in the national ethos.

Those who clung to the abolitionist vision were on the defensive and articulated what could be labeled a theology of "racial nonrecognition" against racial segregation. This minority perspective argued that, in light of growing evidence that racial minorities were assimilating into Anglo-Protestant culture, racial difference was of no consequence. Thus racial segregation was neither socially necessary nor economically efficient. But it would not be until the mid-twentieth century that racial nonrecognition became a central component of religious interracial relations.[32]

THE COSTS AND BENEFITS OF SEPARATION

When the modernist-fundamentalist controversy reached its peak of intensity, most mainline Protestant seminaries embraced the emerging social sciences (which these churches largely sponsored and facilitated). The Social Gospel, leaning heavily on economic and social theory, transformed the nature of mission work towards a focus on education and social reform. Thus the sociological study of race and ethnicity (which aimed at social harmony) accompanied mainline Protestant mission work among racial minorities. Many fundamentalist Protestants, however, viewed the embrace of social structural analysis as a betrayal of the traditional evangelization of individual souls.[33]

The fundamentalist rejection of modernity included a divestment from social scientific methodologies that eventually helped to undermine white supremacy and segregation. Voluminous social scientific research challenged the Social Darwinist assumptions behind nineteenth-century anthropology, culminating in Gunnar Myrdal's *An American Dilemma* (1962). Furthermore, two devastating world wars diminished faith in Western cultural or moral superiority. The shocking discovery of Nazi concentration camps and, to a lesser degree, the recognition of the racism behind the Japanese American internment camps also contributed to a distaste for the prevailing racial ideology. Thus by midcentury, with the exception of the South, racial integration, buttressed by a theology of racial nonrecognition, gained a moral high ground in the United States.[34]

While mid-twentieth-century mainline Protestants' justification for opposing segregation or exclusionary immigration policy was built, in large part, on the emerging social sciences, fundamentalists could not draw on an intellectual framework that was capable of critiquing racism or engaging multicultural realities. Their exile from mainline Protestant denominations in the early decades of the twentieth century left them vulnerable to uncritical embrace of local mores and a nineteenth-century framework with regard to human relations.

The historian Margaret Bendroth's argument regarding neo-evangelical antipathy to feminism in the mid-twentieth century offers a striking parallel to evangelicals and race and ethnicity. Because neo-evangelicalism inherited an antimodern fundamentalist theology that insisted on hierarchical gender roles, it was predisposed to oppose feminist or gender egalitarian ideas. Similarly, neo-evangelicalism was predisposed to resist sociological categories that have explanatory power with regard to racial-ethnic identity and structural racism.[35]

Furthermore, evangelical institutions remained relatively isolated from racial and ethnic populations (which, admittedly, were still rather small). But even if they wanted to start new cross-cultural missions, evangelicals were at a disadvantage. African American churches were already independent and established institutions. The large majority of Hispanic and Asian congregations were affiliated with mainline Protestant denominations. About the only place to connect was by recruiting racial-ethnics to evangelical Bible schools, seminaries, parachurch organizations, and evangelistic revivals. In such efforts, there was virtually no discussion about race and ethnicity. Although there are some accounts of close interracial friendships in these settings, there is little evidence that unequal racial hierarchies were addressed publicly within evangelical institutions.

If evangelicals wanted advice about relating to racial-ethnics from an institutional and social structural level, they might have studied how mainline Protestantism engaged racial minorities. The Protestant denominations shifted emphasis from racial integration to multiculturalism in the middle decades of the twentieth century. To a large extent this mirrored a social transformation of the United States that few neo-evangelicals understood.

Mainline Protestants, having undergone a revival of the Social Gospel in the 1930s, turned their attention to addressing the "American dilemma" after World War II. Both locally and nationally, mainline Protestants invited racial outsiders into their institutions to effect change. Their initial solution was to work toward racial integration through racial nonrecognition. In March 1946 the Federal Council of Churches renounced "the pattern of segregation in race relations as unnecessary and undesirable and a violation of the Gospel of love and human brotherhood." It committed itself and its member churches to "work for a non-segregated church a non-segregated society." Practically, this policy discouraged the recognition of "racial-ethnic" markers (though it assumed that Anglo-American was not such a marker). Ethnic- and language-based judicatories were phased out. In Texas, the Tex-Mex Presbytery became a transitional "holding presbytery" for Latino congregations until they could become self-supporting and join existing geographic presbyteries. It dissolved in 1955 when all existing Latino churches became self-supporting. Methodist leaders disbanded the Japanese Methodist Conference in 1964 and merged Japanese congregations into geographical conferences.[36]

Furthermore, mainline Protestant leaders discouraged starting new racial-ethnic congregations. They assumed that English-speaking children of immigrants would assimilate into (Anglo) American life. Because they believed that ethnic congregations would eventually disappear, white leaders considered it inappropriate to use funds to start new ministries. Indeed, many denominational leaders encouraged ethnic churches to close and integrate into established white congregations.

Although this policy succeeded for congregations with European roots, it proved ineffective for Asian and Latino congregations in the long run. Early on, a significant number of English-speaking Latinos and Asians embraced this policy and integrated into mainstream congregations or denominational structures. Later, many changed their minds about an integration policy based on racial nonrecognition or Anglo conformity. Most racial-ethnic congregations, however, resisted the integration policy and retained their ethnic identities. When pressed, many left the mainline denominations and became more clearly identified with evangelicals and pentecostals. In the case of Texas Latinos, the denominations with the least rigid organizational structures—Baptists and Pentecostals—have grown the most since the 1960s. By contrast, Methodist growth has been slow, and Presbyterians have experienced no growth at all. Among the Chinese and Japanese (the two largest Asian American populations in the middle decades) and other Asian American Protestants, integration met with limited success. Efforts to eliminate ethnic names and markers from Asian American congregations largely failed.[37]

By the late 1960s racial-ethnic leaders within mainline Protestantism began to advocate for greater racial recognition and representation. They pointed to recent studies that indicated that Asian American Protestant churches were actually thriving. A younger cohort was coming of age in these congregations. Few Asian Americans were joining white churches. Thus integration was failing. They also argued that an integration that erases racial and cultural distinctives is not true integration. Invitation without justice or shared power is also not a real racial integration. Furthermore, liberation, feminist, Third World, and racial-ethnic theologies were flowering within mainline Protestantism. Black, Asian, Hispanic, and other caucuses formed on the rising tide of ethnic consciousness. Many believed that a historical moment had arrived. At last Christianity was becoming de-Westernized and racially diverse.

One result of the caucus debates within mainline Protestantism was the embrace of multiculturalism. Even before the tremendous recent growth of Asian and Hispanic immigration, mainline Protestant denominations had started to respond to demands to better address racial-ethnic diversity in the 1970s. For example, denominations opened more visible leadership roles to racial-ethnic leaders. Denominations created positions and allocated funds to serve race-specific ministries. Several mainline seminaries created African, Asian, and Hispanic American programs to more adequately train leaders for multicultural ministries.

Whereas mainline Protestants maintained a delicate relationship with African Americans and other racial-ethnic groups by embracing multiculturalism, most evangelicals had very little interest in engaging in these conversations. The latter largely stood on the sidelines during the civil rights movement and, with few exceptions, rarely engaged the question of ethnic identity or multiculturalism. Their departure from mainline Protestant mission boards earlier in the century forfeited opportunities to interact more deeply with racial-ethnic people and with the social issues that were relevant to them.

While mainline Protestants focused on civil rights, farmworkers, and immigration policy, evangelicals and Pentecostals were planting churches in the United States and overseas. Ironically, the decentralized evangelical and Pentecostal organizations became fertile soil for the growth of Hispanic and Asian American Christianity. A key factor in their growth was the freedom to create indigenous ministries and congregations that, ironically, resulted from segregationist practices.

Earlier in the twentieth century many evangelical and Pentecostal churches (such as the Salvation Army and Assemblies of God) remained in cities to minister to the disenfranchised and the poor—many of whom were racial-ethnics. Others ministered in rural areas to serve sharecroppers and farmworkers. The Pentecostal movement, in particular, brought unprecedented growth among Hispanics in the United States and Latin America. The leaders of the Azusa Street revival that began in 1906 believed that the modern experience of Pentecostalism would break down racial barriers. During the early meetings in Los Angeles, the movement was very diverse. But the movement was not immune to racial divisions in the United States. For example, when the Assemblies of God formed in 1914, African American leaders such as Bishop Charles Harrison Mason (1866–1961), founder of the predominantly African American Church of God in Christ, were excluded on account of their race.

Eventually racially segregated organizations emerged. Indigenous Latino denominations such the Concilio Latinoamericano de Iglesias Cristianas (CLADIC) and the Apostolic Assembly of the Faith in Jesus Christ formed in 1923 and 1925. Both denominations have transnational ties to Mexico and the United States. The Assembly, a Oneness Pentecostal denomination, was founded because the Oneness denominations decided to organize along racial lines. CLADIC formed, in part, because Latinos were not allowed to take leadership roles in the Assemblies of God denominational structure. Nevertheless, the Assemblies of God continued to engage Latinos by establishing Spanish-language Bible Institutes in California and Texas in 1926. Language-specific and racially segregated congregations became the norm in Pentecostal and evangelical Hispanic churches, which were key factors for their growth.[38]

Pentecostalism did not make strong inroads into the Asian American Protestant communities in the middle decades of the twentieth century. But neo-evangelicalism grew within Asian American mainline Protestant congregations, while fundamentalist congregations were planted alongside as alternative expressions of faith. The Japanese Evangelical Missionary Society (JEMS), founded in May 1950, was an example of this. Evangelical pastors (influenced by Fuller Theological Seminary and the Bible Institute of Los Angeles (BIOLA) sought to rebuild their churches and evangelize their communities in the aftermath of the Japanese American internment camps of World War II. They also wanted to bring the Gospel back to Japan by sending Japanese American missionaries. This coalition of evangelicals from both mainline denominations and independent fundamentalist churches became one of the most influential Asian American Christian organizations in the United States. Among the Chinese, students and pastors trained at Wheaton College, Westminster Seminary, Fuller Seminary, Multnomah, and BIOLA (in the 1960s Dallas Theological Seminary became an influential training center) steered many congregations away from mainline Protestantism or planted new independent congregations. Thus by the 1970s an increasing number of Asian American churches were planted or steered by leaders who were uncomfortable with the seemingly worldly ethos or politicized theology of mainline Protestantism.

The Hispanic and Asian American shift toward evangelicalism was augmented by the growth of global evangelicalism and pentecostalism. The fruit of second-wave evangelical and fundamentalist missions (for instance, faith missions such as Overseas Missionary Fellowship [formerly Chinese Inland Missions] in Asia and Central America Mission) in the early twentieth century yielded strong and growing indigenous and independent movements in Latin America and Asia. The World Christian Database estimates that the global evangelical population grew from 98 million in 1970 to 300 million by 2010. It is expected to grow to 349 million by 2020. (Operation World uses less stringent definitions and estimates the following worldwide evangelical population: 124 million in 1970, 550 million in 2010, and more than 650 million by 2020.) The growth of worldwide pentecostalism is even more astounding. The Center for the Study of Global Christianity at Gordon-Conwell Theological Seminary groups Pentecostals, Charismatics, and Independent Charismatics together under the term "Renewalist." Accordingly, Renewalists are growing from 62.7 million (5.1 percent of all Christians) in 1970 to a projected 709.8 million (27.8 percent of all Christians) by 2020. Renewalists will have grown most rapidly in Asia (9.3 million to 165.6 million) and Latin America (12.8 million to 203.1 million).[39]

Since 1970 second-wave evangelicals and Renewalists from Asia and Latin America have accelerated the Asian and Hispanic realignment from mainline Protestantism to evangelicalism. For example, in politics, many Asian Christian immigrants, who struggled to sustain their faith in countries affected by the Cold War (for example, Korea, the Chinese diaspora, Vietnam, and other areas in Southeast Asia), became fiercely anticommunist and found conservative evangelicalism to be a more tenable ally than they found "liberal" Protestants. Most of these church planters were themselves trained by evangelical, Pentecostal, and fundamentalist missionaries and supported conservative social issues—especially those that defended the traditional family. Latino evangelicals have been influenced by the politics of conservative American evangelicals and have in turn altered American evangelical views on immigration. Asian, Hispanic, and black evangelicals may now be reshaping evangelical discourse on race and ethnicity.[40]

A few progressive evangelical organizations such as Evangelicals for Social Action and Sojourners have included antiracism as part of their ministry priority. African American evangelical leaders such as Tom Skinner (1942–1994) and William Pannell (b. 1929) reminded their fellow evangelicals of the significance of the civil rights vision and advocated for an evangelical black theology. Similarly, Hispanic theologian Orlando Costas (1942–1987) called for social justice for the marginalized and articulated something akin to an evangelical liberation theology. Although these were minority voices within American evangelicalism as a whole, they illuminated paths for engagement with ethnic and racial diversity within and outside the evangelical family.[41]

THE FUTURE OF MULTICULTURALISM IN AMERICAN EVANGELICALISM

As mainline Protestant denominations responded to the call for multicultural ministries and racial justice in the 1970s, they began to experience membership decline. A number of explanations for this development have been provided: spiritual laxity, leftward theological drift, generational change, religious restructuring, the second disestablishment of Protestantism, white flight, conservative backlash, population shifts to the South and Mountain regions, and so forth. The historian David Hollinger argues that "evangelicals triumphed in the numbers game by continuing to espouse several ideas about race, gender, sexuality, nationality, and divinity that remained popular with the white public when these same ideas were abandoned by leaders of the mainline, ecumenical churches as no longer defensible."[42]

Whatever the reasons, evangelicals were clear beneficiaries of mainline decline as they gained numeric dominance and political and cultural prominence in the late 1970s. Ironically, the presence of African Americans, Asian Americans, and Latinos in mainline Protestant denominations did not increase despite efforts to become more inclusive. While African American churches remained comfortably independent because of their history and legacy, most of the newly arriving Asian and Latino populations identified more with evangelicalism than with mainline Protestantism. Historian Juan Martínez quips, "Mainline churches opted for Latino civil rights, but Latinos opted for Pentecostalism."[43]

Despite the changing demography, most white and racial-ethnic evangelicals remained disconnected from one another. Not until very recently did American evangelicals fully realize the dramatic ethnic and racial transformations within their own spiritual household. Once white evangelicals recognized the changes, given their history, few were prepared to respond favorably. As recent as 2006 Robert Putnam's *Social Capital Benchmark Survey* revealed that evangelical young adults (twenty-one to forty-five years old), when compared with their peers, were least welcoming of an increased Asian and Hispanic presence in the United States. Sociologist Robert Wuthnow concluded from these data that though most young adults held favorable views toward Asians and Hispanics, "the fact that a quarter of evangelicals are not welcoming means that evangelicals are a more likely source of mobilized resistance against newcomers than any other religious group is. It also demonstrates, contrary to what some believe, that religion matters. It influences how people think and the kinds of people with whom they associate."[44]

Wuthnow speculates that relatively greater evangelical hostility toward Asians and Hispanics was the product of a lower level of education among white evangelicals and an upbringing in small towns where fewer Asians and Hispanics reside. Evangelicals were more likely to protect their families from social changes that were leading to greater ethnic diversity and exhibited a stronger religious exclusivism in their congregations. Finally, evangelicals shared with political conservatives a greater antipathy towards nonwhites (for example, those who voted for George W. Bush in 2000 were significantly less welcoming toward Asians than those who did not).

At the same time, Wuthnow argues that regular church attendance can also reduce the rate of inhospitality. Whether or not it is ethnically homogeneous, a church that encourages its members to engage the wider community will be a source of trust building and expansion of social networks.

Thus regular attendance at these types of congregations can mitigate ethnocentrism, enhance multicultural awareness, and work toward a common good in the area of race relations.

Furthermore, the surge of racial-ethnic diversity in cities and on college campuses over the past few decades has undoubtedly provided opportunities for many white evangelicals to recognize the value of multicultural discourse and practice. In these settings, white evangelicals who engage racial minorities have a higher likelihood of becoming sympathetic toward racial diversity.

I will highlight three recent evangelical responses to racial-ethnic diversity that may be instructive in considering the future of evangelical multiculturalism. The first is an attempt to read the Bible through the lens of cultural and historical contextualization. The second is a recognition of and response to structural racism in society and institutions. The third is the need to grapple with white privilege and racial equity within congregations and organizations as part of efforts to build intentionally multiracial faith communities. In all three cases, evangelicals have had to abandon a posture of nonrecognition or suspicion toward the social sciences—especially with regard to race. This critical embrace of the social sciences has already taken place in most evangelical institutions of higher education, denominations, and congregations, which has led to a rhetorical support of multiethnicity. Yet there has been little engagement of the power dynamics around race and a subtle tendency to devalue immigrant evangelical experiences.

Biblical Theology in Context

InterVarsity Christian Fellowship is one of the few evangelical organizations that seriously addresses the questions of race and ethnicity in a manner that permits racial-ethnic leaders to shape the discourse. At their triennial missions convention, Urbana 2012, an estimated 40 percent of the 17,000 attendees were Asian and Pacific Islander Americans (30 percent East Asian; 6 percent Southeast Asian; 3 percent South Asian; 1 percent Native Hawaiian/Pacific Islander). Comparatively, 56 percent were White/Caucasian; 8 percent were Black/African American; 6 percent were Hispanic/Latino; 1 percent were Native American, Native Alaskan, First Nations; and 0.6 percent were Middle Eastern. This represents a significant growth of Asian American participation since the previous convention in 2009 (3,849, or 24 percent, of the 15,800 were of Asian or South Asian descent). Furthermore, Urbana 2012 provided "ethnic-specific" lounges for Pan-Asian North Americans and those interested in Black Campus Ministries, Native and Indigenous Ministries, and Latino Ministries.[45]

InterVarsity has made practical responses to the changing demographics of its ministry. By the 1980s InterVarsity recognized that the increasing racial diversity on campuses necessitated attention to questions of race and ethnicity that mainstream evangelicalism had not adequately addressed. Many campus chapters had divided into ethnic subgroups that provided safe haven for ethnic fellowships to grow. Because chapter leadership tended to be dominated by white students, ethnic subgroups gave racial-ethnic students opportunity to serve and lead within their own racial-ethnic contexts. InterVarsity leaders drew on research by Fuller Seminary missiology professor Donald McGavran, who popularized the use of homogeneous units as the most effective way to grow religious groups and organizations. Thus effective evangelistic outreach became a practical justification for maintaining ethnic subgroups.[46]

Yet the reduced opportunities to build cross-ethnic relationships and community became a concern. In the 1990s InterVarsity's staff became increasingly diverse racially. The Asian American growth, in particular, generated some tension among students and staff. In some chapters the Asian American population was so overwhelming that some white students suggested forming a white chapter. At the leadership level, some whites (and some Asians) criticized Asian American staff for ministry among exclusively Asian American chapters. Debates emerged over whether ethnic-specific or multiethnic chapters better aligned with the "biblical" standard.[47]

In 2001 Asian American staff members Collin Tomikawa and Sandy Schaupp wrote a paper in response to this tension. The paper concluded that because racial reconciliation is a biblical mandate, student and staff ought to be encouraged to reach across the racial divide. The authors also concluded that growing awareness and appreciation of ethnic identity are essential parts of the journey to racial reconciliation. All cultures, though fallen, reflect and retain some aspects of the Kingdom of God and should be honored in Christian ministries. Finally, they agreed that ethnic-specific fellowship groups are strategic and therefore should not be dissolved.

Nevertheless, the authors disagreed about whether culture was a pre-Fall or post-Fall reality. They acknowledged that they each gave "a difference of weight . . . to culture" and disagreed about "how much [to] emphasize ethnic identity growth in our ministries." They also disagreed about the ultimate end of ethnic fellowships: were they means to a multiethnic end or do they have theological legitimacy by themselves?[48]

This study helped create space for the inclusion of a more favorable view of "culture" in biblical theology. It rejected "color-blindness" or "racial nonrecognition" because the latter approach usually resulted in the perpetuation of white organizational leadership. This reading of the Bible provided justification for increasing racial representation at IVCF's highest leadership levels.[49]

Recognizing Structural Racism

InterVarsity's level of sophistication regarding race and ethnicity is rare among evangelicals. Another instance where the conviction about achieving racial reconciliation resulted in a practical outcome is in the recent history of the Evangelical Covenant Church. When leaders of this small Swedish American denomination read Michael Emerson and Christian Smith's sociological study, *Divided by Race: Evangelical Religion and the Problem of Race in America* (2000), they felt convicted about the sin of ignoring race.[50]

Emerson and Smith introduced their readers to racialization theory. The problem identified is that the United States continues to be divided racially through a historical sociopolitical process called racialization (which should not be confused with ethnicity or ethnogenesis). Drawing from Howard Winant and Michael Omi's Racial Formation theory, first proposed in their now classic *Racial Formation in the United States* (1986), Emerson and Smith argue that public and private realities are structured along racial lines. Furthermore, the racial formations are fluid and dynamic, responding to and interacting with economic and political change. Even though "race" is a social construct (and therefore not based on any real biological differences), its recurring formations have real impact on people who are perceived to belong to a particular race. Given the social structural nature of racialization, racial integration cannot happen by simply changing individual attitudes or trying to be color-blind.[51]

Most white evangelical informants in *Divided by Race* did not recognize the dynamics of racialization because they did not understand structural racism. They preferred to see racism as a problem with personal attitudes that can be resolved by developing friendships with people of other races. This view is rooted in an individualistic worldview that was earlier noted in the fundamentalist rejection of the social sciences. Such a view refuses to acknowledge the significance of social structures in human experience or cultural and historical contexts in biblical interpretation. According to this "color-blind" theology, salvation in Christ liberates humanity from earthbound affairs, thus rendering matters such as race irrelevant. Critics charge those who draw attention to race with elevating a worldly concern above the "pure" and "cultureless" Gospel. But by universalizing what they believe to be a cultureless Christian faith, many evangelicals have unconsciously imposed their own cultural norms and racial assumptions on others. In this way, Emerson and Smith argue that evangelicals lack the conceptual tools to understand structural racism and thus are unable to relate adequately to the relevance of racial and cultural diversity in the church.[52]

In response to *Divided by Faith*, the Evangelical Covenant Church decided to revise its denominational goals in order to address racial reconciliation. The Covenant then prioritized ethnic church planting and programs of racial justice and reconciliation. As a result, racial minority ministries (Asian American ministries, in particular) are among the fastest growing in the denomination. Furthermore, like IVCF, the Covenant has made a commitment to increasing racial-ethnic representation in its organizational leadership. Particularly noteworthy is its "Five-Fold Multi-Dimensional Test" for ethnic ministry and diversity. In it, the level of participation, power, and purposeful narratives of diverse perspectives (especially racial minorities) are measurements of progress toward a genuine and not just multiethnic culture within the denomination and its local expressions.[53]

The Covenant's recognition of and conscious effort to overcome structural racism is, when compared with other evangelical denominations, likely the most overt embrace of the social theory of racialization.[54] This does not diminish the fact that almost all evangelical denominations have experienced significant growth among their racial-ethnic members over the last thirty years. The Southern Baptist Convention, the largest Protestant denomination in the United States, for example, has the largest number of racial-ethnic congregations. In 1986 C. Peter Wagner, the church-growth expert at Fuller Theological Seminary, asserted that "Southern Baptists are the most ethnically diverse denomination, worshiping in 87 languages in more than 4,600 language-culture congregations every Sunday." Some analysts challenged Wagner's assertion because he based it on absolute numbers alone. A U.S. Congregational Survey in 2002, for instance, revealed that Southern Baptists were "less diverse than worshipers as a whole and less diverse than the U.S. population" but comparable with the Evangelical Lutheran Church in America. According to the Southern Baptist supplement to the survey, Asian or Pacific Islanders constituted 1 percent of the total population. Black or African Americans made up 4 percent, Hispanics and Latinos 3 percent, Indian (American)/ Alaska Native Americans 2 percent, White or Caucasian 91 percent, and "other race" 1 percent. By 2011, after the historic apology in 1995 for its past racism and opposition to civil rights legislation, and after the election of its first black vice president (Fred J. Luter Jr., who was elected president in 2012), the percentage of racial-ethnic Southern Baptists had risen to 19 percent while white membership was in decline. In 2013 an estimated 10,000 of the 46,000 Southern Baptist congregations were "ethnic in some shape, form or fashion," making the Southern Baptists "by far the most ethnic convention in the nation."[55]

There are clear indications that the swelling ranks of racial-ethnics within the Southern Baptist Convention are pressing for ways to address structural racism. Familiar calls for public discussions about race and increased racial-ethnic representation echo the recent efforts of the Evangelical Covenant Church. For instance, on November 6, 2013, Thom Rainer, president and CEO of Southern Baptist retailer LifeWay Christian Resources, publicly apologized for publishing a Vacation Bible School curriculum in 2004 called "Rickshaw Rally." Asian American evangelical leaders spoke out against what they perceived to be offensive racial stereotypes, but received no response from LifeWay until 2013, after another Asian American evangelical backlash against prominent evangelical leaders who publicly repeated similar stereotypes. "LifeWay will continue to train our staff to be aware of and sensitive to ethnic and cultural differences so that our materials continue to respectfully represent all people groups," Rainer said. Furthermore, he pledged to "lead our executive leadership staff to engage in dialogue and conversation with ethnic leaders that we might go forth together to strengthen believers and reach people in North America and around the world."[56]

Because racialization and racism are embedded in America's social structure, InterVarsity, the Evangelical Covenant, Southern Baptists, and several other evangelical organizations and denominations are beginning to engage in familiar (but cutting-edge for evangelicals) models of racial reconciliation and justice beyond building friendships across ethnic and racial lines. One might say that some evangelicals today are repeating the 1970s efforts of mainline Protestants to secure racial justice for their minority constituency. The broad evangelical support of comprehensive immigration reform is potentially another instance of a more favorable response to multiethnic diversity. It is a hopeful sign that more white evangelical leaders and organizations are prepared to engage a deeper and more realistic conversation about race.

Grappling with White Privilege and Racial Equity for Intentionally Multiracial Organizations

Another area of promise for American evangelicalism is in efforts to build intentionally multicultural congregations, organizations, and communities. This is especially popular among younger and better-educated evangelicals. The authors of *Against All Odds: The Struggle for Racial Integration in Religious Organizations* (2005) conducted studies of six multiracial evangelical organizations in the Midwest and California (four congregations, a campus ministry, and a Christian college). The authors begin with several important premises. The first, as articulated in *Divided by Faith*, is that America continues to be divided racially through racialization. The second is that religious organizations are mediating institutions between the private and public spheres. As such, multiracial religious organizations have the potential to draw people out of their private, racially segregated lives and into a social space where human interactions are more intimate than in the public arena. The new interracial relationships that are created can model a future American society.[57]

One of the key factors for creating healthy interracial organizations is to intentionally recruit leaders who reflect and understand a particular target group. Thus a predominantly white congregation would need to appoint Asian staff in order to attract Asian members. But the authors argue that this alone would not bring about necessary and healthy change: "The importance of minimizing the costs of being in interracial organizations is greatest for those who are racial minorities in the larger society... because they pay the costs of both numerical and minority statuses daily in the larger society." In other words, racial minorities pay a higher "cultural tax" than racial majorities and therefore have a greater need to avoid paying these taxes in the religious organizations in which they invest their social capital. By contrast, as the racial majority, white people experience less "cultural taxation" in American society than they do in interracial organizations. This creates a dynamic some have labeled as the problem of "white privilege." The study enumerates multiple examples of unconscious white privileging. "Whites are accustomed to being in control in social contexts," claim the authors. Their norms and values in most cases prevail without challenge. Thus whites enjoy far greater opportunity, relative to racial minorities, to live in, establish, and reproduce social spaces that accommodate their preferences, culture, and superior status."[58]

Against All Odds illustrates how white privilege operates in multiethnic evangelical organizations. White people are more likely than racial minorities to leave interracial religious organizations if their particular preferences and interests are not being met. Despite their desire to attend an interracial church and their belief that this membership holds intrinsic benefits for them, white adults are unwilling to sacrifice the potential experiences, privileges, and opportunities of their children to do so. Finally, maintaining legitimacy within the dominant group is of greater priority for whites than are the desires and needs of fellow nonwhite organization members.

The behavior of white people becomes a major destabilizing factor for interracial churches. According to *Against All Odds*, whites are "not necessarily aware of their privileged status as the dominant racial group, nor are they aware how their own actions perpetuate it." The authors conclude that "unless whites are conscious of the status and privileges afforded them through whiteness, and unless they act to dismantle the structure that sustains that privilege, they will by default reproduce the racialized social order." Whereas white privilege tends to destabilize an interracial organization, interracial marriages bring stability. But this is further evidence that building friendships and trust across racial lines—even within the same organization—is extraordinarily difficult when racial identities are so clearly demarcated.[59]

Despite the struggles to work around white privilege, sociologists such as Michael Emerson (one of the authors of *Against All Odds*) believe that efforts to build multiracial congregations are well worth it. In *People of the Dream: Multiracial Congregations in the United States* (2006), Emerson argues that multiracial congregations are "bridge organizations that gather and facilitate cross-race social ties." Members of interracial congregations have many more racially diverse social ties at every level than do Americans who do not regularly attend a religious congregation or who attend uniracial congregations. Emerson calls these people "Sixth Americans" (that is, people who are less tethered to one of the five major racial groups and more interracially connected). He believes that given their extensive interracial social ties, Sixth Americans and multiracial congregations "are building considerable bridging capital, that is, resources that accrue from cross-racial social ties." This bridging capital can be used for gaining access to better schools, higher education, health care, neighborhoods, jobs, and access to many other forms of information and action. Without resources gained from these cross-racial ties, such access would likely be curtailed. Although Emerson is not certain that Sixth Americans and multiracial congregations will have a major impact in reducing racial inequality, he believes they have potential to become harbingers of future race relations in the United States.[60]

The interracial practices and relationships that Emerson describes are emerging among some American evangelicals. They are present and growing in a number of denominations and parachurch organizations. In regions with significant ethnic and racial diversity, many evangelical congregations are consciously seeking to become multiracial. There is reason to be cautiously optimistic. When "majority-race America" disappears, it is possible that white privilege will end and racial equity will be closer to the norm. But many changes still need to be embraced more fully in American society as a whole and within evangelicalism before the privileges of even a minority white population are dismantled.

EXIT POLLS AND THE FUTURE OF AMERICAN EVANGELICALISM

According to Southern Baptist Theological Seminary president Al Mohler, the U.S. elections in 2012 were a "catastrophe" and a "disaster" for evangelicals. "The entire moral landscape has changed," he said, since "an increasingly secularized America understands our positions, and has rejected them." Evangelical leaders such as Mohler bemoaned the reelection of President Obama, the outcomes of four same-sex marriage ballot initiatives, and losses by social conservative candidates in red states. The future of evangelicalism and the United States now seemed to them in peril.[61]

The loss was not because of a lack of effort on the part of white evangelicals, it would seem. According to a postelection poll conducted by the Pew Research Center, 79 percent of white evangelicals voted for Republican candidate Mitt Romney and only 20 percent for Barack Obama (compared with 59 percent of all white Americans who voted for Romney). White evangelical Protestants constituted 23 percent of the 2012 electorate (compared with 23 percent in 2008 and 21 percent in 2004).[62] By comparison, nonwhite voters made up 28 percent of all voters in 2012, up from 26 percent in 2008. Obama won 80 percent of these votes.

The exit polls highlight an emerging color-line dilemma in the United States and for American evangelicalism. Some 93 percent of African Americans, 71 percent of Latinos, and 73 percent of Asians voted for Obama. Minority Christians—consisting of black, Asian, Hispanic, and mixed-race Americans—made up 31 percent of Obama's coalition, the largest religious group. A pre-election poll indicated that 50 percent of Latino evangelicals preferred Obama, while 39 percent favored Romney. Pre-election surveys noted that Asian American evangelicals were mostly Republican and more likely to be Republican than other Asian Americans, but less likely than white evangelicals to be Republican. Romney's campaign did not reach out to black and Latino evangelicals who oppose abortion and same-sex marriage. Would that have garnered more evangelical votes? Perhaps not. Such efforts may have encouraged more Asian and Latino evangelicals to vote Republican, but it is evident that Asian and Latino evangelicals, minorities within their racial groups, were not as sold on the Republican candidate during this election.[63]

It may be too early to declare that the Christian Right has fallen from the mainstream. But it is possible that, as one news reporter observed, "white Christians are simply too old and too few in number to control the outcome of a nationwide election." Political alliances with the nonwhite electorate will now be necessary in national elections.[64]

Although most African American, Hispanic, and Asian American evangelicals and pentecostals agree with white evangelicals on personal social issues such as opposition to abortion and same-sex marriage, they diverge sharply on public social policy such as health care, affirmative action, poverty alleviation, educational equity, and immigration reform. Thus the traditional "white" base must adjust to these issues if there is to be any hope of building a new evangelical moral agenda. Some evangelical leaders, such as Sojourners' president Jim Wallis, argue that the elections were not a disaster for evangelicals per se, just those who "had again tied their faith to the partisan political agenda of the Republican Party." To him, "evangelical" is too often equated with "conservative white evangelical." The postelection efforts of a broad range of evangelicals to advocate for "just and humane immigration laws" is one indication that American evangelicalism is no longer defined by one demographic group. Wallis may be correct in his analysis that "there is a new evangelical agenda for a new evangelical demographic."[65]

CONCLUSION

Just as neo-evangelicals repudiated their fundamentalist exclusivity and stepped into a very different post–World War II society, twenty-first century evangelicals are also stepping into an unfamiliar world. The racial landscape along with other social realities have changed dramatically over the past three decades. But this time the transformations have occurred within the evangelical family.

This chapter has suggested that the American evangelicalism that white theological and social conservatives have dominated has been both uninterested in and ill-equipped to partner with racial minorities until very recently. This was largely due to their separation from mainline Protestantism during the early twentieth century and the formation of culturally isolated organizations in the middle decades. Although mainline Protestants engaged interracial social issues and exhibited some concern about racial integration, most fundamentalists and evangelicals paid little attention and uncritically imbibed the prevailing norms about race and ethnicity. This was also true of most racial-ethnic evangelicals whose theological perspectives developed in mainstream evangelical institutions. But despite American evangelicalism's seemingly unchanging racial ethos, its racial-ethnic demographics underwent a remarkable transformation over the past forty years.

Those who engaged racial minorities soon realized that cooperative interracial mission or effective evangelistic outreach required adjustments within the prevailing evangelical ethos. Such changes necessitated biblical and theological reinterpretations that were sensitive to cultural and historic contexts, recognition of structural racism in society and institutions, and a relentless commitment to grapple with white privilege and racial equity within congregations and organizations.

The promise of American evangelicalism will be fulfilled only when white evangelicals are no longer hesitant to seek a multicultural and multiracial future characterized by racial equity. Although much work remains, there are promising signs that American evangelicals are willing to allocate resources to face, embrace, and shape a racially diverse future. Indeed, as the 2012 elections illustrated, that future has arrived. So, too, have new opportunities to build a global and multiracial evangelical future.

NOTES

1. While recognizing that pentecostalism is a distinct religious movement, this chapter adopts the view that there is enough commonality to include it within the American evangelical label.

2. Barry A. Kosmin and Ariela Keysar, *The American Religious Identification Survey (ARIS 2008): Summary Report* (Hartford, Conn.: Trinity College, 2009), http://commons.trincoll.edu/aris/files/2011/08/ARIS_Report_2008.pdf, accessed August 6, 2015.

3. Luis Lugo et al., *U.S. Religious Landscape Survey* (Washington, D.C.: Pew Research Center, February 2008), 40, http://religions.pewforum.org/pdf/report-religious-landscape-study-full.pdf, accessed August 6, 2015; Pew Research Center, "America's Changing Religious Landscape," May 12, 2015, http://www.pewforum.org/2015/05/12/americas-changing-religious-landscape/, accessed August 6, 2015; Kosmin and Keysar, *ARIS 2008*, 15.

4. Albert G. Miller, "The Rise of African-American Evangelicalism in American Culture," in *Perspectives on American Religion and Culture*, ed. Peter Williams, 259–

69 (Oxford: Blackwell, 1999); "National Black Evangelical Association," in *Encyclopedia of African American Culture and History*, ed. Jack Salzman, David Lionel Smith, and Cornel West (New York: Macmillan Reference Library, 1996).

5. American Immigration Council, "African Immigrants in America: A Demographic Overview," Immigration Policy Center, June 28, 2012, http://www.immigrationpolicy.org/just-facts/african-immigrants-america-demographic-overview; Randy Capps, Kristen McCabe, and Michael Fix, "New Streams: Black African Migration to the United States," Migration Policy Institute, 2011, http://www.migrationpolicy.org/pubs/africanmigrationus.pdf; Helina Faris, "5 Fast Facts About Black Immigrants in the United States," Center for American Progress, December 20, 2012, www.americanprogress.org/issues/immigration/news/2012/12/20/48571/5-fast-facts-about-black-immigrants-in-the-united-states/; Sam Roberts, "More Africans Enter U.S. Than in Days of Slavery," February 21, 2005, http://www.nytimes.com/2005/02/21/nyregion/21africa.html?_r=0; all accessed August 6, 2015.

6. Roberto Suro et al., *Changing Faiths: Latinos and the Transformation of American Religion* (Washington, D.C., Pew Research Center, 2007), http://www.pewforum.org/uploadedfiles/Topics/Demographics/hispanics-religion-07-final-mar08.pdf, 3, 7, 29; Juhem Navarro-Rivera, Barry A. Kosmin, and Ariela Keysar, *U.S. Latino Religious Identification 1990–2008: Growth, Diversity & Transformation* (Hartford, Conn.: Institute for the Study of Secularism in Society & Culture, 2010), http://commons.trincoll.edu/aris/files/2011/08/latinos2008.pdf, 1; Pew Research Center, "Religious Tradition by Race/Ethnicity (2014)," http://www.pewforum.org/religious-landscape-study/compare/religious-tradition/by/racial-and-ethnic-composition/; all accessed August 6, 2015.

7. United States Census Bureau, *U.S. Census 2010*, http://www.census.gov/2010census/, accessed August 6, 2015.

8. Juan Francisco Martínez, *Los Protestantes: An Introduction to Latino Protestantism in the United States* (Santa Barbara, Calif.: Praeger, 2011), 10–18.

9. Ibid., 18–27.

10. Suro et al., *Changing Faiths*, 3; Barbara Bradley Hagerty, "U.S. Hispanics Choose Churches Outside Catholicism," NPR, October 19, 2011, http://www.npr.org/2011/10/19/141275979/u-s-hispanics-choose-churches-outside-catholicism, accessed August 6, 2015.

11. Suro et al., *Changing Faiths*, 29.

12. Ibid., 2.

13. Ibid., 4.

14. Cary Funk et al., *Asian Americans: A Mosaic of Faiths* (Washington, D.C.: Pew Research Center, July 19, 2012), http://www.pewforum.org/files/2012/07/Asian-Americans-religion-full-report.pdf, 43, accessed August 6, 2015.

15. The majority (53 percent) of American Buddhists are white. Only 32 percent of Buddhists in America are Asian; Lugo et al., *U.S. Religious Landscape Survey*, 45; Funk et al., *Asian Americans*, 11; Kosmin and Keysar, *ARIS 2008*, 15.

16. Andrew Kohut et al., *The Rise of Asian Americans*, updated ed. (Washington, D.C.: Pew Research Center, April 4, 2013), http://www.pewsocialtrends.org/files/2013/04/Asian-Americans-new-full-report-04-2013.pdf, 185, accessed August 6, 2015.

17. Ibid., 13.

18. Ibid., 174. The Pew study of Asian Americans as a whole and media coverage of it have been criticized on multiple grounds. Critics are especially concerned that the report was too focused on "one-dimensional narratives of exceptionalism" and not enough on the challenges facing subgroups such as Cambodians and Bangladeshis, who have relatively low rates of educational attainment. See Rebecca Trounson, "Advocacy Groups Concerned About New Asian American Study," *Los Angeles Times*, June 19, 2012, http://latimesblogs.latimes.com/lanow/2012/06/study-on-us-asians.html, accessed August 6, 2015; Joyce Moy et al., "Letter to Pew Research Center," Asian American and Pacific Islander Policy Research Consortium, June 22, 2012, http://www.aapiprc.com/home-1/pressreleases/pewopenletter, accessed August 6, 2015; Pew Research Center, "Religious Tradition by Race/ethnicity."

19. Kohut et al., *Rise of Asian Americans*, 170.

20. Ibid.

21. Ibid., 178.

22. Ibid., 17.

23. Ibid., 187.

24. Ibid., 167.

25. Janelle S. Wong and Jane Naomi Iwamura, "The Moral Minority: Race, Religion, and Conservative Politics in Asian America," in *Religion and Social Justice for Immigrants,* ed. Pierrette Hondagneu-Sotelo, 35–49 (New Brunswick, N.J.: Rutgers University Press, 2007).

26. George Marsden, *Fundamentalism and American Culture*, 2nd ed. (New York: Oxford University Press, 2006); Mark Noll, *America's God: From Jonathan Edwards to Abraham Lincoln* (New York: Oxford University Press, 2002); Joel A. Carpenter, *Revive Us Again: The Reawakening of American Fundamentalism* (New York: Oxford University Press, 1999); Margaret Lamberts Bendroth, *Fundamentalism and Gender: 1875 to the Present* (New Haven, Conn.: Yale University Press 1996).

27. Martínez, *Los Protestantes*, 29–31; Mark T. Banker, *Presbyterian Missions and Cultural Interaction in the Far Southwest, 1850–1950* (Urbana: University of Illinois Press, 1993).

28. Timothy Tseng, "Ministry at Arms' Length: Asian Americans in the Racial Ideology of Mainline American Protestants, 1882–1952" (Ph.D. diss., Union Theological Seminary, 1994); Jennifer C. Snow, *Protestant Missionaries, Asian Immigrants, and Ideologies of Race in America, 1850–1924* (New York: Routledge, 2007).

29. Robert H. Keller, *American Protestantism and United States Indian Policy, 1869–82* (Lincoln: University of Nebraska Press, 1983); Frederick Hoxie, *A Final Promise: The Campaign to Assimilate the Indians, 1880–1920* (Lincoln: University of Nebraska Press, 1984).

30. Najia Aarim-Heriot, *Chinese Immigrants, African Americans, and Racial Anxiety in the United States, 1848–82* (Urbana: University of Illinois, 2003); Lisa Yun, *The Coolie Speaks: Chinese Indentured Laborers and African Slaves in Cuba* (Philadelphia: Temple University Press, 2008).

31. Edward J. Blum, *Reforging the White Republic: Race, Religion, and American Nationalism, 1865–1898* (Baton Rouge: Louisiana State University Press, 2005), 3.

32. Henry Yu, *Thinking Orientals: Migration, Contact, and Exoticism in Modern America* (New York: Oxford University Press, 2002), and Tseng, "Ministry at Arms' Length," both make the case that the Chicago sociological theory of assimilation associated with Robert Park was an outgrowth of Protestant urban missions to European immigrants, Asians, and, later, black migrants to northern cities.

33. William Hutchison, *Errand to the World: American Protestant Thought and Foreign Missions* (Chicago: University of Chicago Press, 1993).

34. Gunnar Myrdal, *An American Dilemma: The Negro Problem and Modern Democracy* (New York: Harper & Row, 1962); Pamela E. Klassen, *Spirits of Protestantism: Medicine, Healing, and Liberal Christianity* (Berkeley: University of California Press, 2011).

35. Bendroth, *Fundamentalism and Gender*.

36. David W. Wills, "An Enduring Distance: Black Americans and the Establishment," in *Between the Times: The Travail of the Protestant Establishment in America, 1900–1960*, ed. William R. Hutchison, 172 (New York: Cambridge University Press, 1989).

37. Martínez, *Los Protestantes*, 25–27; Lester Suzuki, "Persecution, Alienation, and Resurrection: History of Japanese Methodist Churches," in *Churches Aflame: Asian Americans and United Methodism*, ed. Artemio R. Guillermo, 113–34 (Nashville, Tenn.: Abingdon, 1991). Martínez notes that "Latino Protestantism in Texas looks very different in 2010 than it did in 1910. The Baptists have almost 1,500 Latino congregations in the state, whereas the Assemblies of God have over 400. The Methodists and the Presbyterians each have fewer than 100 Latino congregations in the state. And both Baptists and Assemblies of God have more Latinos in their 'non-Latino' churches than either mainline denomination."

38. Martínez, *Los Protestantes*, 31–33.

39. Gina A. Bellofatto and Todd M. Johnson, "Key Findings of *Christianity in Its Global Context, 1970–2020*," *International Bulletin of Missionary Research* 37, no. 3 (July 2013): 157–64.

40. I trace the evangelical transformation of a formerly mainline Chinese American Protestantism in Tseng, "Trans-Pacific Transpositions: Continuities and Discontinuities in Chinese North American Protestantism," in *Revealing the Sacred in Asian and Pacific America*, ed. Jane Naomi Iwamura and Paul Spickard, 241–71 (New York: Routledge, 2003).

41. The National Black Evangelical Association, organized in 1963 by African American evangelicals, championed an evangelical black theology. NBEA, "Welcome," http://www.the-nbea.org/home-3/, accessed August 6, 2015; William E. Pannell, *My Friend the Enemy* (Waco, Tex.: World Books, 1968); Tom Skinner, *How*

Black Is the Gospel (Philadelphia: Lippincott, 1970); Orlando E. Costas, *Christ Outside the Gate: Mission Beyond Christendom* (New York: Orbis, 1982).

42. David A. Hollinger, *After Cloven Tongues of Fire: Protestant Liberalism in Modern American History* (Princeton, N.J.: Princeton University Press, 2013), 18.

43. Martínez, *Los Protestantes*, 39.

44. Robert Putnam, *Social Capital Benchmark Survey* (2006), http://www.ropercenter.uconn.edu/2006-social-capital-community-benchmark-survey/, accessed August 6, 2015; Robert Wuthnow, *After the Baby Boomers: How Twenty- and Thirty-Somethings Are Shaping the Future of American Religion* (Princeton, N.J.: Princeton University Press, 2007), 196.

45. Thanks to Nikki Toyama-Szeto, former program director of the Urbana Conference for InterVarsity Christian Fellowship, conversation with author, 2013. "Number of Asian Americans at Urbana 2009 Missions Conference," http://djchuang.wordpress.com/2012/12/19/number-of-asian-americans-at-urbana-2009-missions-conference/; Neil Rendall and Pete Hammond, "The History of InterVarsity's Multiethnic Journey," http://mem.intervarsity.org/mem/about-mem/history, and "Ethnic Specific Lounges at Urbana," http://mem.intervarsity.org/mem/urbana; all accessed August 6, 2015.

46. Donald A. McGavran, *Understanding Church Growth* (Grand Rapids, Mich.: Eerdmans, 1980), 95.

47. InterVarsity Multiethnic Ministries, "Asian American Ministries: Vital Stats," http://mem.intervarsity.org/aam/our-mission/vital-stats, accessed August 6, 2015.

48. Collin Tomikawa and Sandy Schaupp, "Two Views Regarding Ethnic Specific and Multi-ethnic Fellowships," paper written for the National Asian American Staff Conference, March 2001, Madison, Wis., InterVarsity Christian Fellowship/USA, 17.

49. Contrast this with the majority of evangelical scholarship that seems to equate racial or ethnic recognition with racism. For example, J. Daniel Hays, *From Every People and Nation: A Biblical Theology of Race* (Downers Grove, Ill.: InterVarsity Press, 2003).

50. Michael Emerson and Christian Smith, *Divided by Race: Evangelical Religion and the Problem of Race in America* (New York: Oxford University Press, 2000).

51. Howard Winant and Michael Omi, *Racial Formation in the United States: From the 1960s to the 1990s*, 2nd ed. (New York: Routledge, 1994).

52. J. Kameron Carter, *Race: A Theological Account* (New York: Oxford University Press, 2008), argues that a purported cultureless approach to theology is more akin to Gnosticism, an early heresy, which resulted in the formation of racial hierarchies in Western history; thus an orthodox rejection of this heresy can lead to a greater appreciation of difference.

53. Thanks to Rev. Gregory Yee, superintendent of the North Pacific Conference of the Evangelical Covenant Church, conversation with author, 2013.

54. The Covenant appeared more willing than other evangelicals to engage what Hollinger calls "demographic diversification" and "cognitive demystifica-

tion," that is, what mainline Protestants had engaged in since the nineteenth century as a means of accommodating the Enlightenment and modernity. Thus mainline Protestants were self-consciously modern, which meant "an increasingly generous opinion of foreign peoples and their inherited religions, a revulsion toward the persistence of antiblack racism in their own country, a recognition that the American nation was as much the possession of non-Protestants as of Protestants, a positive response to secular psychology and sociology, and a growing receptivity to theologies that rejected or downplayed the role of supernatural power." Hollinger overgeneralizes this point in order to draw a sharp contrast with neo-evangelicals; Hollinger, *After Cloven Tongues of Fire,* 11.

55. C. Peter Wagner, "A Vision for Evangelizing the Real America," *International Bulletin of Missionary Research* (April 1986): 62; Phillip B. Jones and Cynthia Woolever, *Southern Baptist Congregations and Worshipers Supplement to A Field Guide to U.S. Congregations* (Alpharetta, Ga.: North American Mission Board, 2002), 4; Erick Eckholm, "Southern Baptists Approve Steps Aimed at Diversity," *New York Times,* June 15, 2011, http://www.nytimes.com/2011/06/16/us/16baptist.html, accessed August 2, 2015; Becky Perlow, "Southern Baptists Elect First Black President," CNN *Belief Blog,* June 12, 2012, http://religion.blogs.cnn.com/2012/06/19/southern-baptists-to-elect-first-black-president/, accessed August 6, 2013; Erin Roach, "Ethnic Leaders Affirm Value of Southern Baptist Diversity," *Baptist Press,* June 18, 2013, http://bpnews.net/bpnews.asp?ID=40558, accessed August 6, 2015.

56. Sarah Pulliam Bailey, "Southern Baptists' LifeWay Apologizes for 'Offensive' Curriculum," *Religious News Service,* November 6, 2013, http://religionnews.com/2013/11/06/lifeway-president-apologizes-decade-old-rickshaw-rally-offended-asian-american-christians/, accessed August 6, 2015.

57. Brad Christerson, Korie L. Edwards, and Michael O. Emerson, *Against All Odds: The Struggle for Racial Integration in Religious Organizations* (New York: New York University Press, 2005), 158, 172, 168, 170, 171.

58. Ibid., 158, 172.

59. Ibid., 172.

60. Michael O. Emerson, *People of the Dream: Multiracial Congregations in the United States* (Princeton, N.J.: Princeton University Press, 2006), 162–63.

61. Tobin Grant, "Post-Election Fight Over the 'Evangelical' Brand," *Christianity Today,* November 20, 2012, http://www.christianitytoday.com/ct/2012/november-web-only/post-election-fight-over-evangelical-brand.html, accessed August 6, 2015.

62. Pew Research Center, "How the Faithful Voted: 2012 Preliminary Analysis," November 7, 2012, http://pewforum.org/2012/11/07/how-the-faithful-voted-2012-preliminary-exit-poll-analysis/#rr, accessed August 6, 2015.

63. Pew Research Center, "Changing Face of America Helps Assure Obama Victory," http://www.people-press.org/2012/11/07/changing-face-of-america-helps-assure-obama-victory/; CNN, "Election 2012: Results," http://www2.cnn.com/election/2012/results/main; Dan Merica, "Survey: Religiously Unaffiliated, Minority Christians Propelled Obama's Victory," November 15, 2012, http://religion.blogs

.cnn.com/2012/11/15/survey-religiously-unaffiliated-minority-christians-propel-obamas-victory/; Paul Taylor et al., *Latinos, Religion and Campaign 2012: Catholics Favor Obama, Evangelicals Divided* (Washington, D.C.: Pew Research Center, October 18, 2012), http://pewforum.org/Race/Latinos-Religion-and-Campaign-2012.aspx; all accessed August 6, 2015.

64. Bob Smietana, "Christian Right Falls from the Mainstream: Election Signals America's Cultural Shift as White Evangelicals Lose Power," *Tennessean*, November 25, 2012, http://theaquilareport.com/christian-right-falls-from-mainstream/, accessed August 6, 2015.

65. Grant, "Post-Election Fight"; Melissa Steffan, "New Efforts by Barna Group, NAE, Others Aim to Reach—and Understand—Hispanics," *Christianity Today*, November 15, 2012, http://www.christianitytoday.com/ct/2012/november-web-only/nae-barna-latinos-hispanics.html?paging=off, accessed August 6, 2015.

Conclusion

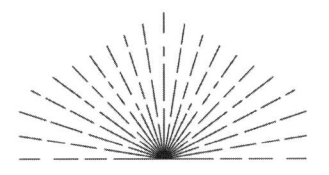

Candy Gunther Brown

The story of American evangelicalism is far from simple. From the 1970s to the present, the plot has indeed thickened. Whether one considers cultural characteristics, spirituality, theology, politics, or race and ethnicity, it becomes apparent that the story of evangelicalism is closely entwined with the American narrative, and that there are multiple stories within the story. This book's chapters vary in tone from relatively neutral description to optimism to pessimism about what the future holds. This concluding chapter steps back to construct a composite portrait from the sketches produced in the preceding chapters. As of 2016 American evangelicalism can be characterized by its biblicism, nondenominationalism, magnetic leadership, selective adaptation to popular culture, pentecostalization, globalization, ethnic diversification, political realignment, and generational change. After examining each of these themes in turn, this chapter gestures toward the future. Evangelicalism has once again become the normative form of non-Catholic Christianity in the United States, and evangelicals and nonevangelicals alike will be well advised to consider the implications.

BIBLICISM

The Bible has always been, and remains today, at the center of evangelical culture. Not only do evangelicals read the Bible on their own; ARIS 2008 shows that 77 percent strongly agree that it is very important to participate in prayer or Bible study groups, and 73 percent (versus 43 percent of mainline Protestants) participate in such a group at least monthly.

Evangelicals esteem the Bible as uniquely authoritative—indeed as the final authority on all matters of Christian faith and practice—although some people debate whether the text must be considered inerrant or taken literally word for word. Although frequently insisting that biblical principles are unchanging, evangelical interpretations and applications of biblical principles do vary by historical and cultural context. The Bible is a lengthy, complex book, and evangelicals inevitably give more or less emphasis to certain kinds of biblical passages.

During the sixteenth-century Reformation, Protestants rejected the authority of the Catholic hierarchy to regulate doctrine and practice, instead affirming the right and responsibility of every Christian—who together constitute the "priesthood of all believers"—to use the Bible to navigate questionable matters. Rejecting a single, authoritative interpretation of the Bible yielded a proliferation of "Christian" viewpoints on many issues. Because the Bible alone, rather than a centralized institution, governing board, or individual leader, is considered indisputably authoritative, there is no single evangelical position or means of enforcing the boundaries of who or what counts as "evangelical."

Evangelicals do care a great deal about safeguarding doctrinal orthodoxy and may accuse one another of erring on the side of "fundamentalism" or "liberalism." Evangelicals envision themselves as "earnestly contending"—often against other self-identified evangelicals—"for the faith once delivered to the saints" (Jude 1:3). Certain evangelicals may claim that there is only one reasonable interpretation of the Bible and that those who disagree are unfaithful to the Bible itself. Yet evangelicals who highly regard biblical authority may be found on opposite sides of important doctrinal questions. Despite the Reformation principle of *sola scriptura*, tradition plays an important role in theological debates. Some evangelicals argue that the Bible should be read on its own without undue deference to tradition, whereas other evangelicals argue that church tradition provides a crucial check on the legitimacy of novel biblical interpretations.

Generational change poses new questions about the importance of tradition and the meanings of evangelical biblicism. For instance, until recently there was little disagreement among evangelicals that the Bible explicitly prohibits sex outside of marriage and homosexuality whether or not a couple is married. As American public opinion on sexual practices shifted, younger evangelicals became more likely to interpret sex outside of marriage and same-sex marriage as consistent with biblical principles. If younger evangelicals can read their Bibles in a way that reverses traditional evangelical views of issues that the Bible appears to address directly, it seems unclear how much the biblical text itself will matter to biblical justifications the rising generations use to authorize adaptations to American culture.

NONDENOMINATIONALISM

Denominationalism is less useful as a way of understanding evangelicalism today than was the case a century ago. As evangelicalism came to dominate the nineteenth-century American religious landscape, evangelicalism's institutional center of gravity was located in denominations. Adjacent to denominational structures, nineteenth-century evangelicals participated in informal networks of nondenominational voluntary societies to address particular reform causes such as temperance or distribution of tracts and Sunday school literature.[1]

Over the course of the twentieth century, Americans' attachments to denominations waned. The process began when theologically liberal factions took over denominational leadership structures, prompting fundamentalists to withdraw and form rival institutions. The informal, anti-institutional ethos of the 1960s counterculture and the ecumenical enthusiasm of the 1960s–1970s Charismatic movement hastened the shift away from denominationally organized religion. Mainline Protestant denominations have been losing members for decades, and especially since the turn of the twenty-first century. But even evangelical denominations have shared in the declining fortunes of denominational Christianity. The largest Protestant denomination in America—the evangelical Southern Baptist Convention—now counts fewer than 16 million members. After continuous growth from its founding in 1845, membership plateaued in 2004 and declined every year from 2007 to 2011. In 2012 the annual convention elected its first black president and voted to allow affiliated churches to rename themselves Great Commission Baptists in an effort to broaden the denomination's appeal beyond white southern culture.[2] Although denominational bureaucracies have not disappeared, individuals and congregations feel freer to move between denominations or leave them altogether, or retain denominational affiliations while participating in larger-than-denominational alliances.

Rather than form new denominations, Christians are increasingly joining "nondenominational" churches that express an evangelical and/or pentecostal ethos. Protestants are less likely to declare allegiance to any one denomination and increasingly likely to self-identify more simply as "Christian," "Protestant," "Pentecostal," "Charismatic," "born again," or "evangelical." Of the evangelicals surveyed by ARIS 2008, 44 percent described themselves as "Baptist," 13 percent "Christian," 11 percent "nondenominational," 8 percent "Pentecostal," and 6 percent "Protestant." The ARIS survey series shows that nondenominational Christian identity has been trending upward, particularly since 2001. Fewer than 200,000 people favored the term "nondenominational" in 1990; in 2008 it accounted for over 8 million Americans. The Pew Religious Landscape Studies confirm that the trend toward nondenominational identification has continued: with the number of Pew-defined evangelicals further identifying as Baptists falling from 41 percent in 2007 to 36 percent in 2014, while the share claiming a nondenominational affiliation rose from 13 percent to 19 percent. Even when denominational labels are used, they mean less than they once did. There are, for instance, pentecostal Presbyterians and de facto cessationists in the Pentecostal Assemblies of God. On the whole, however, it is more likely that one will find pentecostals in a nondenominational than a Baptist congregation.

As denominationalism collapsed, some individual churches went off in their own directions, allowing for an increasing range of doctrinal positions within evangelicalism. Other local congregations joined relatively loose associations or nonhierarchical networks of churches united by shared values and relational connections. It is not uncommon or looked down on for ministries to forge explicit ties with multiple network hubs. Affiliated churches remain institutionally autonomous and self-governing. Itinerating speakers, books, audiovisual materials, websites, and conferences regularly rearticulate a common vision. Relational networks are not anarchical but organized on the model of family relationships. In any family there are implicit, and to an extent explicit, lines of authority. Leaders and churches not only can be invited to join but can be disfellowshipped for failing to bring doctrines or practices into line with accepted norms. It is, however, difficult to enforce accountability, since renegades can simply align with (or initiate) a new relational network.³

The move away from denominationalism is not complete and may not prove permanent. Sociologists have observed a pattern of churches birthing higher-commitment sects that progressively reify into churches. Associations that begin as nondenominational networks sometimes take on characteristics of a denomination. For example, the pentecostal Association of Vineyard Churches formed in 1985 as a network of churches with the same "spiritual DNA." As of 2015 Vineyard USA still calls itself a movement, but it no longer shies away from being classed alongside other denominations. The Toronto Airport Christian Fellowship (TACF), which hosted the "Toronto Blessing" revivals of 1994–2006 that led to its disfellowshipping from the Vineyard, came to provide "apostolic leadership" for an international "fellowship of churches," a "family of churches, a network of people." This network, Partners in Harvest, serves many of the same functions as a denomination—by providing a "primary relational affiliation and covering"—but seeks to avoid the institutionalizing tendencies of formal denominational structures. In 2009 TACF was renamed Catch the Fire Toronto!, and it has planted other churches (each of which bears the name Catch the Fire!) in Canada, the United States, Great Britain, and continental Europe. One might ask whether this move marks a key moment in the transformation of a relational network into a denomination, and whether neo-institutionalization will inevitably lead to the "routinization of charisma" theorized by sociologist Max Weber.⁴

Routinization is not all bad. Denominations have served a stabilizing function for evangelicalism by filling in as proxies for the leadership that established church hierarchies once exercised. As institutions, denominations operate through regularized leadership structures and decision-making processes that slow the rate of change in doctrine and practice. The decline of denominational structures intensifies the problem of determining who speaks authoritatively for evangelicals or regulates orthodoxy and also makes it possible for evangelicalism to adapt (for good or for ill) more quickly to cultural change. In the face of denominational decline, individual leaders and parachurch ministries, although not new to evangelicalism, are carrying more of the weight of evangelical entrepreneurialism and activism.

Conclusion

MAGNETIC LEADERSHIP

Because there is no official evangelical magisterium, hierarchy, or headquarters, evangelicals look up to organizations and individuals whose claim to leadership rests squarely on their ability to attract and keep a following. Institutions such as the National Association of Evangelicals and *Christianity Today* magazine and individuals such as Billy Graham provided the post–World War II evangelical movement with informal leadership.

Declining denominational authority is creating a leadership vacuum filled by magnetic individuals whose claim to authority is not ascribed but must be won by following the lead of popular culture. Insisting that the Bible alone is authoritative paradoxically heightens the authority that magnetic leaders exercise informally. Throughout evangelicalism's history, individual (mostly male) leaders have attracted followers and unified the evangelical movement: Martin Luther (1483–1546), John Calvin (1509–1564), George Whitefield (1714–1770), John Wesley (1703–1791), Jonathan Edwards (1703–1758), Charles Grandison Finney (1792–1875), Phoebe Palmer (1807–1874), Dwight L. Moody (1837–1899), Billy Sunday (1862–1935), Aimee Semple McPherson (1890–1944), Billy Graham (b. 1918), Kathryn Kuhlman (1907–1976), Oral Roberts (1918–2009), Benny Hinn (b. 1952), and Rick Warren (b. 1954).

Evangelical leaders are entrepreneurs who know how to read what their audience wants, and who take the initiative to meet popular demands in creative ways. Leadership must be exercised by means of persuasion since there is no mechanism for enforcing obedience on particular issues or guaranteeing continued allegiance. Leaders who push their followers too hard risk losing their following. Evangelical pastors, parachurch ministry leaders, and songwriters are all most likely to win and keep a following if they revert to a simplified, Bible-only, sometimes clichéd, common-denominator message that minimizes potential for offending segments of the evangelical world. There are also self-appointed evangelical watchdogs, typically labeled "discernment ministries," such as Hank Hanegraaff's (b. 1950) Christian Research Institute, who see themselves as exposing heretical threats to Christianity coming from popular culture and even from within the Christian fold. But no one has to accept or even listen to warnings issued. These groups' authority is diffused when different discernment ministries reach opposite conclu-

Conclusion

sions about what is legitimate and even the same ministries issue self-contradictory verdicts.[5]

Although magnetic leaders and parachurch ministries can mobilize support for causes and motivate personal piety, they do not cultivate loyalty or deference in the same way that denominations once did. Denominationally supported preachers in nineteenth-century America did not mince words in preaching against presumed heresies such as Christian Science or hesitate to eject church members for dabbling in practices labeled "occult." Today evangelical megachurches model a "seeker-sensitive" style designed to appeal to consumers in a pluralistic society. The seeker-sensitive model of church growth limits the degree of leadership that pastors can exercise because they serve at the pleasure of the people. If pastors take unpopular positions, at odds with popular culture, they risk losing their flocks and forfeiting cultural influence. Some evangelical pastors are willing to compromise even on moral issues out of a pragmatic concern to keep their platform.[6]

POPULAR CULTURE

Since the first century Christianity has contained within it twin impulses: appropriation of "non-Christian" means for "Christian" purposes and boundary setting or proscription of particular beliefs and actions that seem inherently corrupting. Which specific ideas and activities fall in or out of favor at a given time or place depends on cultural and historical factors in addition to religious factors. At the core of the evangelical movement is a tricky balancing act—speaking to without being corrupted by culture. Unlike liberals or fundamentalists, evangelicals seek to neither conform to nor remain aloof from culture but exert a transformative influence by combining theological conservatism with cultural adaptability.

Evangelicalism has long been a populist movement oriented toward ordinary people more than social elites and as such takes its cues from popular culture. In recent decades evangelicals have become better educated, wealthier, and more globally aware and cosmopolitan in their engagements with culture. Modern evangelicals have experimented with evangelistic tattoos and surfboarding ministries and are media-savvy, aggressively using print, radio, satellite television, cell phones, and the Internet to compete with what the world has to offer. In borrowing resources from the surrounding culture, evangelicals pick up on the most popular cultural trends as offering the greatest opportunities for achieving evangelical goals. First, they seek to evangelize non-Christians by creatively presenting the Gospel in culturally relevant ways. Second, Christians want to help one another grow spiritually. Finally, evangelicals may be least vocal about, but most motivated by, a third goal: finding a legitimate way to access perceived benefits without compromising Christian identity.[7]

Although always claiming biblical support for their positions, in their pragmatism, evangelicals sometimes seem to borrow more than they challenge in their cultural surroundings. One key trajectory of American culture since the 1970s holistic health-care movement is the embrace of self-fulfillment, psychological therapy, emotional well-being, and holistic care of body/mind/spirit. In this cultural milieu evangelicals have been particularly concerned to guard against "Eastern" religions and the "New Age," often keeping their distance from nonwhite immigrants whom they associate with intellectual threats to Christian orthodoxy. At the same time evangelicals have enthusiastically embraced recently popular forms of complementary, alternative, and integrative medicine inspired by selective interpretations of non-Christian religions, including Hinduism, Buddhism, Taoism, and Western metaphysical spirituality (such as yoga, mindfulness meditation, acupuncture, and chiropractic). Paradoxically, fear of investigating unfamiliar beliefs has made it more likely that evangelicals will participate in health and wellness activities that embody the very worldviews they find suspect, sometimes leading participants to embrace progressively less evangelical worldviews.[8]

Because evangelical clergy have often devalued the body and its senses, blamed the sick for their afflictions, or discouraged prayer for miraculous healing, people in the pews have sometimes viewed Christianity as irrelevant to daily health needs and looked elsewhere for help. Although evangelicals are in principle committed to shunning religious eclecticism, they can be just as eclectic as anyone else when healing is at stake. When people, evangelical Christians included, need healing or want better health, the urgent—and legitimate—question of which health-care choice works best overshadows theoretical concerns about why therapies work. If evangelicals experience cognitive dissonance, desire for benefits can prompt them to rationalize, rather than change, therapeutic choices. It is paradoxical when groups that strenuously eschew theological pluralism embrace

Conclusion

therapeutic pluralism, when doing so may lead them to engage in the very theological combinativeness they so assiduously sought to avoid.[9]

PENTECOSTALIZATION

Since the 1960s a pentecostal emphasis on spiritual gifts and expressive worship has infused growing segments of Protestant and Catholic Christianity. Alongside the practice of spiritual gifts (such as healing), pentecostal worship music has contributed to the spread of pentecostal influences beyond the bounds of pentecostal denominations. Contemporary praise and worship styles, which emerged in part from pentecostal revivals, emphasize an experience of a deeply personal, emotional, therapeutic connection between the individual worshipper and God.

The ARIS survey series suggests that the growth of pentecostal denominations during the 1990s seems to have leveled off in the 2000s. However, membership in specific denominations is only part of the story. More survey respondents describe themselves as Pentecostal or Charismatic than the numbers who belong to pentecostal denominations. The method of ARIS researchers was to classify respondents by the denominational affiliation they listed first, even if they also listed other identifiers. Evangelicals accustomed to thinking in terms of denominational identity may have first named their local Baptist or Methodist church, although their congregation or they as individuals also identify with the pentecostal movement or engage in healing or worship practices influenced by pentecostalism. Whereas ARIS 2008 categorized 11 percent of evangelicals as pentecostal based on denomination, 24 percent described themselves as Pentecostal and 38 percent as Charismatic. If these categories do not fully overlap and some respondents selected one but not the other category (which seems likely given the finding of another nationwide survey that only 7 percent of those who self-identify as either Pentecostal or Charismatic identify with both labels), then pentecostals could account for more than half of American evangelicals.[10]

As the center of global Christianity shifts to the global South, American evangelicalism can be expected to follow the lead of evangelicals in the two-thirds of the world where pentecostalism is spreading rapidly. Hispanic, Asian American, and immigrant black African evangelicals are already more likely than non-Hispanic white evangelicals to embrace

Conclusion

pentecostalism. The ethnic diversification of American evangelicalism may be accompanied by its further pentecostalization.

GLOBALIZATION

Although American evangelicalism has always been part of a transatlantic religious culture, fueled by revivals and transatlantic print and relational networks, pentecostalism was from the outset a truly global phenomenon. Internationally disseminated reports of supernatural outpourings, including divine healing, glossolalia, and prophecy, fueled pentecostal growth.

Since the mid-twentieth century, American evangelicals have participated in thickening global networks characterized by multidirectional cultural flows among diverse local contexts, no one of which exerts a dominant influence. Leaders from the global South have increasingly conducted evangelistic campaigns in North America, cultivated friendships with North American ministry leaders, and marketed their books, CDs, and DVDs in the United States and Canada. The relative cheapness and ease of international travel and the technologically mediated transmission and linguistic translation of texts and music, a growing proportion of which originate in Africa, Latin America, and Asia, facilitate cross-cultural communication. Modern evangelicals are more prone to travel than their forbears, but modern technology also means that physical travel is less necessary for identifying as members of a global Christian community.[11]

No longer is America unsurpassed as a missionary sending country. Immigrant evangelicals from countries such as South Korea, Brazil, and Ghana, whose ancestors may have been evangelized by American missionaries, now undertake "reverse missions" to America through which they seek to counteract the rising tide of secularism that they perceive as infecting even America's Christian culture. Meanwhile, the contents of American missionary activities have shifted from evangelizing unreached people groups toward humanitarian relief and development. "Short-term" missions have become increasingly popular among American evangelicals, with the result that North Americans often learn at least as much as they teach when hosted by two-thirds-world evangelical churches.

North American evangelicals continue to export democratized models of religious practice, but they also import more starkly supernatural worldviews. A growing number of North American evangelists have taken note that Latin American and African evangelistic services are much larger and boast much higher retention rates for new converts than do North American services. This has led some evangelicals to seek to combine Billy Graham's interdenominational networking and follow-up through local churches with supernaturalist strategies such as using healing and deliverance from demons as evangelistic tools; this is true, for instance, of the German-born evangelist Reinhard Bonnke (b. 1940), who spent most of his evangelistic career in Africa before beginning to itinerate across the United States in 2013, hosting Gospel Crusades under the banner "America Shall Be Saved!"[12] By contrast to the highly intellectual forms of evangelicalism cultivated by Calvinism, the evangelicalism of the global South is more experiential and prominently features the practice of spiritual gifts and expressive worship. Rather than ask whether claims of divine intervention are credible given the discoveries of modern science, people in the global South are more likely to ask which source of supernatural aid is the most powerful. Evangelical and pentecostal Christianity has spread through the global South as people evaluate it as a more effective religion than competitors in meeting practical, everyday needs.[13]

The globalization of American evangelicalism has contributed to a heightened expectation of divine intervention in the natural world, particularly through healing. Globalization heightens both the actual threat and the fear of disease. For people suffering from endemic poverty and poverty-related infirmities, for any religion to be taken seriously as representing a God who is a true God, it must not simply provide theological explanations and hope for the afterlife, but it must also serve existential needs in the here and now. Where sickness is pervasive and most people lack even basic medical care, healing is not subsidiary but integral to salvation and appears to provide tangible evidence that the Gospel is good news. Yet even where biomedical science is the most sophisticated, convenient, and affordable, people continue to suffer lifelong, debilitating conditions and to die from disease. A U.S. national survey in 1998 reported that 75 percent of Americans prayed for their health, and 22 percent prayed for the improvement of specific conditions. A Centers for Disease Control (CDC) survey noted a dramatic increase in the use of prayer as a therapeutic intervention between 1990 and 2002; 43 percent of those polled had prayed for their own health in 2002, and 24 percent had solicited intercessory prayer for their health from others. A global, pentecostalized version of American evangelicalism that prominently features prayer for healing may indeed be the wave of the future.[14]

RACIAL AND ETHNIC DIVERSIFICATION

Since the mid-1960s immigration has fundamentally altered the composition of the American population and of American evangelicalism. ARIS 2008 found that the most significant change since 1990 both statistically and demographically was rapid growth of the Hispanic population and to a lesser extent the Asian population. Hispanics have replaced African Americans as the nation's largest minority. The census showed in 2010 that of the total U.S. population, 16 percent are Hispanic, 14 percent black or African American, and 3 percent Asian. If current trends continue, by 2040 the non-Hispanic white population will no longer be in the majority. The Asian population is projected to more than double to 8 percent of the total population by 2060.[15]

In its formal institutional presence, American evangelicalism remains largely Anglo, but on the ground it is increasingly diverse. In racial and ethnic composition, evangelicals are less black, Asian, and Hispanic than America as a whole—but this gap seems to be narrowing, and non-Hispanic whites may soon constitute a minority among the ranks of evangelicals. Based on the 2008 Future of Religion in America Survey silos, out of all "born again or evangelical Christians"—including members of African American, mainline, and Catholic churches—61 percent are non-Hispanic white, 20 percent are black, 13 percent are Hispanic, 1 percent are Asian, and 1 percent are Native American.

Differences can be observed between how first-generation immigrants and their offspring negotiate ethnic and religious identity. Spanish speakers are more likely to be Catholic, while English-speaking Hispanics are more likely to identify as Baptists or mainliners. As generational and cultural change occurs within the Hispanic population, we can expect more Hispanics to reaffiliate from Catholic to Protestant churches. Although Hispanics account for just 28 percent of American Catholics, of those Catholics who identify as born again or evangelical, 39 percent are Hispanic compared with 47 percent who are non-Hispanic white. In other words, Hispanic Catholics are disproportionately more likely than other Catholics to identify as born again or evangelical. As the Hispanic

Conclusion

population grows, we can expect the further evangelicalization of American Catholicism. Moreover, since many Hispanic Protestants and Catholics embrace pentecostal practices, the Latinization of American evangelicalism may accelerate its pentecostalization.

Asian Americans are substantially more likely to indicate no religious identity than other racial or ethnic groups, but Christians are the largest religious group of Asian Americans. Compared with white Christians, Asians are more likely to attend church, affirm that their faith is the only true one, and insist that there is only one way to interpret the teachings of their faith; at the same time, they are less likely to be word-for-word biblical literalists. Although Asian Americans still constitute a very small percentage of the total U.S. population and an even smaller percentage of evangelicals, this minority is disproportionately influential because they are strategically positioned in higher education to influence evangelical elite culture.

The experiences of pre–World War II white evangelicals ill prepared them for the post-1970s explosion of racial and religious diversity. While mainline Protestants embraced diversity as part of a broader, socially progressive agenda, white fundamentalists and evangelicals kept their distance from minorities and focused on building their own, white-controlled institutions. As the memberships of evangelical institutions became more diverse, leadership remained predominantly white and largely out of touch with needs and priorities of minority members.

Since the 1960s nonwhite evangelicals have been working within evangelical institutions to advocate for racial recognition, representation, and shared leadership. As part of a larger turn toward social justice and humanitarian concerns, both white and nonwhite evangelicals are becoming increasingly involved in urban and overseas ministries, where cross-cultural interaction is more likely. Likewise, as evangelicals become better educated and more cosmopolitan, they are more likely to forge relationships across ethnic and racial lines, for instance, in Christian fellowship groups on college campuses.

Since 1945 evangelical educational attainments have grown, but so too have those of the national population. Evangelicals are still less likely to have graduated from college and/or attended graduate school (20 percent) than are nonevangelical Catholics (31 percent) and mainline Protestants (37 percent), or the total U.S. population (27 percent of those age twenty-five and over), and about as likely to have a college degree as religiously affiliated African Americans who do not identify as born again or evangelical (21 percent).[16] Second- and third-generation Asian American and Latino evangelicals are a surging presence in universities and campus fellowships, constituting a majority of some chapters of national groups such as Cru and InterVarsity Christian Fellowship. Evangelical young adults tend to be less welcoming of Hispanics and Asians than are nonevangelical young adults. But campus ministries have some of the best track records of any evangelical institutions for recruiting minority leaders and cooperatively shaping discussions of the issues that diversification raises.

It remains to be seen how well the evangelical movement as a whole will adapt to its growing racial and ethnic diversity. White evangelicals will have increasing opportunities to move beyond racial nonrecognition and colorblind arguments to listen to the priorities and agendas of minority evangelicals. Evangelicals may work to build more intentionally multicultural churches and organizations with leaders recruited from underrepresented groups. Immigrants may bring their global perspectives on Christianity to the evangelical movement and encourage treating America as a mission field. At stake in whether evangelicals make the most of opportunities presented—and turn their entrepreneurial instincts toward creating new opportunities—is the long-term coherence of the evangelical movement.

The racial-ethnic diversification of American evangelicalism has already had profound political implications, as visibly displayed in the outcome of the 2012 presidential election. Shaped by different histories and cultures, the social and political priorities of Latino and Asian American immigrants diverge from those of white evangelicals. Although just as theologically conservative, recent immigrants are less likely to embrace individualistic social and political values and shrinking government and to vote Republican. Most black, Hispanic, and Asian American evangelicals side with white evangelicals in opposing abortion and same-sex marriage, but minority evangelicals take a different view of, and often give more weight to, public policies for universal health care, affirmative action, poverty alleviation, educational equity, and immigration reform.

In 2012 most Anglo Americans voted Republican, but large majorities of African Americans, Asians, and Latinos voted Democratic. Although Latino and Asian American evangelicals are minorities within their ethnic-racial groups, minority Christians are President Barack Obama's largest group of religious supporters. Hispanic evangelicals are twice as likely as Hispanic Catholics to identify with the Republican Party, but in 2012 more Hispanic evangelicals voted for Democrat Obama than for Republican Mitt Romney. Asian American evangelicals are closer to white evangelicals in their political and social priorities than are either African American or Hispanic evangelicals; a majority of Asian American evangelicals voted for Romney in 2012. Even so, Asian American evangelicals are less Republican than white evangelicals though more Republican than nonevangelical Asian Americans, who favored Obama in 2012. As evangelicalism becomes more ethnically and racially diverse, one important implication may be a shift away from the recent alliance between the evangelical movement and the Republican Party.

POLITICAL REALIGNMENT

Media portrayals notwithstanding, evangelicalism is not a synonym for the religious Right, Republican politics, and social conservatism. Evangelicals' political profile has risen since the 1970s, but evangelical involvement in American public life is nothing new. It is easy to forget that nineteenth-century evangelicals pioneered social-reform movements, early twentieth-century evangelicals largely eschewed party politics, and when neo-evangelicals reentered the political fray, they sided with the Democrats up through the 1970s. After all, the Year of the Evangelicals, 1976, marked the election of a *Democratic* Southern Baptist. More recently, only one religious group, white evangelicals, has constituted a consistently strong Republican voting bloc. ARIS 2008 shows that for non-black members of evangelical denominations, 36 percent self-identified as Republicans, 24 percent as Democrats, and 30 percent as Independents. By comparison, for the total U.S. population, 24 percent identified as Republicans, 34 percent as Democrats, and 29 percent as Independents. The percentage of Independents is roughly equal between these groups, but white evangelicals are much more likely than other Americans to align with the Republican Party.

Yet evangelicalism is primarily a religious rather than a political movement. Some evangelicals have always been and continue to be thoroughly apolitical, believing that spiritual means are best suited to accomplishing spiritual ends. When evangelicals do become involved in politics, they often do so for religious reasons and/or make political decisions based on religious values. The Puritans who established Massachusetts Bay colony as a "city on a hill" in the seventeenth century worried that if government pursued unrighteous policies, it risked divine judgment against the entire body politic. This same concern motivates many of today's evangelicals who crusade against abortion and same-sex marriage as moral wrongs that court divine judgment.[17]

The evangelical policy agenda is broadening and shifting. Evangelicals who view Republican policies on abortion and same-sex marriage as aligning with biblical teachings may also care deeply about the environment, homelessness, and world hunger and perceive Democratic policies as more in line with biblical values on these issues. It matters which parts of the Bible one attends to most closely. Determining how to vote, for evangelicals as for other Americans, often involves weighing priorities. Because party politics demands compromise and alliances among diverse constituencies, voters will rarely love everything about their chosen party or its platform. Voters must decide what matters to them most. Religious as well as social and cultural factors and personal needs play into the decision of how to apply the Bible to politics—as can be illustrated by the difference in how white and minority evangelicals voted in 2012. White, and to a lesser extent Latino, biblical literalists are more likely to identify with the Republican than the Democratic Party, but black biblical literalists remain staunchly Democratic. It is revealing to compare the political allegiances of "born again or evangelical Christians" in the four ARIS religious silos: of nonblack members of evangelical denominations, 42 percent are Republican compared with 7 percent of born-again African Americans, 19 percent of born-again Catholics, and 32 percent of born-again mainliners. Regular attendance at religious services, whether Christian, Jewish, or Islamic, can also be correlated with voting Republican. Clearly more than theological identity goes into political identity.

Although some white evangelicals have opted to join the religious Left and campaign for the Democratic Party, many others question whether either major political party can solve America's seeming social and moral malaise. When, for instance, evangelicals call for renewed concern with social justice and global poverty, they often mean that the church, rather than government, should shoulder more responsibility for meeting human needs. Evangelicals may also become more likely to build coalitions with nonevangelicals. It is striking that widespread evangelical support of Romney—a Mormon—in 2012 (including an endorsement from Billy Graham) represented a reversal of evangelicals' long-standing denial that Mormons belong within the Christian fold.[18]

GENERATIONAL CHANGE

First-generation leaders of the post–World War II neo-evangelical movement are passing from the scene through deaths and retirements. The icon of twentieth-century evangelicalism, Billy Graham, is, as of 2015, in his late nineties. Generational change inevitably means some important new directions for American evangelicalism—although the multiple contributors to this volume emphasize diverse possibilities for where younger evangelicals are taking this movement. The rising generations defy easy classification as conservatives or liberals. Some are attracted to the immediacy of pentecostal spirituality, whereas others look back toward the early church or sixteenth-century Reformers for spiritual and theological resources. The younger generations are socially more cosmopolitan. They are better educated and more advanced professionally, have more cross-cultural relationships, and are more apt to view social justice, environmentalism, and global humanitarian aid as biblical mandates. They are more permissive on same-sex marriage, premarital sex, cohabitation, and pornography yet less permissive on abortion. Younger evangelicals may be more likely than their elders to express vague theological ideas, but they believe the Bible is the literal or inspired word of God, describe born-again conversion experiences, and actively share their faith with others.

Evangelicalism has long been a youth-oriented movement that adapts ways of doing church to popular culture. Today's younger generations incorporate contemporary worship styles, visual arts, dance, and drama and are reinserting once-abandoned liturgies. They are experimenting with their own forms of Christian worship and community, and their own language for describing themselves. Of all the Christian groups enumerated by ARIS 2008, the generic Christian category has the most youthful adherents. Younger evangelicals are more likely to describe themselves as nondenominational Christians, emerging Christians, or missional Christians—and less likely to describe themselves as "evangelical."

FUTURE

If, as this volume has argued, evangelicalism has since the mid-twentieth century re-emerged as the normative form of non-Catholic Christianity in the United States, but evangelicalism itself remains a contested and unstable category, what is the future of American evangelicalism?

The increasing preference of Americans to describe themselves as generic Christians does not necessarily indicate growing Christian unity. The rapprochement between evangelicals and Catholics can be expected to continue, while fault lines within evangelicalism deepen. "Church" may look much different in the twenty-first century. Evangelical worship services may bifurcate, on the one hand, into even more highly mediatized megachurch performances, and, on the other hand, into multiracial, intentional communities and small-group meetings that emphasize personal experiences of God and the practice of spiritual gifts. The divide between pentecostal and cessationist (especially Baptist) evangelicals may replace older divides between evangelical and mainline or Protestant and Catholic Christians. As old conflicts between Calvinists and Arminians resurface with new force, the upstart pentecostal movement may outstrip them both, propelled by healing and expressive worship. Indeed, it seems likely that evangelicalism as a whole will become increasingly Latinized and pentecostalized. Immigration and American participation in globalized cultural flows may reinvigorate evangelicalism or heighten cultural and theological conflicts within the evangelical movement.

American evangelicalism can still be described as united by biblicism—as well as conversionism, activism, and perhaps to a lesser degree crucicentrism—but far less so by denominationalism. Denominations may experience further decline in membership and influence, while nondenominational churches, magnetic leaders, and parachurch ministries pick up the slack. Growing ranks of evangelicals looking for a more stable center may join a Catholic or Orthodox church or ascribe renewed authority to historic Christian interpretations of the Bible. Time will tell whether

Conclusion

the net impact will be an attenuation of evangelicalism or the evangelicalization of other Christian branches.

Religion in America has become a chosen rather than an ascribed identity. Globally, this has worked to evangelicalism's advantage—as seen, for instance, in dramatic religious shifts in Latin America as people raised Catholic choose to affiliate with an evangelical and/or pentecostal church. In the United States as well, an evangelical tradition that emphasizes making a decision for Christ can prosper by nudging people to choose a born-again and/or evangelical identity instead of conforming to the norms of popular culture. But if mainline Protestant denominations lost members because of their liberalizing theologies whereas higher commitment churches won members, then to the extent that evangelicals seek to accommodate rather than direct popular culture, they too may fail to motivate commitment and lose adherents. Given a shifting emphasis from evangelism to humanitarianism, evangelical "activism" may become harder to distinguish from secular philanthropy. Evangelical cultural—and theological—distinctiveness from popular culture may diminish as evangelicals continue to embrace and be shaped by America's therapeutic culture and in particular by the rise of complementary, alternative, and integrative medicine. We may see novel cultural polarizations as, for instance, functional naturalism draws together cessationist evangelicals and Nones, while pursuit of holistic health for body/mind/spirit unites pentecostal Protestants and Catholics with metaphysical healers. Evangelicalism may fragment as a political movement as individuals and constituencies within evangelicalism embrace a widening array of agendas that do not neatly match the platforms or methods of any political party.[19]

The label "evangelical" may come to mean so many different things that it becomes no more useful than denominational labels are now in predicting theological, spiritual, social, or political views. Conversely, usage of the term "evangelical" may narrow to such a degree that a majority of Christians who consider themselves "born again" and share beliefs and values long associated with evangelicalism will object to being called evangelicals. From the vantage of 2016, evangelicalism is an affinity group, a movement, and an ethos that has in the past and continues in the present to shape American religion, culture, society, and politics in ways that cannot be responsibly ignored. Today's evangelicals confront new challenges and new opportunities as they strive to balance purity from and transformative presence in American culture. Evangelicals may reinvent themselves in myriad ways, but <u>evangelicalism is not about to disappear. The future of American evangelicalism must unfold at its own pace, but it is a future that remains closely tied to the future of America.</u>

NOTES

1. Candy Gunther Brown, *The Word in the World: Evangelical Writing, Publishing, and Reading in America, 1789–1880* (Chapel Hill: University of North Carolina Press, 2004), 36.

2. Lillian Kwon, "Southern Baptists Experiencing Accelerating Decline in Membership," *CP Church & Ministries*, June 13, 2012, http://www.christianpost.com/news/so-baptist-membership-drops-for-fifth-straight-year-baptisms-are-up-76608/; Kathy Finn, "Southern Baptists Accept New Name to Expand Reach," *Reuters*, June 20, 2012, http://www.reuters.com/article/2012/06/20/us-usa-religion-baptists-idUSBRE85J10220120620; both accessed August 6, 2015.

3. Candy Gunther Brown, *Testing Prayer: Science and Healing* (Cambridge, Mass.: Harvard University Press, 2012), 43–46.

4. Roger Finke and Rodney Stark, *The Churching of America, 1776–1990: Winners and Losers in Our Religious Economy* (New Brunswick, N.J.: Rutgers University Press, 1992), 44–45; Vineyard USA, "Vineyard Core Values," http://www.vineyardusa.org/site/about/vineyard-values, accessed August 6, 2015; Partners in Harvest: Spreading the Fire, "A Little Bit About Us," http://partnersinharvest.org/about, accessed August 6, 2015; Catch the Fire, "About," http://catchthefire.com/about, accessed August 6, 2015; Max Weber, *The Theory of Social and Economic Organizations*, trans. A. M. Henderson and Talcott Parsons (New York: Simon & Schuster, 1947), 358–92.

5. CRI, "Ask Hank: Because Truth Matters," http://www.equip.org/basic-christian-thought/ask-hank-because-truth-matters/, accessed August 6, 2015; Candy Gunther Brown, *The Healing Gods: Complementary and Alternative Medicine in Christian America* (New York: Oxford University Press, 2013), 69.

6. Brown, *Healing Gods*, 159.

7. Kate Netzler Burch, "Jesus Freaks, Sacred Ink, Holy Yoga, and Other Tales from the Margins of Pop Culture: A Theory of Evangelical Identity Construction," unpublished paper, May 5, 2010.

8. Philip Rieff, *The Triumph of the Therapeutic: Uses of Faith after Freud*, 2nd ed. (Chicago: University of Chicago Press, 1987), 30; Brown, *Healing Gods*, 89.

9. Brown, *Healing Gods*, 17–18; Leon Festinger, *A Theory of Cognitive Dissonance* (Stanford, Calif.: Stanford University Press, 1957), 3; Robert Wuthnow, *After the Baby Boomers: How Twenty- and Thirty-somethings Are Shaping the Future of American Religion* (Princeton, N.J.: Princeton University Press, 2007), 106.

Conclusion

10. In a nationwide sample of 4,001 Americans collected in 1992 by the Survey Research Center of the University of Akron, out of 487 respondents who self-identified as Pentecostal or Charismatic, only 34 (7 percent) chose both labels (Corwin E. Smidt et al., "The Spirit-Filled Movements in Contemporary America: A Survey Perspective," in *Pentecostal Currents in American Protestantism*, ed. Edith L. Blumhofer, Russell P. Spittler, and Grant A. Wacker [Urbana: University of Illinois Press, 1999], 118).

11. Candy Gunther Brown, ed., *Global Pentecostal and Charismatic Healing* (New York: Oxford University Press), 9, 20.

12. Jennifer Leclaire, Reinhard Bonnke: All America Shall Be Saved!," *CharismaNews*, February 4, 2013, http://www.charismanews.com/us/38095-reinhard-bonnke-all-america-shall-be-saved, accessed August 7, 2015.

13. Brown, *Global Pentecostal and Charismatic Healing*, 353.

14. Ibid., 6–7, 19; Miroslav Volf, "Materiality of Salvation: An Investigation in the Soteriologies of Liberation and Pentecostal Theologies," *Journal of Ecumenical Studies* 26, no. 3 (1989): 447–67; David M. Eisenberg et al., "Trends in Alternative Medicine Use in the United States, 1990–1997: Results of a Follow-Up National Survey," *Journal of the American Medical Association* 280 (November 11, 1998): 1569–75; Patricia M. Barnes et al., "Complementary and Alternative Medicine Use Among Adults: United States, 2002," *Advance Data from Vital and Health Statistics* 343 (May 27, 2004): 1–20.

15. United States Census Bureau, *United States Census 2010*, http://www.census.gov/2010census/; United States Census Bureau, "U.S. Census Bureau Projections Show a Slower Growing, Older, More Diverse Nation a Half Century from Now," December 12, 2012, https://www.census.gov/newsroom/releases/archives/population/cb12-243.html; both accessed August 6, 2015.

16. Looking only at nonblack members of evangelical denominations versus all self-identified evangelicals across silos (used for the figures in the text), the percentages of evangelicals and African Americans with a college education are nearly identical—at 19 percent and 18 percent, respectively.

17. Sacvan Bercovitch, *The American Jeremiad* (Madison: University of Wisconsin Press, 1978), 93.

18. David Badash, "Breaking: Billy Graham Endorses Romney Then Scrubs Site Calling Mormonism A 'Cult,'" *New Civil Rights Movement*, October 12, 2012, http://www.thenewcivilrightsmovement.com/breaking-billy-graham-endorses-romney-then-scrubs-site-calling-mormonism-a-cult/politics/2012/10/12/51106, accessed August 6, 2015.

19. Roger Finke and Rodney Stark, "The New Holiness Clubs: Testing Church-to-Sect Propositions," *Sociology of Religion* (Summer 2001): 176.

APPENDIX A

American Religious Identification Survey: Research Design

ARIS 2008 is the third in a landmark time series of large, nationally representative surveys that track changes in the religious loyalties of the U.S. adult population within the forty-eight contiguous states from 1990 to 2008. The surveys conducted in 2001 and 2008 are replicas of the survey in 1990 and were led by the same academic research team using an identical methodology of random-digit-dialed telephone interviews (RDD) and the same unprompted, open-ended key question, "What is your religion, if any?" Interviewers did not prompt or offer a suggested list of potential answers. Moreover, the self-description of respondents was not based on whether established religious bodies or institutions considered them to be members. To the contrary, the surveys sought to determine whether the respondents regarded themselves as adherents of a religious community. The surveys tap subjective rather than objective standards of religious identification. The U.S. Bureau of the Census has recognized the value of this unique series of national surveys, which allows scientific monitoring of change over time. The bureau itself is constitutionally precluded from such an inquiry into religion and so has incorporated NSRI/ARIS findings into its official publication, the *Statistical Abstract of the United States*, since 2003.

The key religion question is part of an inquiry that also probes a range of sociodemographic, political, social, and life-cycle issues, as well as attitudes that add richness to the main findings. These responses reveal the nation's pattern of religious beliefs, behaviors, and belonging. The ARIS 2008 survey was carried out from February through November 2008 and collected answers from 54,461 respondents who were questioned in

Appendix A: ARIS: Research Design

English or Spanish. To fill the information gap on the growing number of people who do not have a landline but use cellular telephones mainly or exclusively, we supplemented the traditional RDD sample with a separate national cell phone survey. Results for the ARIS key open-ended question on religious self-identification indicate no statistically significant differences between the RDD sample and the cell phone sample. ARIS 2001 interviewed 50,281 respondents, and the NSRI in 1990 interviewed 113,713 respondents. The huge number of cases in these surveys provides unparalleled, in-depth profiles of the social makeup of religious groups and detailed geographical coverage with a high degree of statistical precision and a standard error of under 0.5 percent for the full sample in 2008.

As one might expect with more than 220,000 interviews recorded over three surveys, the ARIS respondents offered a vast number of theological, religious, and denominational responses to our key question. These open-ended answers have to be aggregated down to a manageable number of categories for analytical purposes. This requires using a simplified aggregation that helps highlight the major trends in religious sentiments across five major theological blocs as utilized in tables 1, 2, and 12 of the full ARIS 2008 summary report. The category Catholic comprises (1) Roman Catholics, (2) Eastern Rites Catholics, and (3) all others who used the term "Catholic" in their response. The "Other Christians" bloc is composed of all non-Catholic respondents who self-identified with a religious group that claims to be Christian, as well as any theological term that related to Christianity. The "Other Religions" bloc comprises all the other faiths, world religions, and religious groups that are not Christian. The "Nones" are an amalgamation of all the respondents who provided answers to our key question that identified them as having no religious identity or connection. The most common response was "None" or "No Religion." This bloc can be described as the nonreligious, irreligious, and antireligious bloc. It includes anticlerical theists, but the majority are nontheists. For reasons of scientific integrity we have also included data on the "Unknown" category, composed of those who said they did not know the answer to our key religion question and those who refused to reply to our key question. We have no religious identification data on this population, but we do have demographic and attitude data.

A further reclassification of the responses that offers a finer-grained taxonomy identifying twelve religious traditions and some of the larger re-

Appendix A: ARIS: Research Design

ligious groups is provided in table 3 and other subsequent tables of the full ARIS 2008 summary report. However, this summary is just the tip of the iceberg of statistical data on a much larger number of religious groups than can be handled here and many more social variables than are highlighted here. The studies in 1990 and 2001 were fully analyzed and reported in *One Nation Under God: Religion in Contemporary American Society* (1993) and *Religion in a Free Market: Religious and Non-Religious Americans* (2006).

APPENDIX B

American Religious Identification Survey: Future of Religion in America Survey

EVANGELICAL SURVEY QUESTIONNAIRE

EV-1. Do you consider yourself a born-again or Evangelical Christian?

1   Yes
2   No
D   (DO NOT READ) Don't know
R   (DO NOT READ) Refused

FO-1. Did you have a religious initiation ceremony, such as a baptism, Christening, circumcision, confirmation, bar mitzvah or naming ceremony?

1   Yes
2   No
D   Don't know
R   Refused

Are you: (READ LIST)

1   Single, that is never married
2   Single, living with a partner
3   Married
4   Separated
5   Widowed, or
6   Divorced
R   (DO NOT READ) Refused

FO-2. Were you married in a religious ceremony?

Appendix B: ARIS: Future of Religion in America Survey

(INTERVIEWER: IF RESPONDENT SAYS THEY HAVE BEEN MARRIED MORE THAN ONCE ASK IF ANY OF THOSE WERE RELIGIOUS MARRIAGE)

1	Yes
2	No
D	Don't know
R	Refused

FO-3. When you die, do you expect to have a religious funeral or service?

1	Yes
2	No
D	Don't know
R	Refused

FO-4. Aside from weddings and funerals, how often do you attend religious services? Would you say . . . ?

(READ LIST)

4	More than once a week
3	Once a week
2	Once or twice a month
1	A few times a year, or
N	Never
D	(DO NOT READ) Don't know
R	(DO NOT READ) Refused

EV-2. Next, I will read a series of statements. Please tell me if . . . ?

4	Strongly agree
3	Somewhat agree
2	Somewhat disagree
1	Strongly disagree
D	(DO NOT READ) Don't know
R	(DO NOT READ) Refused

(ROTATE)
a. The Bible is the actual word of God
b. The Bible is a human composition that reveals the word of God
c. The Bible is a reliable guide for faith
d. The Bible is a reliable guide for morality
e. It is very important to share your faith with nonbelievers
f. It is very important to participate in prayer or Bible study groups

Appendix B: ARIS: Future of Religion in America Survey

g.   Jesus Christ is the only way to salvation
h.   You prefer a liturgical or traditional worship style
i.   You prefer a contemporary worship style

EV-3.   How often do you (INSERT)? Would you say . . . ?

1   Everyday
2   At least once a week
3   Monthly
4   Once or twice a year, or
5   Never
D   (DO NOT READ) Don't know
R   (DO NOT READ) Refused
(ROTATE)
a.   Share your faith with nonbelievers
b.   Read the Scripture outside of worship
c.   Participate in prayer or Bible study groups
d.   Volunteer in church programs and activities
e.   Volunteer for a charitable or community organization not connected to a church

EV-4.   As I read from a list, please tell me IF YOU THINK EACH WORD DESCRIBES YOU OR NOT. What about (INSERT ITEM) . . . ?

1   Yes
2   No
D   Don't know
R   Refused
(ROTATE)
a.   Pentecostal
b.   Charismatic
c.   Liberal or Progressive Christian
d.   Evangelical
e.   Fundamentalist
f.   In the Emerging Church

APPENDIX C

American Religious Identification Survey: Typology of Religious Groups

RELIGIOUS GROUP NAME	RELIGIOUS CLUSTER
Advent Christian Church	Evangelical Protestant
African Methodist Episcopal Zion Church	African American
Albanian Orthodox Archdiocese of the Orthodox Church in America	Mainline Protestant
Albanian Orthodox Diocese of America	Mainline Protestant
Allegheny Wesleyan Methodist Connection	Mainline Protestant
American Baptist Association	Evangelical Protestant
American Baptist Churches in the USA	Evangelical Protestant
American Carpatho-Russian Orthodox Greek Catholic Church	Mainline Protestant
Amish; Other Groups	Evangelical Protestant
Antiochian Orthodox Christian Archdiocese of North America	Mainline Protestant
Apostolic Catholic Assyrian Church of the East, North American Dioceses	Mainline Protestant
Apostolic Christian Churches (Nazarean)	Evangelical Protestant
Apostolic Christian Church of America, Inc.	Evangelical Protestant
Apostolic Lutheran Church of America	Mainline Protestant
Armenian Apostolic Church / Catholicossate of Cilicia	Mainline Protestant
Armenian Apostolic Church / Catholicossate of Etchmiadzin	Mainline Protestant
Assemblies of God	Evangelical Protestant
Associate Reformed Presbyterian Church	Evangelical Protestant
Bahá'í	
Baptist General Conference	Evangelical Protestant
Baptist Missionary Association of America	Evangelical Protestant

Appendix C: ARIS: Typology of Religious Groups

Barren River Missionary Baptists	Evangelical Protestant
Beachy Amish Mennonite Churches	Evangelical Protestant
Berean Fundamental Church	Evangelical Protestant
Bible Church of Christ, Inc.	Evangelical Protestant
Brethren Church (Ashland, Ohio)	Evangelical Protestant
Brethren in Christ Church	Evangelical Protestant
Bruderhof Communities, Inc.	Evangelical Protestant
Buddhist	
Bulgarian Orthodox Diocese of the USA	Mainline Protestant
Calvary Chapel Fellowship Churches	Evangelical Protestant
Catholic Church	Catholic
Central Baptist Association Ministries	Evangelical Protestant
Christ Catholic Church	Evangelical Protestant
Christian and Missionary Alliance	Evangelical Protestant
Christian Brethren	Evangelical Protestant
Christian Church (Disciples of Christ)	Mainline Protestant
Christian Churches and Churches of Christ	Evangelical Protestant
Christian Methodist Episcopal	African American
Christian Reformed Church in North America	Evangelical Protestant
Christian Union	Evangelical Protestant
Church of Christ, Scientist	
Church of God (Anderson, Indiana)	Evangelical Protestant
Church of God (Cleveland, Tennessee)	Evangelical Protestant
Church of God (Seventh Day)	Evangelical Protestant
Church of God General Conference	Evangelical Protestant
Church of God in Christ	African American
Church of God in Christ, Mennonite	Evangelical Protestant
Church of God, Mountain Assembly, Inc.	Evangelical Protestant
Church of God of Prophecy	Evangelical Protestant
Church of Jesus Christ of Latter-day Saints	
Church of the Brethren	Evangelical Protestant
Church of the Lutheran Brethren of America	Mainline Protestant
Church of the Lutheran Confession	Mainline Protestant
Church of the Nazarene	Evangelical Protestant
Church of the United Brethren in Christ	Evangelical Protestant
Churches of Christ	Evangelical Protestant
Churches of God, General Conference	Evangelical Protestant
Community of Christ	Mainline Protestant
Congregational Christian Churches, Additional (not part of any national CCC body)	Evangelical Protestant
Congregational Christian Churches, National Association of	Evangelical Protestant

Appendix C: ARIS: Typology of Religious Groups

Conservative Baptist Association of America	Evangelical Protestant
Conservative Congregational Christian Conference	Evangelical Protestant
Conservative Mennonite Conference	Evangelical Protestant
Coptic Orthodox Church	Mainline Protestant
Cumberland Presbyterian Church	Mainline Protestant
Duck River and Kindred Baptists Associations	Evangelical Protestant
Eastern Pennsylvania Mennonite Church	Evangelical Protestant
Enterprise Baptists Association	Evangelical Protestant
Episcopal Church	Mainline Protestant
Estonian Evangelical Lutheran Church	Mainline Protestant
Evangelical Bible Churches, Fellowship of	Evangelical Protestant
Evangelical Congregational Church	Evangelical Protestant
Evangelical Covenant Church	Evangelical Protestant
Evangelical Free Church of America	Evangelical Protestant
Evangelical Lutheran Church in America	Mainline Protestant
Evangelical Lutheran Synod	Mainline Protestant
Evangelical Mennonite Church	Evangelical Protestant
Evangelical Methodist Church	Evangelical Protestant
Evangelical Presbyterian Church	Evangelical Protestant
Fire Baptized Holiness Church (Wesleyan)	African American
Free Lutheran Congregations, Association of	Mainline Protestant
Free Methodist Church of North America	Mainline Protestant
Free Will Baptists, National Association of	Evangelical Protestant
Friends (Quakers)	Mainline Protestant
Fundamental Methodist Conference, Inc.	Mainline Protestant
General Six Principle Baptists	Evangelical Protestant
Greek Orthodox Archdiocese of America	Mainline Protestant
Greek Orthodox Archdiocese of Vasiloupoulis	Mainline Protestant
Hindu	
Holy Orthodox Church in North America	Mainline Protestant
Hutterian Brethren	Evangelical Protestant
Independent, Charismatic Churches	Evangelical Protestant
Independent Free Will Baptists Associations	Evangelical Protestant
Independent Fundamental Churches of America	Evangelical Protestant
Independent, Non-Charismatic Churches	Evangelical Protestant
International Church of the Foursquare Gospel	Evangelical Protestant
International Churches of Christ	Evangelical Protestant
International Council of Community Churches	Evangelical Protestant
International Pentecostal Church of Christ	Evangelical Protestant
International Pentecostal Holiness Church	Evangelical Protestant
Interstate & Foreign Landmark Missionary Baptists Association	Evangelical Protestant

Appendix C: ARIS: Typology of Religious Groups

Jain	
Jasper Baptist and Pleasant Valley Baptist Associations	Evangelical Protestant
Jehovah's Witnesses	
Jewish	
Landmark Missionary Baptists, Independent Associations and Unaffiliated Churches	Evangelical Protestant
Latvian Evangelical Lutheran Church in America	Mainline Protestant
Lutheran Churches, American Association of	Mainline Protestant
Lutheran Church—Missouri Synod	Mainline Protestant
Macedonian Orthodox Church: American Diocese	Mainline Protestant
Malankara Archdiocese of the Syrian Orthodox Church in North America	Mainline Protestant
Malankara Orthodox Syrian Church, American Diocese of the	Mainline Protestant
Mennonite Brethren Churches, U.S. Conference of	Evangelical Protestant
Mennonite Church USA	Evangelical Protestant
Mennonite; Other Groups	Evangelical Protestant
Midwest Congregational Christian Fellowship	Evangelical Protestant
Missionary Church	Evangelical Protestant
Moravian Church in America—Alaska Province	Evangelical Protestant
Moravian Church in America—Northern Province	Evangelical Protestant
Moravian Church in America—Southern Province	Evangelical Protestant
Muslim	
National Baptist Convention	African American
Netherlands Reformed Congregations	Evangelical Protestant
New Hope Baptist Association	Evangelical Protestant
New Testament Association of Independent Baptist Churches and other Fundamental Baptist Associations/Fellowships	Evangelical Protestant
North American Baptist Conference	Evangelical Protestant
"Old" Missionary Baptists Associations	Evangelical Protestant
Old Order Amish Church	Evangelical Protestant
Old Order Mennonite	Evangelical Protestant
Old Order River Brethren	Evangelical Protestant
Old Regular Baptists	Evangelical Protestant
Open Bible Standard Churches, Inc.	Evangelical Protestant
Original Free Will Baptists	Evangelical Protestant
Orthodox Church in America: Bulgarian Diocese	Mainline Protestant
Orthodox Church in America: Romanian Orthodox Episcopate of America	Mainline Protestant

Appendix C: ARIS: Typology of Religious Groups

Orthodox Church in America: Territorial Dioceses	Mainline Protestant
Orthodox Presbyterian Church	Mainline Protestant
Patriarchal Parishes of the Russian Orthodox Church in the USA	Mainline Protestant
Pentecostal Church of God	Evangelical Protestant
Presbyterian Church (USA)	Mainline Protestant
Presbyterian Church in America	Mainline Protestant
Primitive Advent Christian Church	Evangelical Protestant
Primitive Baptist Churches—Old Line	Evangelical Protestant
Primitive Baptists Associations	Evangelical Protestant
Primitive Baptists, Eastern District Association of	Evangelical Protestant
Primitive Methodist Church in the USA	Evangelical Protestant
Progressive National Baptist Convention	African American
Protestant Conference (Lutheran)	Evangelical Protestant
Protestant Reformed Churches in America	Evangelical Protestant
Reformed Baptist Churches	Evangelical Protestant
Reformed Church in America	Mainline Protestant
Reformed Church in the United States	Evangelical Protestant
Reformed Episcopal Church	Evangelical Protestant
Reformed Mennonite Church	Evangelical Protestant
Regular Baptist Churches, General Association of	Evangelical Protestant
Regular Baptists	Evangelical Protestant
Romanian Orthodox Archdiocese in America and Canada	Mainline Protestant
Russian Orthodox Church Outside of Russia	Mainline Protestant
Salvation Army	Evangelical Protestant
Schwenkfelder Church	Evangelical Protestant
Separate Baptists in Christ	Evangelical Protestant
Serbian Orthodox Church in the USA	Mainline Protestant
Serbian Orthodox Church in the USA (New Gracanica Metropolitanate)	Mainline Protestant
Seventh-day Adventist Church	Evangelical Protestant
Seventh Day Baptist General Conference, USA and Canada	Evangelical Protestant
Sikh	
Southern Baptist Convention	Evangelical Protestant
Southwide Baptist Fellowship	Evangelical Protestant
Strict Baptist	Evangelical Protestant
Syrian Orthodox Church of Antioch	Mainline Protestant
Taoist	
Truevine Baptists Association	Evangelical Protestant

Appendix C: ARIS: Typology of Religious Groups

Two-Seed-in-the-Spirit Predestinarian Baptists	Evangelical Protestant
Ukrainian Orthodox Church of the USA	Mainline Protestant
Unitarian Universalist Association of Congregations	Mainline Protestant
United Baptists	Evangelical Protestant
United Christian Church	Evangelical Protestant
United Church of Christ	Mainline Protestant
United Methodist Church	Mainline Protestant
United Reformed Churches in North America	Evangelical Protestant
Universal Fellowship of Metropolitan Community Churches	Mainline Protestant
Vineyard USA	Evangelical Protestant
Wayne Trail Missionary Baptist Association	Evangelical Protestant
Wesleyan Church	Evangelical Protestant
Wisconsin Evangelical Lutheran Synod	Mainline Protestant
Zoroastrian	

Contributors

CHRIS R. ARMSTRONG (Ph.D., Duke University) is professor of theology at Wheaton College in Illinois; founding director of Wheaton's institute on faith and vocation, Opus: The Art of Work; and senior editor of *Christian History* magazine. He is the author of *Patron Saints for Postmoderns: 10 from the Past Who Speak to Our Future* (Downers Grove, Ill.: InterVarsity, 2009) and *Medieval Wisdom for Modern Christians: Finding Authentic Faith in a Forgotten Age with C. S. Lewis* (Grand Rapids, Mich.: Brazos, 2016).

AMY E. BLACK (Ph.D., Massachusetts Institute of Technology) is professor of political science at Wheaton College in Illinois. She is the author of *Honoring God in Red or Blue: Approaching Politics with Humility, Grace, and Reason* (Chicago: Moody, 2012); *Beyond Left and Right: Helping Christians Make Sense of American Politics* (Grand Rapids, Mich.: Baker, 2008); and *From Inspiration to Legislation: How an Idea Becomes a Bill* (Upper Saddle River, N.J.: Pearson Prentice Hall, 2007); and the editor (with Douglas L. Koopman and Larycia Hawkins) of *Religion and Politics: Classic and Contemporary Perspectives* (New York: Pearson Longman, 2011).

CANDY GUNTHER BROWN (Ph.D., Harvard University) is professor of religious studies at Indiana University–Bloomington. She is the author of *The Healing Gods: Complementary and Alternative Medicine in Christian America* (New York: Oxford University Press, 2013); *Testing Prayer: Science and Healing* (Cambridge, Mass.: Harvard University Press, 2012); and *The Word in the World: Evangelical Writing, Publishing, and Reading in America, 1789–1880* (Chapel Hill: University of North Carolina Press, 2004); and the editor of *Global Pentecostal and Charismatic Healing* (New York: Oxford University Press, 2011).

MICHAEL S. HAMILTON (Ph.D., University of Notre Dame) is associate professor of history and department chair at Seattle Pacific University in Washington. He has published numerous articles and chapters on evangelicalism and is working on two books on the roles of Calvin College and Wheaton College in evangelical higher education.

Contributors

ROGER E. OLSON (Ph.D., Rice University) is Foy Valentine Professor of Christian Theology and Ethics at Baylor University in Texas. He is the author of eighteen books, most recently *The Journey of Modern Theology: From Reconstruction to Deconstruction* (Downers Grove, Ill.: InterVarsity, 2013); *Against Calvinism* (Grand Rapids, Mich.: Zondervan, 2011); *How to Be Evangelical Without Being Conservative* (Grand Rapids, Mich.: Zondervan, 2008); *Questions to All Your Answers: The Journey from Folk Religion to Examined Faith* (Grand Rapids, Mich.: Zondervan, 2008); and *The Pocket History of Evangelical Theology* (Downers Grove, Ill.: InterVarsity, 2007).

MARK SILK (Ph.D., Harvard University) is director of the Leonard E. Greenberg Center for the Study of Religion in Public Life and professor of religion in public life at Trinity College in Hartford, Connecticut. He is the author of (with Andrew Walsh) *One Nation Divisible: How Regional Religious Differences Shape American Politics* (Lanham, Md.: Rowman & Littlefield, 2008); (with Leonard Silk) *Making Capitalism Work* (New York: New York University Press, 1996); *Unsecular Media: Making News of Religion in America* (Urbana: University of Illinois Press, 1995); *Spiritual Politics: Religion and America Since World War II* (New York: Simon & Schuster, 1988); and (with Leonard Silk) *The American Establishment* (New York: Basic, 1980); and the editor of eleven books.

TIMOTHY TSENG (Ph.D., Union Theological Seminary) is pastor of English ministries at Canaan Taiwanese Christian Church in San Jose, California, and founder and former executive director of the Institute for the Study of Asian American Christianity. He has served as a professor of Christianity at three seminaries. He is the author of *Asian American Religious Leadership Today: A Preliminary Inquiry* (Durham, N.C.: Duke Divinity School, 2005) and editor (with Viji Nakka-Cammauf) of *Asian American Christianity: A Reader* (Castro Valley, Calif.: Pacific Asian American & Christian Education Project and Institute for the Study of Asian American Christianity, 2009); and (with D. J. Chuang) of *Conversations: Asian American Evangelical Theologies in Formation* (Washington, D.C.: Foundation, 2006).

Index

abortion: compared with other issues, 218; evangelicals favoring restrictions on, 128, 134, 139, 218; pragmatic approaches to, 138, 142; racial-ethnic evangelical views on, 174, 194, 195, 216; religious Right and, 40, 141, 143, 150; younger evangelical views on, 43–44, 148, 219
acculturation, religious affiliation and, 164, 171
activism. *See* social activism
African Americans: Christianity of eighteenth century and, 175; education and religious affiliation, 223n16; exclusion from AG, 182; NBEA and theology of, 199n41; post-1990 immigration total, 163; Protestant percentages for, 15n7, 175; reason for not including in evangelical silo, 3; survey findings and percentages for, 6, 15n7, 162. *See also* blacks
AG. *See* Assemblies of God
Against All Odds: The Struggle for Racial Integration in Religious Organizations (Emerson), 191, 192, 193
Alliance of Confessing Evangelicals, 115

American Dilemma, An (Myrdal), 178
American Family Association, 42
American Religious Identification Survey (ARIS): classification and categories in, 154n1, 226–27; denominational identity issues and, 211, 223n10; evangelicalism definition and, 3, 6–8, 15nn7–8; evangelicals identified by Pew compared to, 48n4; findings, 3–5, 15n3, 15n5, 15n7, 66, 127–28, 162–63, 203–4, 206; funding for, 2; key question asked in, 225, 226; methods, 2–3, 16n9, 225–26; number of respondents, 225–26; number of times conducted, 162; project overview, 2–5; research design, 225–27; self-identification approach in, 48n4, 66, 225; survey results for racial minorities, 162–63; surveys comprising, 2, 15n2; years conducted, 225
ancient-future church, 79–86; Bapto-Catholicism and, 85, 91n63; ressourcement movement and, 79–80, 83; Webber on sacraments and, 85–86
Anderson, John, 135

Index

Anglo evangelicals: Latino American evangelicals compared to, 158; missionary focus of, 159–60
ARIS. *See* American Religious Identification Survey
Arminians, 101, 108; Pinnock's "Arminian option," 105
Arminius, Jacobus, 6
Asian Americans: acculturation in religious affiliation, *171*; Christianity of, 215; evangelical hostility toward, 185; failure of racial integration of, 181; on InterVarsity Christian Fellowship staff, 187–88; mid-twentieth-century segregation and, 182–83; Pew survey on, 168, *169*, 170, 198n18; politics of evangelical, 172–74; population projection for, 214; religious affiliation of, 168–74, *169*, *171*, *172*; religious intermarriage among, 170; shift toward evangelicalism, 183–84; subgroups, 168, *169*; survey on religion of Latinos and, 163–64
Assemblies of God (AG), 72, 73, 182
assimilation theory, Chicago, 199n32
Augustine of Hippo, 68, 70
Azusa Street revival, 16n11, 63, 182

Bakker, Jim, 138
Baptism, 55; evangelical theology and, 95, 113–14; re-, 113–14; Spirit, 73
Baptists, 9, 23, 25
Bapto-Catholicism, 85, 91n63
Barna Group survey, 12, 17n22
Barth, Karl, 103, 104, 117, 118
Battle for the Bible, The (Lindsell), 98
Baylor Religion Survey, 15n2
Bebbington, David, 6–7, 16n8, 20, 62, 94; evangelical typology defined by, 67, 88n26
Beecher, Henry Ward, 177
Bell, Rob, 106

Bendroth, Margaret, 175, 179
Berkouwer, G. C., 102, 117
BGEA. *See* Billy Graham Evangelistic Association
Bible, 9; as God's word, 7, 20, 21, 26; higher criticism of, 9–10, 117; inerrancy of, 95, 98–99, 101–2, 103, 104, 109, 110, 111, 112, 117, 204; institutes, 28, 159, 160, 182; literal interpretation of, 16n9, 21, 94, 129, 130, 172, 204, 205, 218, 219; new ways of reading, 42–43, 205; racial-ethnic diversity in context of, 186–88; simplified versions of, 41; study groups, 30, 35, 36, 37, 41, 55, 66, 79, 203; Wycliffe Bible Translators, 30, 38–39, 97
Bible Made Impossible, The (Christian Smith), 110–11
Bible Study Fellowship, 30, 36
biblical inerrancy, 95, 98–99, 104, 108; Henry's stance on, 112; progressives and, 117; tradition and, 110
biblicism, 7, 8, 13, 203–5, 220; definition of ethos and, 94; Christian Smith on traditional, 110–11
Billy Graham Evangelistic Association (BGEA), 28, 36
BIOLA (Bible Institute of Los Angeles), 182, 183
blacks: evangelical movement among, 163, 199n41; literalist, 218; Protestants, 127, 154n1, 175
Bloesch, Donald, 117–18
body, devaluing of, 210
Bonhoeffer, Dietrich, 36
Bonnke, Reinhard, 213
books, subgenre of spiritual, 85
born-again Christians: ARIS question about, 3, 228; Carter as, 133; conversion experiences of, 55, 56, 61, 219; defined, 8; identification as, 1, 6, 206, 221

Index

Bright, Bill, 34, 40, 55
Bright, Vonette, 34
Brow, Robert, 105–6
Brunner, Emil, 103, 104, 117
Bryant, Anita, 132
Buddhists, American, 168, *169*, 170, 172, 173, 197n15, 210
Bureau of the Census, U.S., 225
Bush, George W., 129, 130, 139–42, 144, 148

Calvin, John, 6, 12, 208
Calvinists, 95, 106–7, 108, 213
Cambridge Declaration, 115
Campolo, Tony, 143–44
Campus Crusade for Christ (Cru), 27, 28, 32, 34, 40, 55, 82–83, 159, 216
Carmines, Edward, 135–36
Carpenter, Joel, 175
Carrasco, Rudy, 75
Carson, D. A., 106
Carter, Jimmy, 56, 133, 134, 135
Cash, Johnny, 55
Catholics: abortion and, 134; African American, 162; Asian American, 174; Bapto-, 85, 91n63; distribution of, 127; Eastern Rites, 226; election to presidency of, 82; evangelical engagement with, 79, 82–83, 84, 113; evangelicalization of, 214–15; Graham and, 39; Hispanic, 163, 164, 165, 167–68, 214, 217; identifying as evangelicals, 1, 4, 6, 19; number of, 31, 127, 162; rapprochement between evangelicals and, 19, 38–41, 52n46; rift between Protestants and, 8, 12, 68; Roman, 226; voting and party alignment of, 128–29, 172
CCM. *See* Contemporary Christian Music
CDC. *See* Centers for Disease Control
cell groups, 37

Census. *See* Bureau of the Census, U.S.
Census Bureau Statistical Abstract, U.S., 15n3
Centers for Disease Control (CDC) prayer survey, 213
cessationism, 6, 12, 206, 220, 221
charismata, 8, 16n11
Charismatic movement: African Americans in, 6; Catholic acceptance of, 11; defined, 8, 16n11; distinguished from Weberian charisma, 16n11; ecumenical, 11, 39, 82, 205; emergence of, 58; evangelical status of, 98; heart religion of, 68, 70; Hispanic Catholics in, 164, 167; identification with, 206, 211; megachurches, 73; musical influence of, 58, 60, 68, 69; service structure and, 65; spiritual gifts and, 6, 11, 60, 65, 71–72
charitable giving, 32–33, 51n30
Chicago Declaration of Evangelical Social Concern, 144
Chicago sociological theory of assimilation, 199n32
Children of the Nations (COTN), 34
Chinese Americans, *169*, *173*
Christ, deity of, 100, 108, 117
Christian Coalition, 138–39, 156n21; founding of, 137; membership, 137, 156n20
Christianity Today, 28, 30, 75, 77, 79, 81, 97, 111, 112, 115, 120, 208; founding editor of, 104; 1990 debacle, 105–6; as unifying force, 104
Christian Right: during Bush years, 140–41; emergence of, 132–33, 154; generational change and, 148–49; Left activism compared with, 143–44; 1980s and 1990s changes for, 136–38; organizations, 133, 142; public engagement and, 131; public policy organizations, 142; Republican Party alliance of, 133–35

Christians/Christianity, 27, 30; African American, shaping of, 175; Asian American, 215; born-again, 3, 8; Hispanic American, attributes of, 167–68; immigration and, 11; 1990 percentages compared to 2012, 4; pentecostals distinguished from other, 12; percentage of evangelical, 162; twin impulses within, 209; 2007 percentages compared to 2014, 5; World Christian Database on, 183
Christian Worship Music (CWM), 59
churches: attendance, 130, 185–86; new paradigm for, 71; nondenominational, 31, 205–7; online, 77–78; pentecostal, 29; racial integration in, 180. *See also* ancient-future church; megachurches; *specific churches*; *specific organizations*
Church Growth Institute, 22–23
Civic Forum on the Presidency, 18, 22, 25, 47n1, 152
civil rights movement, 181, 185
CLADIC. *See* Concilio Latinoamericano de Iglesias Cristianas
Claiborne, Shane, 74, 144–45
Clarkson, Margaret, 23–24
Clinton, Bill, 138–39
Colson, Charles, 40, 56, 153
Concilio Latinoamericano de Iglesias Cristianas (CLADIC), 182
conservative denominations, 29
Contemporary Christian Music (CCM), 59
continuationists, 6
Contract with America, 138
conversion: emphasis on, 10, 20, 31, 38, 45, 62, 95, 125; experiences, 9, 27, 55, 56, 61, 67, 72, 140, 219; racial-ethnic groups and, 167, 168, 176

conversionism: definition of, 7, 20, 94; Galli on social activism and, 76; as heart religion, 67–70
cosmopolitanism, 41–44
Costas, Orlando, 184
COTN. *See* Children of the Nations
Cru. *See* Campus Crusade for Christ
crucicentrism, 7, 88n26
crusades, evangelistic, 36, 39, 58, 213
Cuba, 165, *165*
Cuban Americans, 166
culture: biblical theology of, 188; cultural tax, 192; popular, 13, 19, 23–24, 209–11; youth, 56
Cushing, Richard, 39
CWM. *See* Christian Worship Music

Dayton, Donald, 96
Democratic Party, 149; evangelical Left and, 143; Hispanic Catholics identified with, 167; 1970s, 133–34; religious group alignment with, 128, 129, 218; religious outreach in 2008, 146
democratization, 60–61, 63–64
demographics, 4, 19–20, 48n4, 127–28; new evangelical, 160–74, 196n1; racial minorities population growth since 1970, 161; source for racial minority, 162. *See also* religious affiliation
denominations: in ARIS survey, 211, 223n10; conservative and pluralist, 29; decline in, 26, 28, 206, 208; development of, 8–9; largest Protestant, 189; parachurch network and, 29–31; racial minorities in Protestant mainline, 184–85; transdenominational movement, 104; trends crossing boundaries of, 82
discernment ministries, 208–9

Index

diversity: neo-evangelicals' doctrinal and spiritual, 101. *See also* racial-ethnic diversity
Divided by Race: Evangelical Religion and the Problem of Race in America (Emerson and Christian Smith), 188–89, 191
divine healing. *See* healing, divine
Dobson, James, 141
Dominican Republic, 46, *165*
Dominicans, 166
Dorrien, Gary, 120
Douglass, Frederick, 177
Drucker, Peter, 26
dual-mindedness, 24–25
DuBois, W. E. B., 177
Dulles, Avery, 74

EAPE. *See* Evangelical Association for the Promotion of Education
Eastern Orthodoxy. *See* Orthodoxy, Eastern
"easy issues," in politics, 135–36, 153
ECFA. *See* Evangelical Council for Financial Accountability
ECT. *See Evangelicals and Catholics Together*
education, religious affiliation and, 127, 215–16, 223n16
Edwards, Jonathan, 208
elections. *See* presidential elections
Emergent Church, 42, 79
emerging church, 43, 79, 90n48, 106, 109, 120, 220
Emerson, Michael, 188–89, 191, 193
emotional responses: AG and, 72–73; in heart religion, 69–70
entrepreneurialism, 26–27
environmentalism, 43, 145, 218, 219
Episcopal Church, Webber's endorsement of, 114
Episcopalians, 95
ESA. *See* Evangelicals for Social Action

ethnicity. *See* race/ethnicity; racial-ethnic diversity
ethos, evangelical, 93, 94–95
ETS. *See* Evangelical Theological Society
euaggelion, 8
Eucharist, 85–86
Eurocentrism, 75
Evangelical Association for the Promotion of Education (EAPE), 143–44
Evangelical Council for Financial Accountability (ECFA), 31–32
Evangelical Covenant Church, 188, 189, 190, 191, 200n54
"Evangelical Manifesto, An: A Declaration of Evangelical Identity and Public Commitment," 150
"Evangelical Megashift: Why You May Not Have Heard About Wrath, Sin, and Hell Recently" (Brow), 105
Evangelicals and Catholics Together (*ECT*), 40
evangelicals/evangelicalism: ARIS and Pew identification of, 48n4; Bebbington's analysis of, 6–7, 16n8, 62; beginning of, 99; black, 163, 199n41; born-again Christians as, 3; Catholic, 19; change trajectories in, 33–46; changing face of, 158–202, 196n1; character, function and changes in, 18–47; classifying, 93; congregations of, 3–4; criticism of, 69; definitions of, 3, 6–8, 15nn7–8, 92–94, 125–26; distribution of Protestant, 127; dual-mindedness in, 24–25; early prevalence of, 1; ethos of, 93, 94–95; *evangelical* as contested concept, 92–93; exit polls and future of, 194–95; expansion of, 5, 7; four elements in, 62;

evangelicals/evangelicalism (*continued*)
future concerns for, 71–73, 220–22; generosity of, 32; global, 44–46, 183, 212–14; Hispanic and Asian American shift toward, 167, 183–84; historical backdrop of, 8–13; hostility toward Asians and Hispanics, 185; misunderstanding of emotion and feeling in, 69–70; new demographic of, 160–74; new directions in spirituality, 54–91; 1960s revitalization of, 11; nonwhite young, 174; number of, 1; online, 77–78; percentage of Christians identifying as, 162; personal choice and, 10–11; personal needs and, 35–38, 88n24; political realignment of, 217–19; population of 1979, 56; post-Jesus movement, 66; predominance of white, 1; progressive, 102, 117–18, 120; promise of, 196; Protestant, 19, 127; Protestantism and race before, 174–78; public policy agenda of, 150–51, 218–19; racial-ethnic diversity acceptance by Protestant mainliners compared to, 200n54; rapprochement between Roman Catholics and, 38–41, 52n46; reasons for growth of, 10–11; regional variations of survey findings and, 4; retention rates, 212–13; rise and development of movement, 95–98; rising generation and, 13; separation costs and benefits, 178–84; signatures of, 20–22; six common meanings of term, 93; social policy divergence between white and nonwhite, 195; subgenre of spiritual books read and written by, 85; term as Protestant synonym, 9; themes and characteristics of contemporary, 203–23; themes interrelated in trends of, 14; typical worship service, 64–65; typology, 67, 88n26; Webber's phases of, 78–79. *See also* American Religious Identification Survey; surveys; *specific topics*

Evangelicals for Social Action (ESA), 144

Evangelical Theological Society (ETS), 101, 104, 109

evangelical theology: definition of, 92; descriptive understanding of, 119–20; disconnect between spirituality and, 83; division over tradition, 110–17; emerging divide in, 92–123; fragmentation perception of, 104–10; future shifts possible in, 120–21; Hispanic liberation theology, 184; liberal theology and fundamentalism, 125–26; magisterium issue and, 97–98, 111–17, 118, 151–52; NBEA, 199n41; 1990s controversies, 109–10; open theism and, 107–9, 111, 112, 115, 119; postconservative, 118–19; process theology and, 107–9; tribes and types, 99–104. *See also* orthodoxy, doctrinal

evolution, 10
exclusive truth claims, 172
exit polls, 194–95
Explo '72, 55, 57

Falwell, Jerry, 40, 97, 133, 138
Family Research Council (FRC), 137
Federal Council of Churches, 10, 96, 99, 179–80. *See also* National Council of Churches
Fellowship of Christian Athletes, 28
feminism, 179
Filipino Americans, 168, *169*, *173*
Finney, Charles Grandison, 63, 208
Five-Fold Multi-Dimensional Test, 189

Index

Forum on Religion & Public Life, Pew Research Center, 15n2
Foster, Richard, 79, 82, 83
FRC. *See* Family Research Council
Freedom Council, 136
Fromm, Chuck, 58
Fuller Theological Seminary, 22, 73, 79, 97, 98, 99, 102–3, 117, 119, 182, 183, 190; Church Growth Institute, 22–23
fundamentalists, 116; cheap grace theology and, 81; development/emergence of, 10, 125–26; modernity and, 178; neo-evangelicals and, 96, 104, 195; public engagement by, 155n9; social activism by, 10, 79
Future of Religion in America Survey, 214, 228–30

Galli, Mark, 62, 75–76, 77
Gallup Poll, 22
gay rights. *See* homosexuality
gender, 20
General Social Survey, 15n2
generational change, 146–49, 159, 184, 204, 219–20
Gillquist, Peter, 84–85
globalization, 44–46, 212–14
global population, evangelical, 183
global South, 211, 212
Gnosticism, 200n52
God, 21, 26, 107, 108; immediate access to, 66; individual relationship with, 64, 67–69; tradition and direct inward experience of, 90n49
God, Revelation, and Authority (Henry), 112
God gap, 130, 145
godspel, 8
God's Politics (Wallis), 144
Good News Bible, 41
Gordon-Cornwell Theological Seminary, 28, 73, 79, 183

Gospel as Center, The (Carson), 116
Gospel Coalition, 116
Graham, Billy, 28, 36, 57, 70, 77, 97, 102, 208; Catholics and, 39; denomination boundaries crossed by, 82; endorsement of Romney, 219; evangelical definition and, 92; magisterial voice of, 111; as Southern Baptist, 93–94; World Vision and, 33–34
Grant, Ulysses S., 176
Great Awakening, 9
Green, John, 131
Grenz, Stanley, 109–10, 118
Guinness, Howard, 36

Hansen, Collin, 77
"hard issues," in politics, 136
Hauerwas, Stanley, 79
healing: complementary and alternative, 210–11, 221; divine, 8, 11, 12, 71, 210, 211, 220
Hearst, William Randolph, 57
heart religion, 60–61; conversionism as, 67–70
Henry, Carl F. H., 81, 97, 101, 104, 111–12
High Churchmen, 9
Hinduism, 168, *169*, 170, 173, 174, 210
Hinn, Benny, 208
Hipps, Shane, 78
Hispanic Americans: Christianity of, 167–68; conversion to evangelicalism among, 167; diversity, 166; evangelical hostility toward, 185; liberation theology, 184; political party alignment of, 167, 217; religious affiliation by country of origin, *165*; religious affiliation by level of acculturation, *164*; shift toward evangelicalism, 183–84
Hispanic Catholics, 164, 167–68, 214

Holiness movement, 12, 29, 35–36, 72, 101, 102
holistic health. *See* healing
Hollingsworth, Jane, 36
homosexuality: evangelical acceptance of, 98, 145, 148, 173, 174, 204–5; evangelical rejection of, 128, 132, 138, 143, 173, 204–5. *See also* marriage, same-sex
Horton, Michael, 115
Houston, James, 79
humanitarianism, 19, 33–35, 44, 212, 215, 219, 221
Hunter, Joel, 152–53

immigration: Christians and, 11; post-1990 African American, 163; racial-ethnic diversity and, 214; reform, 151, 157n35, 191, 216; U.S. policy variation on, 166
Immigration Act of 1965, 11
incomes, evangelical demographics on, 127–28
Indian Americans, religious affiliation of, *169*, *173*
Institute for the Study of Secularism in Society and Culture (ISSSC), 2
International Congress of World Evangelization, 37
InterVarsity Christian Fellowship (IVCF), 28, 36, 41, 186–88, 189, 191, 216
ISSSC. *See* Institute for the Study of Secularism in Society and Culture
IVCF. *See* InterVarsity Christian Fellowship

Japanese Americans, religious affiliation of, *169*, *173*
Japanese Evangelical Missionary Society (JEMS), 182
Japanese Methodist Conference, 180

JEMS. *See* Japanese Evangelical Missionary Society
Jesus people movement, 54–56, 68, 87n21; antecedents, 62–63; characteristics of post-, 66; future of, 71–73; heart religion and, 67–70; music emerging out of, 11, 55–60; spiritual gifts in, 11; spirituality in, 60–61, 80; worship practices in, 58–61
Jews, 129
Jim and Jane Crow, 177
John Paul II, 39

Kerry, John, 129, 130
Keysar, Ariela, 2
Koop, C. Everett, 134
Korean Americans, religious affiliation of, *169*, *173*
Kosmin, Barry, 2
Kuhlman, Kathryn, 208

Latin America, 166; pentecostals in, 72
Latino Americans: Anglo evangelicals compared to evangelical, 158; politics of, 184; racial integration and congregations of, 179–80, 199n37; segregation and, 182; self-supporting churches of, 180; survey on religion of Asian Americans and, 163–64
leadership: Campus Crusade, 82–83; magnetic, 208–9; racial-ethnic, 180–81, 186, 216; small group, 66; vacuum, 208
lecto divina, 79, 84, 85
Left, rise of evangelical, 143–45
Leonard E. Greenberg Center for the Study of Religion in Public Life, 2
Lewinsky, Monica, 139
Lewis, C. S., 70, 89n31
liberal theology, fundamentalism as reaction to, 125–26

Index

liberation theology, 184
Lindsell, Harold, 98, 104, 111
Lindsey, Hal, 134
literalists, 37, 172, 215; black, 218; percentages, 21
Living Bible, 41
Luther, Martin, 8, 67, 93, 208

magisterium, for evangelicals, 97–98, 111–17, 118; megachurch pastors as new, 151–52
mainliners. *See* Protestant mainliners
mainstreaming trend, 71–73
marriage: interracial, 193; religious inter-, 170; same-sex, 41, 139, 141, 148, 150, 168, 194, 195, 205, 216, 218; sex outside of, 43, 204–5, 219
Marsden, George, 95, 104, 116, 175
Marsden consensus, 96
McAteer, Ed, 133
McCain, John, 18, 19, 22, 129, 130
McIntire, Carl, 100
McLaren, Brian, 43, 53n49
McPherson, Aimee Semple, 208
media, 10, 11, 174
megachurches, 37–38, 77, 151–52; definition of, 27; leadership style of today's, 209; number of, 27
Message, The: The Bible in Contemporary Language (Peterson), 41, 80
Methodists, 5, 9, 23, 25, 100, 180
methods, ARIS, 2–3, 16n9
Mexican Americans, 75, 165, *165*, 166, 176
Mexicans, deportation of, 166
Mexico, 165, *165*
Millennial Values survey of 2012, 147–48
missional movement, 120, 220
missions, 182, 196; agencies, 28, 97, 104; Catholics and, 38–39; effectiveness of, 44, 175, 183–84; emphasis on, 62, 95; experience of evangelical leaders, 36, 37; financial support of, 30; hymns expressing theology, 23–24; racial/ethnic diversity and, 159–60, 175, 176, 178, 179, 181, 182, 186; reverse, 46, 212, 216; short-term, 30, 32, 45–46, 144; Wycliffe Bible Translators, 30, 38–39, 97
Mohler, Al, 194
Moody, Dwight L., 27–28, 63, 80, 177
moralistic therapeutic deism (MTD), 76, 78
morality, 43–44; personal, 6, 143; politics, 135–36, 141
Moral Majority, 40, 133, 138
Mormons, 32, 219
movement politics, 131
MTD. *See* moralistic therapeutic deism
multiculturalism, 75–76; evangelical resistance to, 181; future of, 184–96; missionary work and, 176–77; Protestant mainline embrace of, 177, 181; Protestant shift to, 179
multiracial organizations, 191–93
music, praise and worship, 11; contemporary, 35, 42–43, 58–60, 64; globalization of, 212; heart religion and, 68–69; Jesus people, 55, 61; pentecostal, 13, 35, 39, 60, 65, 71, 211; revival, 63; rock, 24, 35, 55, 58, 64; spectrum of, 64–65; youth, 56–58, 64. *See also* worship
Myrdal, Gunnar, 178

National Association of Evangelicals (NAE), 73, 97, 104, 208; formation of, 10, 96, 125–26; immigration reform statement by, 151, 157n35; tradition concern of, 79
National Black Evangelical Association (NBEA), 199n41
National Congregations Study, 15n2

National Council of Churches, 10, 29, 96, 99
Native Americans, 176
NBEA. *See* National Black Evangelical Association
Neighbour, Ralph W., 37
neo-evangelicalism, 10, 100, 120–21; antipathy to feminism in, 179; birth of, 96; doctrinal, ecological diversity within, 101; Ockenga's influence on, 99; as postfundamentalism, 96; Social Gospel and, 179; two branches of, 101
neo-orthodoxy, 103–4, 117
networks, relational, 206–7
Neuhaus, Richard John, 40
New Christian Right, 132. *See also* Christian Right
New Monasticism movement, 74, 145
Newsweek, 10, 56, 133
New Testament, terminology and history in light of, 8, 16n11
Niebuhr, Reinhold, 100
Nixon, Richard, 133
No Child Left Behind, 140
Noll, Mark, 7, 44, 94, 175
nondenominationalism, 31, 205–7
Nones, 3, 4, 15n5, 66; growth of, 127, 162; percentage of, 127; voting and partisanship of, 129
Norman, Larry, 55, 59, 64
Nouwen, Henri, 82

Obama, Barack, 18, 19, 22, 129, 130, 146, 147, 194
Ockenga, Harold John, 99–100
Oden, Thomas, 108, 113
Omi, Michael, 188
omniscience, God's, 107, 108, 111
Oneness Pentecostals, 95, 98, 182
online evangelicalism, 77–78
Openness of God, The (Pinnock), 107, 108

open theism, 112; ETS investigation of, 109; manifesto of, 107; omniscience redefined by, 108; process theology and, 107–9; tradition and, 111, 112, 115, 119
Orthodoxy: defections to, 82–84, 113; Eastern, 82, 84, 113; evangelical interest in, 79, 84; paleo, 108, 113–16
orthodoxy, doctrinal: concern with, 7, 82, 110, 210; defections from, 98, 103, 106; defined, 29, 100, 112; as defining feature of evangelicalism, 93, 94, 95; disagreements about what constitutes, 102–3, 105, 108, 207; neo-, 103–4, 117–18; progressive, 102, 117–18, 120. *See also* evangelical theology
Ortiz, Juan Carlos, 37

paleo-orthodoxy, 108, 113–16
Palmer, Phoebe, 208
Pannell, William, 184
parachurch organizations: denominations and, 29–31; development of network, 27–29; fields of activity, 31–33; individual direct connection with, 30
Park, Robert, 199n32
partisanship, 128–30, 218; of new generation, 147–48
pastors, megachurch, 151–52
patristics, 84
PEACE Plan, 152
Peale, Norman Vincent, 38
Pensacola Outpouring, 72
Pentecostalism: growth of worldwide, 63, 183, 220; mainstreaming trend in, 71; pentecostalization, 211–12
pentecostals, 6, 16n11, 17n22; attracting new adherents, 11–12; Calvinists distinguished from, 12; church examples for, 29, 101; growth of, 11; heart religion of, 68; Hispanic,

Index

164–65, 167, 180, 181, 182, 185, 215; holistic healing and, 221; immigrant, 163; Latin American, 72; NAE and, 100; New Testament and, 8; nondenominational, 206; Oneness, 95, 98, 182; prayers of, 11–12; segregationist practices of, 181; sermons of, 64; Spirit baptism of, 73; worship music of, 13, 35, 39, 60, 65, 71, 211

People of the Dream: Multiracial Congregations in the United States (Emerson), 193

Perkins, John, 75

pervasive interpretive pluralism, 112, 113–17

Peterson, Eugene, 79, 80, 81, 83

Pew Research Center, 127, 155n2; on Asian Americans, 168, *169*, 170, 198n18; evangelicals identified by ARIS compared to, 48n4; Forum on Religion & Public Life, 15n2; recent surveys of Latino and Asian American religion, 163–64; Religious Landscape Studies, 5, 128, 161–62, 206; 2012 post-election poll conducted by, 194

philanthropy, 34–35

Philokalia, 83

Pierce, Robert, 33

Pinnock, Clark, 105, 107, 110, 118–19

pluralism: pervasive interpretive, 112, 113–17; pluralist denominations, 29; theological, 28, 29; therapeutic, 210–11

pneumocentrism, 88n26

polarization, 5

policy. *See* public policy

political parties: evangelical realignment with, 217–19; racial minority alignment with, 167, 216–17; response to religious groups from, 145–46. *See also specific political parties*

politics, 14, 124–25; advocacy think tank as vehicle for influential, 137–38; Asian American evangelical, 172–74; Clinton years, 138–39; of disengagement, 148–49; "easy issues" in, 135–36, 153; evangelicals in contemporary, 139–46; expanding policy agenda, 150–51; future of evangelical engagement with, 147–54; "hard issues" in, 136; Latino American, 184; morality, 135–36; movement, 131; new public advocacy styles and, 151–53; 1990s division of evangelical, 136–37; political party response, 145–46; Protestant mainliner, 149–50; *quiescent*, 131; racial-ethnic diversity implications for, 216–17; regularized, 131, 142, 149–50; religion, voting and presidential elections in light of, 128–30; religious groups in context of, 125–30; roots of evangelical, 130–39; social activism trend and, 74–76; unusual partnerships in evangelical, 153–54; youth, 147–48. *See also* presidential elections; public engagement

Pope John XXIII, 39

Pope Paul VI, 39

popular culture, 13, 19, 23–24, 209–11

population: Asian, 214; growth of racial minority, *161*

populism, 22–24

postconservative evangelical theology, 118–19

pragmatists: definition of, 156n26; divide between purists and, 141–42; popular culture and, 210; social activism and, 80–81; triumph of, 153–54; Webber and, 78, 79

praise and worship movement. *See* music, praise and worship

prayer: contemplative, 79; groups, 35, 37, 66, 203; healing through, 61, 210, 213–14; pentecostal, 11–12; prominence of, 36, 65, 68; public-school, 135
Presbyterian Church USA, 5
presidential elections: 1960, 82; 1976, 133; 1980, 56, 135; 1984, 135; 1992, 138–39; 1996, 137; religion, voting and, 128–30; 2000, 139–41; 2004, 129, 130, 144; 2008, 18, 19, 129, 130, 146, 147, 149, 152, 194; 2012, 129, 130, 146, 152, 159, 194–95, 216–19. *See also* Christian Right; politics
presidential forum, at Saddleback, 18, 22, 25, 47n1, 152
Prison Fellowship Ministries, 40, 44
process theology, 107–9
progressive evangelicals, 102, 117–18, 120
Protestant mainliners, 1; Asian American, 170; decline of, 5; distribution of, 127; evangelical theology fragmentation and, 105; Hispanic, 164, *164*; membership decline of, 184–85; mid-twentieth-century segregation by, 178; multiculturalism embraced by, 177, 181; pluralism of, 29; politics of, 149–50; racial-ethnic diversity acceptance by, 175, 200n54; segregationism paradox of, 177; social sciences embraced by, 178; voting by, 128–29
Protestants/Protestantism: African American percentage as, 15n7, 175; black, 127, 154n1, 175; conservative and pluralist denominations in, 29; distribution of evangelical, 127; evangelical, 19, 127; evangelical term as Protestant synonym, 9; largest denomination in, 189; multiculturalism shift of, 179; multiracial nature of, 174–78; party divisions of, 1, 9–10; rifts between Catholics and, 12; *sola scriptura* tenet in, 114–15. *See also* Reformation, Protestant
public advocacy, new styles of, 151–53
public engagement: methods of, 131; pragmatism feature of new wave of, 153–54
public policy: Christian Right organizations on, 142; divergence between white and nonwhite evangelicals on, 195; expanding evangelical, 150–51, 218–19; white and nonwhite evangelicals on, 195
Puerto Rican American, 165, *165*
purists, divide between pragmatists and, 141–42
Purpose Driven Church, The (Warren), 23, 24
Purpose Driven Life, The (Warren), 23, 24, 152
Putnam, Robert, 185

quiescent politics, 131

race/ethnicity: Protestantism and, 174–78; race factor in segregation, 161; racialization, 188, 191, 200n49, 200n52; racial nonrecognition, 177–78, 186, 216; sociological study of, 178; stereotypes, 190; structural racism recognition, 188–91, 200n49
racial-ethnic diversity, 215–17; Biblical theology context for, 186–88; in Evangelical Covenant Church and, 188, 189, 190, 191, 200n54; evangelicalism changing face and, 158–202, 196n1; failure to engage, 159; Five-Fold Multi-Dimensional Test for, 189; immigration and, 214; leadership and, 180–81, 186, 216; pentecostalization and, 211–12; political implications of, 216–17; Protestant mainliner encounter and

Index

acceptance of, 175, 200n54; racial equity and multiracial organizations, 191–93; recent evangelical responses to, 186; secularization and, 165; in Southern Baptist Convention, 189–90; white privilege challenge to, 191–93. *See also* segregation

racial integration, 192, 193; failure of Asian American, 181; Latinos and, 179–80, 199n37; racialization and, 188, 200n49; resistance to, 180

racial minorities, 163, 195–96; political party alignment of, 167, 216–17; population growth since 1970, *161*; in Protestant mainline denominations, 184–85; source for demographics on, 162; support for legal abortion among, 174; voting in 2012 presidential election, 194. *See also* religious affiliation; *specific groups*

racial reconciliation, 189–91; as biblical mandate, 187–88

Rainer, Thom, 190–91

random-digit-dialed telephone interviews (RDD), 225, 226

Rayburn, Jim, 36

RDD. *See* random-digit-dialed telephone interviews

Reagan, Ronald, 135, 136

rebaptism, 113–14

Reed, Ralph, 137

Reformation, Protestant: fundamentalist misunderstanding of, 81; paleo-orthodoxy and, 115–16; second, 62

regularized politics, 131, 142, 149–50

relational networks, 206–7

religion: categories and survey data on, 126–27, 154n1; heart, 60–61, 67–70; intermarriage, 170; presidential elections, voting, and, 128–30; survey on Latino and Asian American, 163–64; voluntary nature of American, 221. *See also* demographics

religious affiliation: African American education attainment link with, 223n16; Asian American, 168–74, *169*, *171*, *172*, *173*; education attainment and, 127, 215–16, 223n16; of Hispanics, *164*, *165*

Religious Census of the Religious Congregations and Membership Study, U.S., 31

religious groups: Democratic Party efforts to reach, 146; partisan identification of, 128–30, 218; in political context, 125–30; political party response to, 145–46

Religious Landscape Studies, Pew Research Center, 5, 128, 161–62, 206

religious Right. *See* Christian Right

Renewalists, 183

Republican Party, 146, 151; Christian Coalition Clinton-era support of, 138–39; Christian Right alliance with, 133–35; evangelical identification with, 128, 217; Hispanic American alignment with, 167, 217; new generation politics and, 148; religious groups aligned with, 129–30; weakening ties with, 154

ressourcement movement, 79–80, 83

reverse missions, 46, 212, 216

revivals: Azusa Street, 16n11, 63, 182; emotional and physical manifestations during, 72–73; evangelical growth through, 9, 73, 96, 212; Great Awakening, 9, 63; Holiness and Higher Christian Life, 12; Moody, 63; music in, 63, 211; Pensacola Outpouring, 72; pietistic, 9; racial-ethnic participation in, 175, 179; Second Great Awakening, 9, 63; Toronto Blessing, 72, 207; youth, 57

Richards, Larry, 36–37
Roberts, Oral, 208
Robertson, Pat, 56, 136, 137
rock music. *See* music, praise and worship, rock
Rogers, Jack, 103
Roman Catholics. *See* Catholics, Roman
Romney, Mitt, 129, 194, 217, 219
routinization, 207

sacraments, Webber on restoring, 85–86
Saddleback Church, 18, 19, 20–22, 25, 26, 27, 152. *See also* Civic Forum on the Presidency
same-sex marriage. *See* marriage, same-sex
Sanneh, Lamin, 62
Schaeffer, Francis, 40, 134
Schuller, Robert, 37
Scopes "Monkey" Trial, 10, 96
Searching for an Adequate God (Pinnock), 108
Second Vatican Council, 11
secularization, 165–68, 170, 194, 200n54, 212
seculars. *See* Nones
segregation, 160, 161, 175, 182–83; evangelical and pentecostal practices of, 181; Jim and Jane Crow, 177; Protestant mainliners and, 177, 178; renouncement of, 179–80; social science justification for, 178
self-denial, 24
seminarians, disconnect between theology and spirituality in, 83
separation, costs and benefits of, 178–84
September 11, 140
sermons, as main event, 64
Seymour, William J., 63

Sider, Ronald, 74
Sixteenth Annual Theology conference, 83–84
Sixth Americans, 193
Skinner, Tom, 184
small groups, 35–38, 65–66, 77, 88n24, 220
Smith, Christian, 88n24, 110–11, 188–89, 191
Smith, Chuck, 55–56, 58
social activism: defining ethos and, 94; discontents and dangers, 74–76; in evangelical Left compared to Right, 143–44; in fundamentalist movement, 79; future implications of, 221; Saddleback Church, 20–21. *See also* public engagement
Social Darwinism, 178
Social Gospel, 178, 179
social justice, 6, 74–75, 86, 143–45, 215, 218–19
Social Science Research Solutions, 4
social sciences, 178, 186, 199n32
Sojourners, 143, 144, 195
sola scriptura, 8, 110, 114–15, 204
So Send I You (Clarkson), 23–24
South America, 165, 165
Southern Baptist Convention, 26, 31; racial-ethnic diversity in, 189–90, 191; renaming of, 205
Southern Baptists, 102, 217; debate over evangelical status of, 93–94; Graham as, 93–94; Mohler as representing, 97, 194; Spanish-language Bible Institutes, 182
Spirit baptism, 73
spiritual gifts, 6, 8, 11, 60, 65, 71–72, 211, 213, 220
spirituality, 85, 101; disconnect between theology and, 83; Jesus movement worship and, 60–61; new directions in evangelical, 54–91

Index

Springer, Kevin, 59
Stimson, James, 135–36
Stock, Jon, 74
structural racism, recognizing, 188–91, 200n49
structure of service, 65
study groups. *See* Bible, study groups
subculture, 25
surveys, 15n2, 147–48, 214; Barna Group, 12, 17n22; church attendance question in, 130; criticism of, 170, 172, 198n18; early and recent questions used in, 126; first, 21; RDD in, 225, 226; religion categories and data from, 126–27, 154n1. *See also* American Religious Identification Survey; Pew Research Center
Swaggart, Jimmy, 138

TACF. *See* Toronto Airport Christian Fellowship (TACF)
Taoism, 210
tax exemption, 137, 156n21
Tea Party movement, 146, 149
temporary protected status (TPS), 166
theological pluralism, 28, 29
theology, 83–84, 186–88; liberation, 184. *See also* evangelical theology
Time, 54, 55
Toronto Airport Christian Fellowship (TACF), 207
Toronto Blessing, 72, 207
Townsend, William Cameron, 38–39
Tozer, A. W., 81
TPS. *See* temporary protected status
tradition, 90n49; direct inward experience of God in light of, 90n49; Gospel Coalition approach to, 116; paleo-orthodoxy and Reformation approaches, 115–16; rerooting for recovery of, 77–79; *sola scriptura* and, 114–15, 204; theological division over, 110–17; traditionals in Webber's groups, 78, 79
transdenominational movement, 104
Trask, Thomas, 73
Trinity, doctrine of the, 95, 100, 108, 109, 117
Trinity College, 2
Truman, Harry S., 57
Tyndale House, 28

Understanding Fundamentalism and Evangelicalism (Marsden), 104, 116
United States (U.S.), immigration policy variation of, 166

Values Action Team (VAT), 142
Vatican II, 39, 82
Vietnamese Americans, religious affiliation of, 169, 173
Vietnam War, 11
voluntarism, 25–26, 221
voting, evangelical, 128. *See also* presidential elections

Wacker, Grant, 69
Wallis, Jim, 144, 195
Warren, Kay, 41–42
Warren, Rick, 23, 38, 41–42; influence and popularity of, 19, 24–25; PEACE Plan of, 152; presidential forum staged by, 18, 22, 152
Watergate scandal, 133
Webber, Robert, 78–79, 84–86, 90n49; on ancient-future church, 85–86; Episcopal Church endorsed by, 114
"Weight of Glory, The" (Lewis), 70, 89n31
Wells, David F., 115
Wesley, Charles, 63, 69
Wesley, John, 12, 68, 70, 100
Wesleyan Theological Society (WTS), 102

Whitefield, George, 208
whites: in evangelicalism, 1; privilege of, 191–93; racism of, 177
Willard, Dallas, 79, 82–83
Willard, Frances, 177
Williams, D. H., 84
Willimon, William H., 79
Wilson-Hartgrove, Jonathan, 74
Wimber, John, 56
Winant, Howard, 188
Winchell, Walter, 57
Wolfe, Alan, 35
Wolterstorff, Nicholas, 107
Woods, C. Stacey, 36
World Christian Database, 183
World Concern, 45
World Vision, 33–34
World War II, 11, 33, 35, 43, 56
worship: democratized, 61, 63–64, 68; de-radicalized, 71; emotional and physical manifestations in, 72–73; experiences, 11, 61, 68–69, 213; graduate degrees in, 87n11; music and, 55–60, 63, 64–65, 87n11, 211; pentecostalization of, 11, 13, 211; racial-ethnic experiences of, 158, 167, 190; services, 64–66, 72, 77–78, 167, 220; styles, 11, 35, 39, 58, 60, 68, 84, 85, 158, 167, 219. *See also* music, praise and worship
WTS. *See* Wesleyan Theological Society
Wuthnow, Robert, 45, 88n24, 185
Wycliffe Bible Translators, 30, 38–39, 97
Wyrtzen, Jack, 57

YFC. *See* Youth for Christ
YMCA. *See* Young Men's Christian Association
Yoder, John Howard, 74
Younger Evangelicals (Webber), 78–79
Young Life, 28, 30, 36
Young Men's Christian Association (YMCA), 27, 30
youth: culture, 56; evangelical, 54, 219–20; loss of theological understanding in, 76–77; ministries, 56, 57; movement, 13, 63, 66, 71, 219; nonwhite evangelical, 174; politics of evangelical, 147–48; Webber on, 78, 79
Youth for Christ (YFC), 28, 33, 57, 58
Youth with a Mission (YWAM), 30, 32, 45

Zwingli, Huldrych, 67